The Political Economy of Communications

Bradford Studies In European Politics

The Political Economy of Communications

International and European Dimensions

Edited by
Kenneth Dyson and Peter Humphreys

London and New York

First published 1990 by Routledge
11 New Fetter Lane, London EC4P 4EE

Simultaneously published in the USA and Canada
by Routledge
a division of Routledge, Chapman and Hall, Inc.
29 West 35th Street, New York, NY 10001

©1990 Kenneth Dyson and Peter Humphreys

Typeset by NWL Editorial Services, Langport, Somerset TA10 9DG
Printed and bound in Great Britain by Mackays of Chatham PLC, Kent

British Library Cataloguing in Publication Data
The political economy of communications: international and European
    dimensions
    1. Western Europe. Telecommunications services. Political aspects
    I. Dyson, Kenneth H.F. II. Humphreys, Peter
    384.094

ISBN 0-415-03794-8

Library of Congress Cataloging-in-Publication Data
The political economy of communications: international and European
    dimensions / edited by Kenneth Dyson and Peter Humphreys.
        p.   cm. — (Bradford studies in European politics)
    Includes bibliographical references and index.
    ISBN 0–415–03794–8
    1. Telecommunication policy — Europe. 2. Broadcasting policy —
Europe. 3. Telecommunication policy. 4. Broadcasting policy.
I. Dyson, Kenneth H.F. II. Humphreys, Peter. III. Series.
HE8085.P65   1990   90–44187
384'.094 — dc20   CIP

Contents

Contents

Tables

Contributors

Kenneth Dyson is Professor of European Studies and head of the Department of European Studies at the University of Bradford.

Wolfgang Hoffmann-Riem is Professor of Law and head of the Hans Bredow Institute for Radio and Television at the University of Hamburg.

Peter Humphreys is lecturer in Government and resident Fellow of the European Institute of the Media at the University of Manchester.

Megumi Komiya has lectured at the Department of Telecommunications at Michigan State University. She has now joined Nomura Computer Systems Europe as a telecommunications analyst.

Ralph Negrine is Lecturer at the Centre for Mass Communication Research at the University of Leicester.

Stylianos Papathanassopoulos is Research Fellow at the Broadcasting Research Unit in London, and visiting lecturer at City University, London.

Jean-Luc Renaud was Leverhulme Commonwealth/USA Research Fellow of the European Institute of the Media, at the University of Manchester, and is now senior media and telecommunications consultant with Logica Consultancy (UK).

Volker Schneider is Research Fellow with the Max Planck Society in Cologne.

Raymund Werle is also Research Fellow with the Max Planck Society in Cologne.

Preface

This volume is a companion to *Broadcasting and New Media Policies in Western Europe* (Routledge, 1988), from which it differs both in the questions that it asks and in its choice of approach. In the first volume the questions focused on the manner in which West European states were responding to the challenges – economic, cultural and political – of the new communications technologies. New means of service delivery were offered by advanced cable technologies and by satellites as well as by the availability of new terrestrial frequencies; new services were made possible by the convergence of developments in computing with communications, notably value-added networks (VANs) and videotex; and computing companies (like IBM) and publishing companies (like Rupert Murdoch's News International) were emerging as new entrants into the communications markets. In particular, broadcasting and telecommunications were losing much of their distinctiveness and exclusiveness as policy sectors. Their characteristics as public-service and monopoly providers were challenged. Furthermore, national borders seemed no longer to be the appropriate frame of reference for delivering these new types of service. In what ways were the West European states responding, both in terms of the policies that they evolved and in terms of the way that they evolved these policies? The method employed was cross-national comparison, with a consequent emphasis on national institutional structures and policy processes. In the process the cultural and historical context of regulatory policies was given prominence.

In effect, this choice of question and method implied an interest in the distinctive characteristics of regulatory policies and processes in the individual states. The way in which the peculiar histories, cultures and institutions of West European states had moulded their policies and policy processes into different forms was stressed. National policy responses were characterized by their variety; inherited ideas and institutions mediated the impact of the shared challenge of the communications revolution.

The advantage of this approach deserves to be emphasized. Not least, it acts as a corrective to the tendency to slip into the assumption that the combination of a shared challenge with the reality of 'interdependence' dictates a convergence of policies. *Broadcasting and New Media Policies in Western Europe* did not deny that these forces were at work. It was at pains to emphasize, however, that politics and culture mattered and continued to shape differing types of policy response among the West European states. *La vérité reste dans les nuances*.

This volume differs, in the first instance, in the questions that it asks. The focus shifts to international institutions and to the international dimension of national policies and policy making. What do policy changes within international institutions and at the national level reveal about the political economy of communications? In what ways have the relations between international institutions and states changed under the impact of the communications revolution? What impact has the international dimension had on policies and policy processes at the national level? In what ways has 'high politics' impinged on the international political economy of communications? Correspondingly, the organizing perspective is that of theories of the international political economy and their explanatory power. Particular attention is given to 'neo-liberalism', 'neo-mercantilism' and 'neo-pluralism' in the examination of these questions. The questions themselves are timely as the communications sector becomes increasingly internationalized. There has also been a tendency to ignore the role of international institutions that needs to be corrected.

This volume includes five chapters on telecommunications. Three chapters focus on international institutions: the International Telecommunication Union (ITU), Intelsat and the European Community (EC). They ask some important general questions about the nature of these international institutions in the context of the enormous changes affecting the telecommunications sector. In Chapter 2, Renaud addresses the question of whether the ITU is a global actor in its own right or whether it is just an arena within which conflicts of interest and ideology amongst states take place. This question is also central to Chapter 4 on the EC by Schneider and Werle. Both chapters attempt to determine the extent to which these international institutions have created some degree of autonomy from their member states. Have they been able to take advantages of major changes in the telecommunications sector by pursuing organizational aggrandizement? Or has the telecommunications 'revolution' demonstrated their limitations and inadequacies? In Chapter 3 Komiya seeks to show that economic theory can shed light on the nature of Intelsat as an international institution. In particular, she examines the argument of the United States government that Intelsat constitutes a 'monopoly' by contrasting it with the view of international institutions as co-operatives. Behind the intense debates about the future development of Intelsat can be discerned contrasting paradigms, with very different implications for telecommunications policy.

The volume includes, in addition, two chapters that deal with state strategies to deal with the international political economy of telecommunications. These case studies focus on the question of the role of the state in introducing new technologies, in adapting to international market change and in particular in tackling the important issue of deregulation. In Chapter 9 on France Humphreys considers a country with a traditionally 'mercantilist' bias in political economy to explore how the challenges of internationalization and deregulation in telecommunications have been met by government, and with what consequences. Hoffmann-Riem (Chapter 8, which is also relevant to broadcasting) asks a similar question in a rather different national context. He examines how a country with a strongly entrenched 'public-service' ethic and regulatory culture legitimizes policy changes consequent on the changes in the international political economy of telecommunications.

Four chapters in the volume are concerned with broadcasting and the implications of the shift from the cultural concept of broadcasting as 'trusteeship' to the economic concept of broadcasting as a market. Chapter 5 by Papathanassopoulos focuses on the implications for the EC as an international institution and explores the policy changes within the EC and the nature of its relations with member states. In view of the unique strength of the American broadcasting and film industries, based on a huge home market and an established dominance in international programme flows, West European broadcasting markets face the prospect of a flood of American imports with deregulation and internationalization. Papathanassopoulos explores the response of the EC to this challenge. The impact on Eutelsat is also analysed in Chapter 6 by Dyson.

Three chapters are concerned with state strategies to deal with the international political economy of broadcasting. They address similar questions to those in the national case studies of telecommunications policy, in particular the interaction between the international and national dimensions of policy. Emphasis is given to the special West European problems of legitimating deregulation in a policy sector that has a notably strong historical and cultural rationale for strict public-service regulation. In Chapter 7 on Britain Negrine explores the way in which the national broadcasting policy sector has responded to the challenges of the broadcasting 'revolution'. In this case government has sought to alter the rules of the game radically, propelled by a neo-liberal ideology that welcomes deregulation and internationalization. The chapter analyses the consequent tensions and the extent to which fundamental change has taken place in the dominant pattern of relations. In Chapter 8 on West Germany Hoffmann-Riem draws out the problems of legitimation that arise when technological and market forces conflict with a deeply ingrained cultural commitment to public-service provision and strict regulation. A different historical context from Britain has profound implications for the way in which regulatory change is handled. Dyson in Chapter 6 on Luxembourg analyses the policy implications of the internationalization of broadcasting, the nature and degree of politicization of international broadcasting markets in Western Europe and the relationship of corporate strategies to public policies. The Astra satellite project and the established role of CLT/RTL as an international broadcaster mean that this chapter embraces such countries as Belgium, France, West Germany and Britain. In the age of cable and satellite broadcasting, and of new terrestrial frequencies, Luxembourg has sought to exploit its pivotal geographic location, and linguistic advantages, to gain a strong position in the new pan-European markets. The consequence has been an embroilment of Luxembourg broadcasting in 'high politics'.

In essence the book is a critique of neo-liberal and neo-mercantilist interpretations of political economy. It argues for a neo-pluralist perspective in which communication policies are viewed as being shaped by highly complex configurations of forces, international and domestic, within which institutional structures and policy networks play a central role. Institutional structures both shape strategic options and present constraints for strategy, for instance a strategy of liberalization. Accordingly, attention must focus on such factors as the character of the governmental and administrative systems, the consensus requirements of the party system, electoral pressures, the characteristics of policy networks, the nature of international institutions and the organization of markets. One needs to look not just at national political institutions but also at international institutions and sectoral variations. In this way the complex interdependence of markets and states can be better understood and the conditions of successful policy strategy identified.

Kenneth Dyson
Peter Humphreys

Chapter one

Introduction: politics, markets and communication policies

Kenneth Dyson and Peter Humphreys

During the 1980s four key words have come to dominate the communications sector – deregulation, globalization, synergy and convergence. The prestige of these words reflects the concerns of both business corporations, as they seek to position themselves strategically in fast-changing markets, and governments, which are attempting to secure future national wealth by attracting investment. Communications have always been politically significant to governments, but never more economically significant than in the 1980s. The paradox is that governments are under pressure to cede their traditional regulatory controls in this domain in order to maximise wealth on which future national power is ultimately seen to depend. Cherished ideals of public-service provision in order to ensure universal access to communication services are being sacrificed in the name of a more rapid development of specialized communications markets. The concept of telecommunications and broadcasting as 'public goods' that require stringent controls is giving way to a market model of provision. In the process inherited ideas about the proper relationship between government and industry are being challenged. States are being increasingly drawn into competition for world market shares as a means to both wealth and power. In devising new industrial policies for the communications sector governments have proved notably sensitive to the arguments and behaviour of dynamic new entrants, whether out of ideological conviction, the 'hard-headed' pursuit of industrial and commercial leadership or a recognition of the realities of exposure to external pressure. Accordingly, new concepts have come to govern policy formation, and external forces have become internalized within national policy processes. Deregulation means a relaxation of the conditions of entry and operation in communications markets, thereby giving more discretion to companies; globalization involves the attempt by companies to internationalize their output through mergers, acquisitions and joint ventures, driven by a combination of escalating costs of the new communications technologies and an explosion of demand for new communication services; synergy stresses the advantages of both vertical integration and diversification as means of extracting the maximum value from the assets of the company.

At the level of strategy public policy has displayed a complex interweaving of liberalization (notably of services and terminals in telecommunications) with mercantilism. Thus in the 1980s public policy has become embroiled in the rush to create global communications groups. Correspondingly, groups like IBM and Murdoch's News Corporation, AT&T and Maxwell Communications, Alcatel and Bertelsmann, Sony and NEC of Japan have come to occupy an ever more central position in communications policy determination. Governments have sought to use public policy to encourage one or more national groups and to ward off or attract particular foreign groups. In the process they have also had to reconsider their strategy towards and relationships with such international institutions as the European Community (EC), the International Telecommunication Union (ITU) and Intelsat. The result has been a territorial shift in the arenas in which communications policies are made and a destabilization of traditional very cohesive and collusive policy communities in broadcasting and telecommunications in which a very few groups have enjoyed privileged access and legitimacy. Communications policies are being made in increasingly crowded environments, with new foreign actors coming centre stage. This erosion of independence has freed both governments and groups from old restraints. Governments can use external constraints and 'necessities' to force change on domestic groups, whilst groups can in turn shortcircuit their governments by lobbying international institutions or forging their own cross-national strategies. In these respects the influence of external decision-making centres and constraints has become critical to the development of communications policies.

In this volume we explore the implications of this new influence of external decision-making centres for both international institutions and states. First it is necessary to be more specific about the developments affecting, in turn, telecommunications and broadcasting. These developments form the context of the destabilization and restructuring of the respective policy communities. They help us to understand why governments and groups have found it useful to modify the rules of the game and change their relationships. The inchoate nature of these developments, and the conflicting dimensions of change, underline in turn the degree of uncertainty and instability that continues to characterize a policy process that remains an incomplete learning process.

The telecommunications 'revolution'

The driving force behind the 'revolution' in the telecommunications industry has been provided by the combination of technological developments (notably computerization) and market change (in particular, an explosion of demand from corporate service users). In the process traditional boundaries between different areas of the telecommunications sector have been eroded (the phenomenon of 'convergence') and the traditional public-service paradigm of public policy has been challenged. Two consequences have followed in Western Europe. First, new tensions have emerged. In broadcasting the tensions are between economic and industrial policy considerations and cultural and social concerns, reflected for instance in concerns about the American 'Coca-Cola civilization' and the erosion of 'European cultural identity'. In telecommunications the tension is between pressures to liberalize markets in order to remain competitive and the fear that liberalization might lead to American domination, particularly in advanced telecommunications applications. Second, states have faced considerable legitimation problems as they seek to resolve this tension and rebuild consensus.

The dramatic and exponential development of telecommunications has alerted both companies and governments to the strategic significance of the sector as a key industry of the future.[1] It has been called 'the central nervous system of the evolving world economy of the twenty-first century'.[2] In 1985 the world telecommunications market already amounted to no less than US$65 billion. By 1986 this figure had leapt to $83 billion, and, according to one authoritative estimate, would reach $113 billion by 1990.[3] Western industrialized countries accounted for some three-quarters of this market: the United States for about 40 per cent, the EC countries for about 19 per cent and Japan for 6–8 per cent.[4] At the same time markets in Eastern Europe, Asia and the Third World were scheduled for rapid expansion.

This rapid development of the market had been encouraged by a cluster of technological innovations, affecting all three main areas of telecommunications operation – transmission (notably the advent of optic-fibre cable, satellite technology and semiconductors); switching (with the transition from electromechanical to fully electronic digital-switching technology); and terminals (as the microprocessor made 'intelligent' terminals possible). These developments in telecommunications hardware meant much more than the promise of greater cost-effectiveness in the delivery of the old telephone and telex services. Digitalized telecommunications with enormous capacity for transmission and 'intelligent' terminals meant that a new and widening range of highly specialized data and 'value-added' services could be provided. Vast new commercial opportunities were opened up for hardware and service providers: local area networks (LANs), value-added networks (VANs), videotex, videophone, high-speed facsimile, electronic mail and cable and satellite broadcasting joined a whole new list of names denoting newly available services. A new world of 'interactive', two-way communication services was being born. So great was the potential capacity and efficiency of the telecommunications sector that it seemed possible to build an 'integrated services digital network' (ISDN) on a national or international scale that could deliver all services on one network. Telecommunications companies, national telecommunications authorities (PTTs) and telecommunications policy-makers became embroiled in a climate of technological optimism that could verge on hype.[5] The message was the need for huge programmes of investment. Against the background of rapid technological change and of uncertainty about technical and market performance, governments were under pressure to take difficult and complex decisions about priorities for investment – what type of cable, what type of satellite, cable versus satellite, and what type of service? Rival technological projects and rival service providers stood to win or lose, potentially on a grand scale, from governmental decisions.

The spectacular rate of growth of the telecommunications sector has also been demand driven, not just technology led. In particular, the demand for new equipment and new data and value-added services has expanded dramatically as companies have become increasingly dependent for their efficient performance on the quality of their information. The telecommunications 'revolution' is tied into the wider development of the 'information economy'.[6] Companies have wanted to use new telecommunications services (e.g. on financial markets) or to develop their own internal corporate communications networks (often on a global scale) or to sell telecommunications services (e.g. VANs) or equipment (e.g. terminals or switching equipment). Together, they have been a new and mounting source of pressure on governments to relax entry and operating conditions in the telecommunications sector. Their specific demands have varied and conflicted. Thus, the aerospace industry, cable television companies and service companies like financial institutions have emphasized priority to satellite transmission; the traditional telecommunications companies and the PTTs have preferred optic-fibre cable as a means of developing an ISDN. What they have had in common is the attempt to use governmental regulation as an instrument to gain or retain market share. The main pressure for liberalization has come from the large corporate users and from the new equipment manufacturers.

This scale of expansion, technological change and more variegated demand has had two main consequences for the telecommunications policy sector. First, these developments have drawn together those who provide information, those who transmit information and those who manufacture equipment in the search for synergy via vertical integration. For instance, IBM moved into telecommunications; financial institutions like Citicorp moved into telecommunications. Expertise in traditionally different areas could, at least in theory, reinforce each other. The telecommunications sector has, accordingly, been characterized by a high degree of market entrance from actors in the computer and data-processing sector and in the office equipment and service sectors. In this respect the policy sector has become crowded and destabilized, with consequent tensions about the future rules of the game and about future relations and with new doubts about the ability of governments and regulators to implement policies. At the operational level policy seems to be amenable to continuous renegotiation as old and new actors manœuvre to exploit their resources of power. Internationalization of the sector has further enhanced their room for manœuvre, as we shall see later. Members of the policy sector are not in a position to exert optimal control over the external as well as the internal determinants of policy implementation. In this respect the relative influence of actors can shift in the transition from policy making to implementation.

A second and related consequence for the telecommunications policy sector has been the international diffusion of pressures for liberalization of the sector in the interests of consumer choice, efficiency and competitiveness. Amongst experts there was an emerging consensus that greater competition and liberalization in telecommunications were necessary if a country wanted to compete in international markets. Failure to liberalize would involve the cost of diverting investment, particularly by large corporate users, to competitor countries with a 'lighter-touch' regulation. Liberalization was seen as essential for the competitiveness not just of telecommunications manufacturers and operators but also of the great national service industries like banking and financial services and data processing.[7] Mastery of technological change and increased market share are seen to require a much more innovative industrial structure. The fact that deregulation was linked to the pioneering role of the United States in the telecommunications revolution, combined with the international political and economic muscle of that country, and with the size and importance of its domestic market, made deregulation appear as an American export. It seemed that 'Reaganomics', combined in Western Europe with 'Thatcherism' in Britain, was giving an unassailable ideological dimension to this process of diffusion. In order to eliminate distortions in world trade, and to encourage and reward efficient producers, it was essential to 'roll back' intervention by the state (in the form of subsidies, preferential public procurement policies, protectionism, etc.). For many policy-makers in Western Europe this sort of deregulation was synonymous with the interests of American companies. It was to be resisted or at least 'controlled'. Britain and, in the case of broadcasting, Luxembourg were to be distrusted as 'Trojan horses'.

The US government and its most powerful corporations like AT&T seemed to be determined to ensure that the international market would be an extension of the domestic market. A series of regulatory and court initiatives unleashed a new dynamic of competition between powerful world-class high technology companies in the US market. In 1982 the old monopoly Bell–AT &T telephone company was suddenly 'divested' of its local telephone systems (which had served some 80 per cent of the market). AT&T was allowed to retain a dominant position in long-distance services, although this field too was opened to increased competition. AT&T's dominance of the market for equipment (including terminals) as well as services was replaced by a more open and competitive sector. Moreover, AT&T was now allowed to diversify into many areas of data transmission and computing. At the same time IBM was released from its antitrust constraints and allowed to enter into the telecommunications markets. In the field of satellites NASA's (Comsat's) monopoly in space was removed; this field was opened to private commercial competition in both telecommunications and broadcasting. The deregulatory wave was even extended to standards for new technologies.[8] These moves combined to generate a newly assertive behaviour by the United States government and by American corporations in the international arena. Not least, loss of domestic market share in equipment, especially terminals, to overseas suppliers propelled a new demand for reciprocal access to foreign markets. Direct pressure was brought to bear within West European countries, particularly by American companies 'keen to invest' and 'to continue to pay big tax bills'. Deregulation was also the subject of bilateral negotiations with specific countries, for instance West Germany. Also, pressure was exerted through the General Agreement on Tariffs and Trade (GATT) negotiations on freeing international trade in information services, through the ITU and through Intelsat. In this sense, international penetration of domestic policy communities in Western Europe was very much American penetration, allied to pressures for deregulation. American companies were at the forefront of the 'globalization' process within telecommunications, pressing for joint ventures and promising technology transfer from which Western Europe stood to benefit. The corollary was not only diminishing national barriers to entry for foreign suppliers but also the advantage of the enormous opportunities offered by the massive expansion of international trade in telecommunications equipment and services. This internationalization of telecommunications markets made a degree of liberalization inevitable. It also made the politics of telecommunications policy not less important but more complex and difficult.

West European policy makers seemed to be compelled to confront a number of objective imperatives for liberalization, not least the 'juggernaut' of deregulation unleashed by the world's most powerful economy. However, many of these policy-makers were sensitive to the danger that policies of liberalization could be of greatest benefit to American interests. Behind 'neo-liberal' rhetoric might be discerned a strategy, at once commercial and political, to reassert American power. Broadcasting and telecommunications reforms in Western Europe were quintessentially political: who was to benefit and who to lose?[9]

Internationalization and the changing structure of industry and markets

Traditionally, the telecommunications industry has been characterized by a high degree of regulation in the interest of universal access to the service, with priority to the domestic subscriber whose tariffs were kept low. In Western Europe this public-service character has been underwritten by entrusting the network and service provision to public sector monopoly providers (the PTTs). The PTTs sustained in turn an oligopolistic industry of large national equipment manufacturers, which were protected from outside competition by means of nationalistic policies of research and development, procurement, network attachment approval and standardization. As a result, there was only limited scope for international trade in telecommunications equipment and services. This industrial structure had appeared to be adequate on the whole for the requirements of national telephone networks.

As indicated above, technological and industrial 'convergence' means that the telecommunications sector is fast becoming diversified, particularly as it merges with the traditionally much less regulated electronics and computer sectors. Accordingly, it is no longer an obvious case of natural monopoly. The highly diversified and changing needs of the information economy seem to be better met by private service providers, offering value-added services on a commercial basis, and by new private commercial suppliers of satellite systems, network services, switching systems and terminals. Undeniably, the traditional telecommunications sector had a number of glaring weaknesses. It had led to the virtual 'capture' of the PTTs by privileged exclusive domestic producers, resulting in inefficiencies and overpricing. Protected national companies lacked export orientation and international competitiveness. Innovation was more readily attuned to specific PTT requirements than to international ones, whilst restrictive nationalistic PTT certification requirements appeared to be a barrier to innovation in any case.[10]

The combination of 'convergence' with market demand for services and equipment seemed to entail an inevitable process of liberalization. This sense of the inevitability of liberal economics in telecommunications is compounded by the combination of the internationalization of telecommunications markets with the ascendant market ideology of the United States, the one country with the sheer economic power to shape the agenda of international telecommunications decisively. The international dynamism of American telecommunications policy seemed in the case of Britain to coincide with imitative behaviour of the British government under Margaret Thatcher, who was personally pledged to 'roll back the state' and implant an 'enterprise culture' of self-reliance through deregulation and privatization. Telecommunications was first detached from the Post Office as British Telecom (BT); BT was then privatized. A new private commercial company, Mercury, was allowed to compete with BT's network. The promising new field of VANs was deregulated. Also, a new regulatory body, the Office of Telecommunications (Oftel), was created in the interest of promoting greater competition and efficiency in the sector. In short, during the 1980s Britain seemed to represent a Trojan horse for American ideas in Western Europe. Not least, Britain's priority to business communications in service development and tariff policy seemed likely to force the hand of other West European governments as companies threatened to migrate to a more friendly regulatory environment there.[11]

In fact, as this volume reveals, the normative code underpinning West European telecommunications policies could remain remarkably resistant to American-style deregulation in certain key countries. Across Western Europe as a whole, the nature and pace of regulatory change remained uncertain. At times it seemed more appropriate to characterize this change as 're-regulation' rather than deregulation.[12] Measures of liberalization were accompanied by efforts to create new and more formal regulatory systems in place of the traditional mixture of direct governmental administration (notable in telecommunications) and self-regulation (characteristic of broadcasting). Telecommunications regulation was in the process of being readjusted to advantage certain interests and disadvantage others. In this sense it reflected the interplay of group interests and shifting relations of power rather than an ideological, technological or market imperative at work. Also, conflicts about the nature and pace of regulatory change were in significant part displaced to international institutions like the EC and the Conférence Européenne des Administration des Postes et des Télécommunications (CEPT) within Western Europe and the ITU and Intelsat at the global level. These factors of international organization, the complex patterns of relationships in national policy communities and inherited normative codes of policy operated to deny American ideology an ascendant and determining role in telecommunications regulation in Western Europe.[13] They could not, however, other than in the short term, prevent a decisive impact of the internationalization of markets on telecommunications policy.

The forces promoting an internationalization of telecommunications markets are extraordinarily powerful. Telecommunications markets are not only expanding in a giddy fashion but are also increasingly assuming the character and dimensions of a highly competitive 'global' marketplace. In the first place, the 'computerization' of telecommunications has drastically affected the industry's cost structure. The lead times and rapidly escalating costs of research and development in telecommunications hardware, notably digital-switching equipment, has been accompanied by shortening product life consequent on more rapid product innovation. Consequently, once nationally oriented companies are forced to consider means of more rapidly penetrating much larger markets if they are to be able to compete at all. A global presence becomes indispensable also to generate the resources for continuing future investment. The consequence has been a spate of mergers, acquisitions and joint ventures in telecommunications: for instance, the joint ventures of AT &T and Philips in digital-switching equipment and of AT&T and Olivetti. Noteworthy attempts by governments to involve themselves in this process seem to suggest that 'mercantilism' is still at work, as governments continue to pursue 'economic statecraft' in the interests of national wealth and power (see Chapter 9). Telecommunications policy may not always be a matter simply of recognizing the imperatives of the liberal economy but of attempting to influence corporate strategy and industrial structure.

Second, the wider processes of globalization in the international economy have placed new demands on telecommunications policy from multinational companies. The efficiency of their operations is increasingly dependent on fast and secure international communications, using cable and satellite. As they seek a global reach, these companies are less and less aware of the relevance of national boundaries and jurisdictions and less tolerant of the limitations imposed by traditional national policy communities. International businesses are keen to promote more competition, and thus greater choice and lower prices, in telecommunications equipment and services. This powerful international challenge to national policy communities has led to a more fluid, tense and indeterminate policy process and elevated the telecommunications sector to the level of international 'high' politics.

Third, the liberalization of telecommunications policy unleashed by the United States and, in Western Europe, by Britain has produced new issues and tensions on the international agenda. Whilst large corporate users have benefited, the 'liberalizers' have seen positive trade balances in telecommunications equipment turn quickly into deficits. They have accordingly put new pressures on their main trading partners and sought to effect a change in international regimes towards deregulation. What began as economic liberalism is transformed into a new mercantilism, as concerns about national wealth and power and the consequent need for government action reassert themselves.

Fourth, the international telecommunications market has become more crowded in another sense. More supplier countries have emerged in the Third World, and not simply as suppliers of low technology. The relative ease of technology transfer in telecommunications means that they are increasingly more important as exporters of more sophisticated products, at very competitive prices. Their penetration of Western markets has been another factor evoking mercantilist pressures.

A major feature of this process of internationalization has been the emergence of some ten dominant international producers (see Table 1.1). The United States has three: AT&T, IBM and Motorola. Western Europe has four: Alcatel (France), Siemens (West Germany), Ericsson (Sweden) and Philips (The Netherlands). Japan has two: NEC and Fujitsu. Canada has Northern Telecom. At the same time this pattern is by no means fixed. Mergers and acquisitions may easily shuffle the pack, for instance the takeover of Plessey by GEC and Siemens in 1989. Also, these groups can expect to face even stiffer competition from specialist producers, for example in mobile communications or satellite equipment. The field appears to be particularly open in telecommunications services. In these respects an important measure

Table 1.1 The world's leading telecommunication equipment companies

Rank	Company	Home country	1986 sales (US$billion)
1	AT&T	USA	10.2
2	Alcatel	France[a]	8.0
3	Siemens	FRG	5.4
4	NEC	Japan	4.5
5	Northern Telecom	Canada	4.4
6	IBM	USA	3.3
7	Motorola	USA	3.1
8	Ericsson	Sweden	3.1
9	Fujitsu	Japan	2.1
10	Philips	Netherlands	2.0

Source: *Financial Times*, Telecommunications Survey, 19 July 1989, p. 1; data from Arthur D. Little.
Note: [a]A French multinational, Alcatel's headquarters is actually in Belgium. It is a subsidiary of CGE.

of uncertainty about markets and industrial structure is associated with the telecommunications revolution. Indeed, revolutions very often end up by consuming their own children.

The problems of adjustment to the telecommunications revolution have been especially grave for the West European states. Despite the respectable placing of some West European multinational companies in the producers' league, the traditionally highly protected and fragmented ('balkanized') nature of the West European market has meant that in fact these companies were rather ill-prepared for the challenges of internationalization and liberalization. In particular, they have been forced to address simultaneously the twin questions of how to continue to secure their national market shares whilst creating the right conditions (of innovative capacity, competitiveness, 'critical mass' in terms of size and reciprocity of market access) to enable them to expand their international markets. These questions had to be addressed in the context of a rising challenge from powerful and assertive American and Japanese firms. Also, the traditional relative 'comfort' of West European telecommunications companies has proved an increasing handicap as telecommunications 'converges' with fields in which Western Europe is at an even greater comparative disadvantage, namely computing and microelectronics. West European answers have tended to focus on national and international mergers, acquisitions and joint ventures – with or without explicit governmental support. They have been seen as the necessary basis to achieve economies of scale, technology transfer and market access. It has not always been clear, however, that Intra-European mergers, acquisitions and joint ventures have built on complementary strengths rather than joining strength to weakness or even weakness to weakness. A strategy of building on complementary strengths and maximizing technology transfer and market access might well counsel the importance of linkages to American and Japanese companies. In this respect there has sometimes been a tension between industrial logic and the logic of European integration.[14]

For its part, the European Commission has attempted to orchestrate a united 'European' response to the challenge by simultaneously reducing barriers to competition and developing a strategy to strengthen the EC's telecommunications industry (see Chapter 4). This EC response presents a difficult problem of how to 'square the circle'. It underlines the essentially reactive mode of EC and member states' policy towards telecommunications. The critical influence was coming from external decision-making centres, causing turbulence and confusion. In addition, the EC has faced serious difficulties in formulating an external policy against the background of the diversity of national regulatory regimes and of industrial structures in the member states. Compared with what seemed to be the conceptual clarity and anticipatory daring of American liberal economics, the West European response has at times seemed to be characterized by a combination of nervous reaction and muddle. All the time, the United States has been harrying West European countries by various means (outlined above) to depart from traditional protectionist practices, with particular pressure being placed on the West German government. Absence of firm policies and solidarity of attitudes at the EC level opened up opportunities for divide-and-rule tactics. It could be confidently anticipated that individual West European governments would not be able to remain immune to the effects of American penetration into neighbouring states. The major alarm for the United States was the possibility that the EC could evolve towards a 'fortress Europe', especially under French pressure. The Single European Market might be given a secure ring-fence. This prospect acted as a catalyst for American and Japanese companies to gain a pre-emptive foothold in West European industry before '1992', the EC's self-imposed deadline for the completion of the internal market. Also, the American government and American companies lobbied hard for a reinforcement of the neo-liberal elements in the EC's telecommunications policy. An example was provided by the American attempt to place a so-called 'international model' of standardization on the EC's agenda of reform. This proposal from the Federal Communications Commission (FCC) alerted the European Commission to the American aim of securing the most advantageous position for its own business interests in advance of the projected completion of the Single European Market in 1992.[15] The United States also placed its 'international model', for both standardization and procurement policies, on the agenda of the Uruguay Round of GATT, in a clear attempt to pre-empt the threat of a fortress Europe. In short, telecommunications policy became immersed in all the techniques of economic statecraft. The process of internalization was 'politicized'.

The politicization of telecommunications markets

Traditionally, international trade in telecommunications has been characterized by relative peace and stability. This situation has been made possible by an industrial structure that has been overwhelmingly organized on a national basis and characterized by a high degree of self-sufficiency. International linkages involved a limited functional interdependence amongst the developed countries and fairly well-established patterns of dependence of ex-colonial Third World countries on the developed countries. Fierce corporate competition or high-level conflicts within international organizations were little in evidence. By the same token, telecommunications seemed an improbable object of 'high politics'.

The changes in the international trade structure outlined above have led to a great increase in tension not just in the international telecommunications markets but also in intergovernmental relations.[16] There has been a dramatic increase in serious trade disputes which have quickly assumed a quasi-diplomatic character. This new climate of international diplomatic conflict is exemplified in the three-cornered fight between the United States (AT&T), West Germany (Siemens) and Sweden (Ericsson) over the sale of the ailing French telecommunications company CGCT (see Chapter 9). Another major conflict emerged when Cable and Wireless (Britain) attempted (ultimately with a large measure of success) to penetrate the hitherto closely protected Japanese telecommunications market (in the process testing the real nature of Japan's liberalization policy). Both the United States and Britain have become more and more impatient with the notorious protectionism of the West German Bundespost. Indeed, the EC has taken an increasingly aggressive stance *vis-à-vis* not only Japan but also West Germany, one of its leading member states. As is highlighted in this volume, serious intergovernmental conflicts have emerged within international institutions like the ITU and Intelsat as well as the EC over priorities within telecommunications strategy. In the case of Intelsat a battle developed between the United States and the West European states about its future role (see Chapter 3). The potential for such conflicts is, if anything, growing, reflecting the extent to which international telecommunications has become an area of 'high politics'.

The fast-developing international sector of telecommunications touches not just the political economy of wealth creation but also the emotive symbols of sovereignty and national identity. Governmental actors are influenced by symbolic forms as well as utilitarian calculations, and national communications policy communities and the rituals on which they are based are particularly likely to be interpreted as essential bases of social solidarity. In contrast, those actors with an intense commitment to internationalization of telecommunications are likely to appeal to a different symbol – freedom of information. In this sense the symbolic arguments are ambiguous and complex, but none the less heated. They underline the extent to which the issue of liberalization cannot be confined to the level of 'low politics'. Telecommunications policy has become immersed in the complex and different rituals of different societies, as revealed in several chapters of this volume (e.g. Chapters 7, 8 and 9). These rituals have a double-edged quality. They may act as 'safety valves', for instance by an exhaustive use of certain procedures (like committees of inquiry and pilot projects in West Germany) to contain conflict. Alternatively, they can be used to challenge and recreate the telecommunications order (as in Britain). In both cases rituals remain essential to the legitimation of policy innovations.

The broadcasting 'revolution'

The transformation of the telecommunications sector has close parallels in the related field of electronic media. Profound technological and market changes are revolutionizing the broadcasting sector, with major effects on the 'rules of the game' and on relationships within national policy communities.[17] They have involved the emergence of new actors (especially foreign ones), changes in the relative influence of different actors and the new constraint of external pressures. In some cases, notably Britain in Western Europe, major ideological change has also occurred, with its own direct effects on the 'rules of the game' in broadcasting. However, compared with telecommunications, broadcasting policy has been less demand driven. Politicians and industrialists have operated on the assumption that viewers want a new era of diversity and choice in broadcasting and that increased leisure time will mean more consumption of television. In fact, new private commercial channels have accumulated considerable financial losses in the 1980s, several new channels have failed (e.g. Super Channel, Europa TV and Premiere) and overall in Western Europe the market share of the new satellite programmes has risen only slowly. The most likely scenario is a combination of 'audience fragmentation' with an increase in television viewing time of up to 15 per cent (averaged across Western Europe).

The projected scale of expansion of the West European broadcasting market offered the most exciting new opportunities to programme producers (especially of feature films, television series and cartoons) and to advertisers. Key factors were that new technologies (video cassettes, cable and satellite) were reducing the scarcity of means of distributing programmes, that the shift towards a 'leisure society' and an 'information economy' opened up new market opportunities for 'narrowcast' programming (e.g. sports, feature film and news channels) and that encouragement of programme production by means of deregulation was attractive to governments in search of expanding sectors. Since the early 1980s an enormous increase has taken place in the number of television channels available in Western Europe, notably a doubling between 1983 and 1986, mainly of private commercial channels (Table 1.2). In the same

Table 1.2 The major new channels in Western Europe

Channel	Language	Source of Finance	Ownership
Public-service channels			
3 SAT	German	Advertising	ZDF/ORF/SRG[a]
Eins Plus	German	Licence fee	ARD
TV 5	French	State	Public Service[b]
Worldnet	English	US government	US Information Service
Super Channel[c]	English	Advertising	ITV & Virgin
Private commercial channels			
SAT 1	German	Advertising	Predominantly publishers (including Springer) and Leo Kirch
RTL-Plus	German	Advertising	CLT, Bertelsmann
PRO 7	German	Advertising	Thomas Kirch[d]
Tele 5	German	Advertising	KMP/Berlusconi
La Cinque[e]	French	Advertising	Berlusconi/Hersant
M6	French	Advertising	CLT, Lyonnaise des Eaux
Arts Channel	English	Advertising	Various including WH Smith
Children's Channel	English	Advertising	BT, Thames, Central, Thorn EMI, DC Thomson
Lifestyle	English	Advertising	WH Smith, Yorkshire TV, TVS, DC Thomson
Premiere	English	Subscription	Maxwell, Columbia, 20th Century Fox, Showtime, HBO, The Movie Channel
Screen Sport	English	Advertising + Subscription	WH Smith, ABC, RCA, 3ls, ESP
Sky Television[f]	English	Advertising + Subscription	Rupert Murdoch's News International
CNN	English	Advertising	Ted Turner (USA)

Notes: All these channels are supplied to cable systems by means of low-powered satellites. Some, like Sky Television, are being broadcast directly into homes from the Astra medium-powered satellite. In France and West Germany the new commercial channels are also increasingly available by off-air transmission.

[a]West German, Austrian and Swiss public-service broadcasters.

[b]French, Belgian and Swiss public-service broadcasters.

[c]Originally intended to broadcast the 'best of British' public-service broadcasting into Europe, this channel's future is uncertain. Moreover, following Virgin's assumption of total ownership it can hardly be counted any more as 'public-service'.

[d]Half-owned by Leo Kirch's son.

[e]60 per cent of France can receive La Cinque mainly by terrestrial transmission.

[f]Sky Television runs several services, including a film channel and a news service, on the Astra DBS satellite.

period (1983–6) the number of broadcast programme hours more than doubled to some 230,000 hours.[18] The new commercial channels depended above all on the sale of air-time to advertisers and on the use of repeats and cheaply bought programmes. Their hopes were pinned on a relatively affluent market of some 126 million television homes in Western Europe. There were good grounds for thinking that this scale of expansion could not continue: the problems for cross-national broadcasting caused by language barriers; the enormous escalation of programme production costs; the question of the availability of sufficient advertising revenue to support so many competing channels and programmes; and the continuing heavy losses by new channel operators. Long-term potential for increased viewing and advertising was more limited than some enthusiasts assumed. At the beginning of 1989 the forty satellite television channels available in Western Europe reached only 16 per cent of the viewers that technically they could serve. In effect, their share of the total television viewing public represented 1.6 per cent, an average of 0.04 per cent per channel.

Even so, whilst few extra channels were likely to be launched, PROGNOS estimated a doubling of broadcast programme hours between 1986 and 2000.[19] According to CIT Research, the West European television programme market was scheduled to grow from $10.6 billion in 1988 to $16 billion in 1998. Over the same period the revenue of West European broadcasters was likely to increase by over 60 per cent: from $21 billion to $34 billion. The number of programme hours would grow by two-thirds, from 325,000 in 1988 to 535,000 in 1998.[20] Advertisers were also likely to continue to be attracted by the huge growth potential that seemed to be concentrated in the French and West German television advertising markets. The proportion of Western Europe's total expenditure on television advertising accounted for by these two countries was far below what would be expected from their national wealth. Western Europe as a whole represented a wealthy but as yet underdeveloped advertising market compared with the United States and Japan.[21] According to one authoritative study, the potential growth of the television advertising market (in 1985) was very striking indeed: for example, 166 per cent in France, 268 per cent in West Germany, 345 per cent in The Netherlands, and 398 per cent in Belgium. The average potential growth rate in Western Europe was estimated to be 84 per cent.[22]

Again, as in telecommunications, a cluster of technological developments gave a major spur to the broadcasting 'revolution'. Video cassettes and recorders, new 'broadband' cable technologies and satellites were instrumental in removing the scarcity of frequencies. In this way these new media provided companies and policy-makers with an argument with which to attack a traditional rationale for continuing tight regulation of broadcasting – the shortage of frequencies. Important technical developments in the management of the spectrum (notably digital switching and microprocessors) have also made it possible to release new frequencies for terrestrial broadcasting and mobile communications services. The consequence has been a proliferation of initiatives, often based on prestige projects like national cable plans and national direct broadcasting satellites (DBSs). Competing technological lobbies have fought about the relative merits of these projects, and governments have been drawn into uncoordinated, muddled and ill-considered actions. Technological

Table 1.3 The world's leading 'traditional' broadcasting companies

Company	Country	Consolidated turnover (1986 or 1986–7)
CBS	USA	US$4,900 million
ABC	USA	US$4,100 million
NBC	USA	US$2,600 million
ARD	FRG	ECU2,400 million
BBC	UK	ECU1,300 million
Granada	UK	ECU570 million
ZDF	FRG	ECU530 million
Thames TV	UK	ECU260 million
Central TV	UK	ECU250 million
CLT	Luxembourg	ECU230 million

Source: Adapted from André Lange and Jean-Luc Renaud, *The Future of the European Audiovisual Industry*, Media monograph no. 10 (Manchester: European Institute of the Media, 1989), pp. 172–4.

Table 1.4 Major publishing companies diversifying into the audiovisual field (only companies with significant activities)

Company	Country	Consolidated turnover (1986 or 1986–7)
Bertelsmann	FRG	ECU4,400 million
Time Inc.	USA	US$3,800 million
News Corporation (Rupert Murdoch)	USA/UK	US$3,500 million
Pearson	UK	ECU1,300 million
Axel Springer Group	FRG	ECU1,300 million
Maxwell Communications	UK	ECU1,200 million
Hersant	France	ECU900 million
Burda	FRG	ECU450 million
Editions Mondiales	France	ECU280 million
Bauer	FRG	ECU140 million

Source: Adapted from André Lange and Jean-Luc Renaud, *The Future of the European Audiovisual Industry*, Media monograph no. 10 (Manchester: European Institute of the Media, 1989), pp. 172–4.

complexity, uncertainty and change has bedevilled public policy making: for instance, the relative importance of cable and satellite in developing broadcasting, DBSs versus the new medium-powered satellites like Astra, the relationship between all these projects and the release of new terrestrial frequencies, and the relative importance of entertainment programming and of new data and 'interactive' services. Policies that have been made on too narrow a technical and political basis have tended to founder in application, giving way to alternative policies that have been renegotiated more or less informally to accord with the realities of the market.

Table 1.5 Other major interests diversifying into the audiovisual field (omitting huge financial groups such as, for example, Banque Bruxelles Lambert and other European banks backing the Luxembourg Société Européene de Satéllites)

Company	Sector	Country	Consolidated turnover (1986 or 1986–7)
BT	Telecoms	UK	ECU12,900 million
Fininvest (Berlusconi)	Construction	Italy	ECU4,400 million
Bouygues	Construction	France	ECU3,800 million
Disney	Films/leisure	USA	US$2,500 million
Bond Corp.	Various	Australia	US$2,500 million
Lyonnaise des Eaux	Public works	France	ECU2,300 million
WH Smith	Retailing	UK	ECU2,100 million
Havas	Advertising	France	ECU1,700 million
Chargeurs	Finance	France	ECU1,700 million
Viacom	News/Films	USA	US$900 million
Lorimar	Films	USA	US$800 million
Beta-Taurus (Leo Kirch)	Film (wholesale)	FRG	ECU300 million
Virgin	Videoclips/leisure	UK	ECU210 million

Source: Adapted from André Lange and Jean-Luc Renaud, *The Future of the European Audiovisual Industry*, Media monograph no. 10 (Manchester: European Institute of the Media, 1989), pp. 172–4.

The new dynamism in broadcasting had two main consequences for national broadcasting policy communities in Western Europe. First, technological and market change is forcing convergence between not just broadcasting and telecommunications (notably via cable and satellite broadcasting) but also broadcasting and the publishing and film sectors. Tables 1.3–1.5 tell an interesting story. Table 1.3 illustrates the traditional dominance of the world audiovisual industry by the Anglo-Saxons, in particular the Americans whose major networks are essentially commercial operations. These American giants have long been supplemented by a large number of other 'independent' broadcasting interests: for example, MCA Inc. with a consolidated turnover of $2,400 million (1986–7) and Tribune Broadcasting with a turnover of $2,400 million (1986–7). In addition, the world film industry, which supplies the broadcasters with so much of their entertainment programming, is similarly dominated by American companies. Examples include Warner Communications Inc. with a consolidated turnover of $2,800 million (1986–7), Columbia Pictures with $1,500 million (1986–7) and Twentieth Century Fox with $620 million (1986–7). The dimensions of the American threat to European audiovisual markets become clear from a comparison with the modest turnover of the EC's major film producer, the French company Gaumont (ECU120 million).[23]

Table 1.4 illustrates the clear convergence between the publishing sector and the audiovisual sector. With the expansion of the audiovisual sector under the impact of a multiplication of outlets (cable, satellite, videotex, video cassettes and new terrestrial frequencies), publishing interests have been confronted with the threat of a potentially catastrophic erosion of their share of the information market. Moreover, their advertising markets are similarly threatened. From the end of the 1970s a relative decline took place in advertising revenues accruing to the press sector and a corresponding increase occurred in the share of the broadcasters.[24] This trend is exacerbated by the liberalization measures described in this volume. However, the publishers have been particularly well equipped to respond to this threat by diversifying into the audiovisual sector. First, in most countries the press industry has been highly profitable. The giant publishing 'magnates' (Murdoch, Maxwell, Springer and Hersant) and conglomerates (Bertelsmann) have had the necessary massive financial resources. Their resources easily match, and in some cases (Bertelsmann and Murdoch) exceed, those of the richest European public-service broadcasters. Second, publishers have the professional resources to compete. Operating in a closely related field, with huge editorial resources and expertise at their command, they are well endowed to make the leap into the audiovisual sector. Lastly, the strategies of Maxwell, Murdoch, Springer and Hersant can to some extent be explained by their desire to expand their editorial reach and to establish international communications empires.[25]

Table 1.5 draws attention to the diversification of a host of other actors from very diverse sectors into the audiovisual sector. In some cases the synergy is quite obvious, for instance telecommunications operators like BT, film companies like Beta Taurus and leisure companies like Virgin. In other cases, like Bouygues and Fininvest, the synergy is less clear. The shared characteristic of all these companies is that they are 'cash-rich'. A comparison with Table 1.3 reveals that a striking number of these new investors have resources that match those of the leading public-service broadcasters in Western Europe.

Companies are pursuing 'trans-media synergy' by using ownership of publishing, film, video, electronics and broadcasting interests to extract maximum creative value from a few top quality creative assets. The consequence has been a rush of strategic acquisitions, mergers and joint ventures, involving such companies as Sony, Murdoch's News Corporation, Maxwell Communications, Bertelsmann and Time. Examples included Sony's acquisition of CBS Records and of Columbia Pictures; Murdoch's acquisition of Twentieth Century Fox and launch of Sky Television; Maxwell's participation in France's TF1 channel and in MTV (Europe); Bertelsmann's joint ventures with Luxembourg's CLT/RTL in the West German RTL Plus channel and with France's Canal Plus in a pay-television channel for West Germany; the proposed merger of Time and Warner Communications; Havas's participation in

CLT and in Canal Plus; and Hersant's in France's *La Cinque* channel. Often the availability of the necessary huge resources to invest in broadcasting has been more important than a concept of 'trans-media synergy': for instance, the participation of *Groupe Bruxelles Lambert* in CLT or of the French construction company Bouygues in TF1. In all these cases, broadcasting is being colonized by companies that are used to a much more lightly regulated environment in their traditional sectors and that wish to retain as much individual freedom of manœuvre as possible. The consequence has been that national broadcasting policy communities have become more crowded, destabilized and tense than ever before.

A second consequence of new market and technological pressures for national broadcasting policy communities has been pressures for an international diffusion of deregulation in the interests of greater diversity, choice and efficiency. Publishers, film producers and advertisers have been central to this process, and, as with telecommunications, the United States has been a dominant actor. In particular, the United States government lobbied actively, at the highest level, against the quotas on non-EC programmes proposed by the European Commission. Western Europe was the major export market for American television programmes, accounting for some 56 per cent ($675 million in 1987). It was also the fastest growing export market, with an annual growth rate of some 25 per cent between 1983 and 1987. American programmes also accounted for about one-quarter of the broadcasting time in Western Europe.[26] Moreover, between one-third and one-half (in some cases over a half) of fiction programmes broadcast in Europe were of American origin (see Table 1.6).

This American interest in the West European television market was reinforced in the late 1980s by two developments: at home, opportunities for expansion seemed to be exhausted and profits were under pressure, with a consequent major rationalization of the sector; the completion of the Single European Market in 1992 created fears that exporting to the EC might become more difficult. American companies needed access to the rapidly expanding television markets of Western Europe in the 1990s (where the output of programme hours was expected to double by 2000) and had a huge supply of films and series that could be made available at relatively low prices to European channels in need of cheap and plentiful programmes. By 1987–8 such companies as Harmony Gold, Fox Broadcasting and Tribune Broadcasting were actively pursuing a strategy of international joint ventures and coproductions with European partners like Leo Kirch and Silvio Berlusconi in order to secure their future position. These alliances tended to be of European finance and American programme production. Against this background many West European broadcasters and policy-makers feared the loss of European cultural identity by 'wall-to-wall Dallas'. In some countries, notably France, the dread of American 'cultural imperialism' could assume dramatic proportions,

Table 1.6 Origin of fiction programmes as a percentage of the total amount of fiction programmes broadcast in 1985

Broadcaster	Domestic	EC	EC plus domestic	USA	Other
RTBF (Belgium)	–	–	51	49	–
ZDF (FRG)	17	33	50	36	14
ARD (FRG)	(Data not supplied)				
DR (Denmark)	7	43	50	46	4
RTVE (Spain)	23	30	53	35	12
TF1 (France	22	34	56	37	9
A2 (France)	34	26	60	35	5
BBC (UK)	38	7	45	55	–
ITV (UK)	57	5	62	38	–
RAI (Italy)	11	28	39	57	2
NOS (Holland)	7	30	37	56	7
RTP (Portugal)	7	34	42	38	20

Source: EIM, *Europe 2000: What kind of television?*, Report of the European Television Task Force, Media monograph no. 11 (Manchester: European Institute of the Media, 1988), p. 83. More detailed statistics, breaking the figures down into categories (i.e. films, drama, etc.) are supplied in André Lange and Jean-Luc Renaud, *The Future of the European Audiovisual Industry*, Media monograph no. 10 (Manchester: European Institute of the Media, 1989), pp. 111–13.

Note: The figures for the BBC and ITV are for the year 1982; the figures for RTVE are for feature films only.

leading to proposals for urgent measures to create a 'Latin audiovisual space'.[27] More generally, regulatory programme quotas at national and EC levels (to limit the import of film and television programmes from outside the EC) were seen as a means of containing the spread of 'Coca-Cola civilization'. In response the new commercial channels argued that such quotas would destroy their financial position. At least in the medium term they required cheap and plentiful programmes; their initial heavy start-up costs and audience penetration problems meant that there would be very little money to finance programme production. As a consequence, West European regulatory policies for broadcasting became caught up in a vortex of economic and cultural concerns and arguments. Never far beneath the surface was the presence of American capital and culture and the threat of a media trade war.

Internationalization and the changing structure of industry and markets

In a fashion similar to telecommunications, public-service values and public-service provision have traditionally dominated the national broadcasting policy communities of Western Europe. Emphasis has been placed on a regulatory framework that would encourage broadcasters to inform, educate and entertain their audience (and very much in that rank order); sustain high standards of programming; ensure a universality of access and appeal; establish a very special relationship of broadcasters to the sense of national identity and community; distance broadcasting from vested interests, whether the government of the day or agglomerations of commercial power; and cater for minority interests. The licence fee was seen as the most appropriate financing mechanism to maintain these principles. Public-service broadcasting was a European institution *par excellence*; broadcasting and culture were intimately wedded together in the minds of the broadcasting élite.

Public-service broadcasting was vulnerable on a number of scores in the 1980s. In the first place, many politicians were frustrated with its failure, as they saw it, to live up to its own principles. In particular, politicians who had spent long periods in opposition were tempted to see the traditional broadcasting system as at least a partial explanation; they had been badly served by the public-service broadcasters. This situation was apparent in West Germany after 1982 when the Christian Democrats came back to power at the federal level after 13 years in opposition. French public-service broadcasting was vulnerable precisely because governmental interference had not enabled it to establish a credible image of independence and objectivity. When the socialist François Mitterrand came to power as French President in 1981 after over two decades in opposition, he felt little trust or loyalty to the broadcasting system that he inherited.

More importantly still, technological change had, as we have seen, removed another major rationale for public regulation – the scarcity of frequencies. In this respect broadcasting no longer appeared to be a natural monopoly whose supply must be regulated. With so many possibilities for delivering broadcasting – video cassettes, cable, satellite, new terrestrial frequencies – the regulatory issues shifted to competition, efficiency and consumer preference. Broadcasting lost its distinctiveness as a field of activity and became subsumed in wider consideration of the future information economy. In particular, the concept of electronic publishing revealed the force of convergence with other sectors. West European governments of very different ideological persuasions embraced the concept of the information economy as a vehicle of future job creation and growth. In so doing, they were unable to resist the logic of calls for more competition in broadcasting. In effect a 'paradigm change' had occurred. Broadcasting was no longer solely or even primarily cultural policy. It was a commercial service in a market and must accordingly serve the needs of the consumer.[28]

This market model of broadcasting was associated with new entrants to the national policy sectors and a change in the relative influence of different actors, with the traditional public-service monopoly providers now on the defensive. Telecommunications, publishing and advertising interests have been notably prominent. PTTs have been especially keen to develop their new cable and satellite networks and to exploit the commercial value of broadcasting services in the process. Equipment manufacturers have seen major new commercial opportunities from the expansion of broadcasting, including new reception and decoding equipment. As suggested, publishing, entertainment and leisure interests have identified opportunities for 'trans-media synergy', using an established position in one media field to support and reinforce their position in another field. Advertisers have been quick to spot new possibilities for expanding business as more channels compete for advertising revenue. This cluster of developmental possibilities has in turn attracted financial groups which have identified communications and media as strategic areas. Together, these interests have constituted a powerful coalition for change. They have also helped to internationalize the broadcasting policy sectors of Western Europe.

The internationalization of broadcasting has been propelled commercially and politically by the combination of cable with satellite technologies. Initially, low-powered communication satellites, operated by Intelsat or Eutelsat, have provided new broadcasting entrepreneurs with the means of access to an expanding European cable market. A new generation of high-powered DBSs promised direct reception by relatively small domestic dish antennae from satellites placed in geostationary orbit (e.g. France's TDF-1, West Germany's TV-SAT and Britain's BSB). More cost-effective DBS services were soon being provided by medium-powered satellites like Astra (from 1989) and the new Eutelsat generation for the 1990s. They offered a wider geographical coverage, based on improvements in transmission and reception equipment. Satellite 'footprints' (the area of coverage of the earth's surface) meant that programmes could now 'overspill' national frontiers in a wholly new way.[29] In other words, large international broadcasting markets were being created. By the same token, effective regulation would be more difficult for states to achieve by acting independently. International institutions like the EC were forced into a new prominence, as Chapter 5 illustrates.

In the programming sector internationalization of broadcasting markets was an established phenomenon. During the period 1973–83 44 per cent of total television programme imports into Western Europe were American. American programmes accounted for 10 per cent of total transmission time, some 38 per cent of drama and nearly half of cinema films shown on television in 1984. Between 1984 and 1985 the American film industry increased its income from European television and cable by 56 per cent. Behind this phenomenon was the dynamism of the American film industry. American feature films provided 32 per cent of total world film imports and took half of world receipts. In 1986 their share of cinema box-office returns ranged from 92 per cent in Britain to 43 per cent in France. By contrast, in Western Europe the share of domestic films in national cinema markets fell: in Britain from 41 per cent to 20 per cent (1975–80), in Italy from 60 per cent to 44 per cent (1970–81) and in West Germany from 39 per cent to 19 per cent (1970–81). Annual production of European films for the cinema had been in steady decline between 1973 and 1983: from 80 to 31 films in Britain, from 180 to 131 in France and from 250 to 110 in Italy.[30] Overall, the audiovisual sector already constituted one of the five largest American export industries, with a positive trade balance. It was the fourth largest contributor to American foreign trade receipts. With the explosion of media outlets in Western Europe international trade in this sector was scheduled for a new expansion and an intensified politicization.

The politicization of broadcasting markets

As in the telecommunications sector, broadcasting policy has acquired a new dimension of 'high politics' and 'economic statecraft'. Governments have used regulatory revisions to attract investment, jobs and tax revenue, typically by a promise of 'light-touch' regulation (e.g. the Cable and Broadcasting Act of 1984 in Britain); alternatively, they have sought to use the franchising process and programme and ownership regulations to restrict international media conglomerates. Thus Murdoch has been encouraged in Britain and frustrated in France and Spain. Behind this complex regulatory manoeuvring lurked a whole complex of economic, cultural and political calculations of advantage and disadvantage, as Chapter 6 vividly illustrates.

The early development of satellite communications in Western Europe represented a complex compound of economic and industrial policy with considerations of 'high politics'. For the French government in particular the argument was strongly based on a concern about 'economic sovereignty'. The Nora/Minc report of 1978 in France emphasized that satellite communications would have strategic importance for West European countries:

intended as the pivot of communications, the essential link in the development of network systems, and aimed at facilitating the increase in overlapping transmissions, satellites are at the heart of telematics. Eliminated from the satellite race, the European nations would lose an element of sovereignty with regard to NASA, which handles the launching, and with regard to the firms that specialize in managing them, especially IBM. By contrast, if they were capable of launching them, building them, and managing them, the same nations would be in a position of power.[31]

In other words, access to satellite technology was seen as a symbol of national sovereignty and a determinant of national power. Inexorably it was an increasingly important factor in intergovernmental relations, a subject for high politics.

To an even greater extent than telecommunications, broadcasting was politically and culturally sensitive. Politicians could not rid themselves of the view that control of broadcasting was not just a sensitive issue for the quality of a liberal democracy but also of great relevance to their own electoral prospects. If it was not necessarily a matter of ensuring that one's political friends controlled broadcasting, it was certainly a matter of making sure that one's enemies did not have such control. Franchising and regulatory decisions were heavily influenced by such political calculations, as the experience of Murdoch in Western Europe illustrates. Maxwell and Berlusconi were less threatening to the French Socialist government, whilst in West Germany Christian Democratic states used liberalization to offset 'red' public-service channels with the Springer-led SAT 1 channel.[32]

Secondly, concerns about European cultural identity and national 'cultural sovereignty' added further political heat to the debate about international broadcasting. Western Europe seemed badly placed for the impending battle for programme market share. For every twelve hours of American programmes shown on European television, less than one hour of European programmes was transmitted on American television (and then mainly on minority television services like Public Broadcasting System, The Entertainment Channel and the Hispanic services). Of West European television programme imports, only 16 per cent came from Britain, 7 per cent from France and 5 per cent from West Germany.[33] Western Europe's audiovisual presence in the United States was weak; that of the United States in Europe was strong. Within Europe Italy's early deregulation of broadcasting in the 1970s had indicated what could be expected. By 1982 Italy had become the world's largest importer of American television programmes and of Japanese cartoons. Of 390 series broadcast by West Germany's SAT 1 and RTL-Plus in early 1986, 339 were from the United States, 36 from Britain and 15 from Australia.[34] Western Europe seemed to be threatened by American cultural domination.

Against this background of internationalization and politicization, national broadcasting sectors became not just an arena of high politics but also enmeshed in a confusion of symbolism. On the one hand, broadcasting was witnessing an extension of ' liberty', with greater freedom of choice and more diversity of programming. On the other hand, 'standards' were threatened by cheap programming, relying increasingly on repeats; 'community' was undermined by 'audience fragmentation'; and 'identity' (whether national or European) was imperilled by American cultural forms, represented classically by Disney and Dallas. The outcome was perhaps predictable. Governments were occasionally drawn into assertive behaviour patterns, seeking to impose their will on often recalcitrant interests. More typically, however, broadcasting policy resorted to a new ambiguity and vagueness, characteristics that had a certain political virtue as they sought to reunify a fractious policy sector.

Telecommunications reform in Britain: a case study of deregulation

In the 1980s Britain has appeared as the 'flagship' deregulator of Western Europe, as a Trojan horse for the entry of American ideas and capital, and telecommunications reform has been one of the central planks of Thatcherite ideas for 'rolling back' the state and establishing an 'enterprise culture'. In particular, British Telecom (BT) was a showpiece for the privatization strategy of the government. In the context of Western Europe Britain was the first major radical reformer of telecommunications, putting her West European neighbours under a competitive pressure to emulate her. Accordingly, it provides a useful introductory case study of the theory and practice of liberalization.

Several institutional factors combined to make British telecommunications policy more vulnerable to radical reform. Cabinet government and the concept of sovereignty residing in Crown-in-Parliament endowed the political system with a capacity for action that is denied other West European systems with their more decentralized and coalition-based structures. Second, the British PTT did not enjoy the autonomy of action available to the French and West German PTTs. There was not, as in France and West Germany, a special PTT Ministry with a direct managerial self- interest to protect or able to act as an exclusive and dedicated champion of the sector.[35] In other words, the British telecommunications policy sector was less able to insulate itself from the impact of issues in other policy sectors. The Post Office had lost the benefits of its own sponsoring ministry in 1974 when responsibility for most of its affairs had been transferred to the Department of Industry. Also, it lacked its own budget and was therefore dependent on the budgetary policy of the Treasury. Relatively low levels of investment in the 1970s made the Post Office increasingly vulnerable to criticisms of its performance. Compared with the French PTT morale was low. Third, the telecommunications sector was characterized by a greater degree of internal tension and distrust than in France and West Germany. The three major manufacturers – GEC, Plessey and STC – were rivals to an extent that jeopardized their collaboration on the System-X digital switching exchange development.[36] The Post Office was the main victim of this situation and had lost confidence in the established domestic suppliers. Fourth, the major telecommunications users were unusually well organized in Britain. The Telecommunications Managers Association (TMA) was to play an important role in telecommunications reform, providing a single and clearly articulated view to government. Finally, the capacity of the trade unions to resist radical reform was diminished by conflicts of interest between two unions, the Union of Post Office Workers (UPOW) and the Post Office Engineering Union (POEU).[37] These institutional factors combined to make a defence of the status quo more difficult than in France (see Chapter 9) and West Germany (see Chapter 8).

Telecommunications liberalization was the subject of three major legislative acts – the 1981 Telecommunications Act, the 1984 Telecommunications Act and the 1984 Cable and Broadcasting Act. The 1981 Act had two main consequences: it split telecommunications from the postal services and created BT as a separate government-owned corporation; and it made the first inroads into its monopoly. Full competition was introduced into the terminals market, except that BT continued to control the apparatus licensing procedure and retained the right to install the first telephone. More importantly, the Secretary of State for Trade and Industry was given the new power, to be exercised in consultation with BT, to grant licenses to competitive networks and services. Under this power the Secretary of State granted a licence (in February 1982) to Mercury (later to become a wholly owned subsidiary of Cable and Wireless) to provide a basic switched network service, in competition with BT; licensed two national cellular radio networks, one of which was jointly owned by BT and Securicor; and, in October 1982, granted a general licence to VANs operators.

Two legislative acts of 1984 completed this process of liberalization and were notably important in creating new regulatory institutions. The 1984 Telecommunications Act brought BT's monopoly to an end and empowered the government to privatize BT (effected in November 1984).[38] Licensing powers for all telecommunications systems and services passed to the Secretary of State. A new statutory body, Oftel, was to advise the Secretary of State in the exercise of these powers and to police licence provisions, for instance with respect to the provision of 'basic conveyance' services by public telecommunications operators (like BT, Mercury and the national cellular radio networks), managed data networks (MDNs), VANS and private branch systems. The Secretary of State could also delegate licensing powers to Oftel. Finally, the terminal attachment market was completely liberalized, with the power to license attachments moved from BT to the British Approval Board for Telecommunications (BABT).[39] The Cable and Broadcasting Act aimed to create 'light-touch' regulatory conditions for the rapid development of interactive cable systems and services by exploiting the demand for entertainment television programmes, for instance sports, film and children's channels, as a means to attract private sector investment. Regulatory conditions were eased: for instance, a company could combine the functions of cable provider, operator and programmer, and cable operators were given wide discretion to offer the services that they wished, backed in the case of technologically advanced systems by 15-year licences. The Cable Authority was established as a new licensing and regulatory body, independent of both the broadcasting and the telecommunications establishments.[40]

This survey makes clear the radical character of British telecommunications reform in the 1980s. It also shows just how important institutional conditions are for the emergence of a reforming coalition and for the success of governmental policy strategy. The fact that policy reform was so centralized in Whitehall, involving an interaction of No. 10 Downing Street and the Department of Trade and Industry, created a 'window of opportunity' for such a strategy. In the case of the Cable and Broadcasting Act the decisive impetus came from a report, *Cable Systems*, in 1982 from the new Information Technology Advisory Panel (ITAP). ITAP had been established in the Cabinet Office to shortcircuit the traditional processes of Whitehall policy making and provided a channel through which new and assertive electronics companies were able to have a voice at the centre of government. The traditional guardian of public-service broadcasting, the Home Office, was essentially a defensive actor. Telecommunications policy reform was also a testament to the weak representation of the interests of manufacturing industry within the institutional structures of the British state. These weaknesses were further compounded by customer and public dissatisfaction with the performance of industry and made ideas of radical reform more acceptable. In particular, the Conservative government was convinced that inward investment was a major means of improving the efficiency of a British industry that was too wedded to traditional and costly practices. A further factor was the traditionally intimate links of the City of London to Whitehall with mounting concerns about the competitiveness of the British financial sector in new and fast-changing international markets. The development of new telecommunications systems and services and a relative reduction in international business tariffs seemed an essential requirement if one of Britain's most successful sectors was to continue to be successful. In the absence of powerful, cohesive and mutually supportive institutional structures the British telecommunications policy network was vulnerable to pressures from other policy networks that had these institutional characteristics.

At the same time government strategy did not face an institutional *tabula rasa*. Institutional factors qualified the scope and speed of reform and its application. In the case of the Cable and Broadcasting Act, for example, BT seized the new opportunities to seek out corporate alliances in cable operation and in cable and satellite programming, soon emerging as the major player. BT proved to be the one cash-rich company willing to commit itself extensively to this new and risky field, and this commitment was welcomed by the Cable Authority which also saw in BT's engagement a better guarantee that cable systems and services would be technologically advanced. The 1984 Telecommunications Act reveals that government strategy was not simple and coherent in the first place. The government's decision to maintain BT as a dominant and integrated telecommunications company was fundamental to the course of telecommunications reform. In fact the government invested great hopes in BT as a 'flagship' both of its privatization programme and of the British information technology sector internationally. The desire for a successful privatization of BT became the overriding aim of policy and constrained the scope for radical change. Quite simply, the government was concerned to sell shares in BT at the best possible price. Also, elements within the Department of Trade and Industry were able to promote the idea that the expertise and financial resources of BT were crucial motors for the development of the British information technology sector. Regulatory change sought to encourage rather than cripple such a role. Additionally, party and electoral considerations were influential. There were fears of a political reaction if the interests of domestic and small business subscribers in a universal basic telephony service were jeopardized by overhasty regulatory action. It was also felt to be necessary to give Mercury special protection. No further public telecommunications operators were to be licensed before 1990, simple resale was forbidden before 1989, and a very favourable interconnect agreement with BT was enforced. In short, the provision of basic switched services and the use of private circuits remained tightly controlled.

This complexity of governmental strategy meant that the operation of regulatory policy by Oftel and by the Cable Authority became a continuous balancing act. Policy was being made and remade within the regulatory process. Because of the problems of attracting sufficient private-sector investment in cable systems, the Cable Authority shifted increasingly to a promotive rather than a regulatory role. It became a champion of further relaxation of regulatory conditions. Regulation under the terms of the 1984 Telecommunications Act was made complicated by the presence of three aims in the legislation: the maintenance and improvement of the universal provision of basic voice telephony, for all consumers; improved equipment and services for industrial and commercial users by means of liberalization and competition; and a strengthening of the position of the British telecommunications industry in the world market. Both the passage of the legislation and later regulatory practice made it clear that, where these objectives were in conflict, priority was to be given to the requirements of universal service provision over competition. The government's concern for the aim of strengthening British industry in world markets was most evident when it overruled the advice of Oftel, and overlooked the reservations of the Monopolies and Merger Commission, by approving BT's acquisition of Mitel, the Canadian terminal equipment manufacturer – despite the threat that it would reinforce BT's dominance of the British terminal equipment market.

A central characteristic of British telecommunications policy in the 1980s was the *creation* of regulation, focused on new regulatory institutions, to replace direct government administration. For instance, the 1984 Telecommunications Act contained a new telecommunications code and provision for 'notice-and-comment' procedures by Oftel. In practice, however, this process of new institution building remained very incomplete. Only extremely limited provision was made for licensing hearings by Oftel, whilst franchising power was exercised even more secretively and unaccountably by the Cable Authority. Instead of a tightly defined regulatory system on the American model, policy remained subject – as we have seen – to a high degree of governmental discretion. A further characteristic is that liberalization was qualified by other aims of policy reform. In practice, BT emerged as a reinvigorated and dominant actor in the telecommunications sector, without a powerful regulatory body as an effective counterweight in the name of competition. The most vivid effect of liberalization was an explosive growth of private VANs, outpacing the rest of Western Europe. In the period 1981–6 over 700 VANs were licensed, a development that was welcomed by business users and by multinational companies in particular. The new range and quality of telecommunications services and the competitiveness of business tarrifs were judged to be major incentives for multinational companies to relocate their European operations in Britain. However, liberalization proved more of a threat than an opportunity for British equipment manufacturers, for instance in the terminals and cellular radio markets where American and Japanese companies were notably successful. Institutional factors did more than just shape the nature of the reform coalition in British telecommunications policy. They influenced also the nature of the development of the domestic telecommunications markets.

Conclusion

In this introduction several key trends in the development of communication policies in Western Europe have been emphasized: an assault on the legitimacy of 'public- service' principles and 'public-service' provision; the displacement of a cultural by an economic conception of communication; the internationalization and diversification of business operations; the speed of technological development and the undermining of a rationale for regulation based on the scarcity of frequencies; and the impact of ideological change and of political frustrations with the performance of public-service operators. Within public-service operators themselves there have been signs of a loss of faith in public-service principles; a new generation of managers, accountants and technocrats has emerged at the fore. Programming and service policies and financial strategies have increasingly moved towards a market model of provision.

Despite the force of these trends it is not at all clear that communication policies in Western Europe can be accounted for as the outcome of technological or market determinism. A more detailed study of the responses of international institutions and of national policy networks reveals a much more complex picture. Public-service providers continue to have major resources at their disposal, including large networks, an enviable and varied domestic programming capability and, not least, deep roots in national cultures. Values of national sovereignty and cultural identity are readily identified with them and constitute in themselves important resources that they can use (notably their support for the domestic programme production industry). Neither the impact of national institutional arrangements nor the impact of tradition on communication policies should be underestimated. Policy sectors have not been homogeneously internationalized. In this sense national institutional structures and cultures remain important, and public-service providers can have a key role in reasserting their importance and their own role in the maintenance of cultural identity. In effect, whilst considerable destabilization and alteration may have occurred within policy sectors, it is not at all clear that the dominant patterns of relations within these sectors have changed.

Notes

1 M. Snow, 'Telecommunications literature. A critical review of the economic, technological and public policy issues', *Telecommunications Policy* (June 1988), p. 153.

2 Ibid., p. 153.

3 'Telecommunications survey', *Financial Times*, 19 July 1989, p. 1.

4 W. Neu, K.-H. Neumann and T. Schnoering, 'Trade patterns, industry structure, and industrial policy in telecommunications', *17th Annual Conference of the International Institute of Communications*, 11–14 September 1986, p. 1.

5 For an account of this political 'hype' in Britain and France see P. Humphreys, 'Legitimating the communications revolution', in K. Dyson and P. Humphreys (eds), *The Politics of the Communications Revolution in Western Europe* (London: Frank Cass, 1986), pp. 165–74.

6 For examples see D. Bell, *The Coming of Post-industrial Society* (New York: Basic Books, 1973), A. Toffler, *The Third Wave* (New York: W. Morrow, 1980), T. Stonier, *The Wealth of Information* (London: Methuen, 1983), W.P. Dizard, *The Coming Information Age* (New York: Longman, 1982), and V. Mosco and J. Wasko (eds), *The Political Economy of Information* (Madison, WI: University of Wisconsin Press, 1987).

7 See M. Snow (ed.), *Marketplace for Telecommunications: Regulation and Deregulation in Industrialised Democracies* (New York: Longman, 1986).

8 J. Tunstall, *Communications Deregulation: The Unleashing of America's Communications Industry* (Oxford: Basil Blackwell, 1986).

9 For an example of the argument that deregulation by Britain ultimately benefits American interests see J. Hills, *Deregulating Telecoms: Competition and Control in the United States, Japan and Britain* (Oxford: Basil Blackwell, 1986).

10 The Yankee Group, *Report on European Telecommunications* (Rickmansworth: The Yankee Group, 1983), vol. 1, p. 16. For a general overview see OECD, *Trends of Change in Telecommunications* (Paris: OECD, 1987). Illustratively, according to the OECD, the price differential between Western Europe and the United States in the field of switching equipment was of the order of 60–100 per cent.

11 K. Morgan and D. Webber, 'Divergent paths: political strategies for telecommunications in Britain, France and West Germany', in Dyson and Humphreys (eds), op. cit., pp. 56–79.

12 W.H. Melody, 'Telecommunication: policy directions for the technology and information services', in R. Finnegan, G. Salaman and K. Thompson (eds), *Information Technology: Social Issues* (Sevenoaks: Hodder and Stoughton Educational, 1987), pp. 114–28.

13 K. Morgan and D. Webber, 'Divergent paths: political strategies for telecommunications in Britain, France and West Germany', in Dyson and Humphreys (eds), op. cit., pp. 56–79. Also P. Humphreys, 'The state and telecommunications modernization in Britain, France and West Germany', in

U. Hilpert (ed.), *The State and Techno-industrial Innovation* (London: Routledge, 1990).

14 K. Morgan, chapter 8 in A. Cawson, K. Morgan *et al.* (eds), *Hostile Brothers: Competition and Closure in the European Electronics Industry* (Oxford: Clarendon, 1989).

15 European Commission, *Towards a Dynamic Europe: Green Paper on the Development of the Common Market for Telecommunications Services and Equipment*, COM87/290 (Brussels: European Commission, 1987), pp. 161–5.

16 A. Marshall, 'International trade frictions; potent source of conflict', *Financial Times*, European Telecommunications Survey, 11 May 1989, p. IV.

17 K. Dyson and P. Humphreys with R. Negrine and J.-P. Simon, *Broadcasting and New Media Policies in Western Europe* (London: Routledge, 1988).

18 K. Schrape, 'Fernsehprogrammbedarf und Programmversorgung', *Media Perspektiven*, no. 6 (1987) pp. 345–53.

19 K. Schrape and M. Kessler, 'Film–Fernsehen–Video: Programmbedarf bis zum Jahr 2000', *Media Perspektiven*, no. 9 (1988), pp. 541–54.

20 J. Peasey, 'Der Markt fuer Fernsehprogramme in Westeuropa 1988 bis 1998', *Media Perspektiven*, no. 8 (1989), pp. 481–9.

21 J. Tydeman and E. Kelm, *New Media in Europe: Satellites, Cable and Videotex* (Maidenhead: McGraw-Hill, 1984), pp. 64–5. Also, European Advertising Tripartite, *The European Advertising and Media Forecast* (London: NTC Publications, 1985).

22 A. Lange and J.-L. Renaud, *The Future of the European Audiovisual Industry*, Media Monograph no. 10 (Manchester: European Institute of the Media, 1989), p. 148.

23 Ibid., pp. 172–4.

24 Tydeman and Kelm, op. cit., pp. 49–67.

25 Dyson *et al.*, op. cit., pp. 21–3.

26 Ibid., p. 18.

27 A. Mattelart and M. Mattelart, *International Image Markets* (London: Marion Boyars, 1984).

28 For the thesis that a 'paradigmatic change' is occurring in broadcasting policy see W. Hoffmann-Riem, 'Law, politics and the new media: trends in broadcasting regulation', in Dyson and Humphreys (eds), op. cit., pp. 125–46.

29 R. Negrine (ed.), *Satellite Broadcasting: the Politics and Implications of the New Media* (London: Routledge, 1988).

30 K. Dyson, 'Conclusions: patterns of regulatory change in Western Europe', in Dyson *et al.*, op. cit., pp. 319–20.

31 S. Nora and A. Minc, *The Computerization of Society* (Cambridge, MA: MIT Press, 1980), p. 76. Originally published as *Informatisation de la société* (Paris: Documentation Française, 1978).

32 K. Dyson and P. Humphreys, 'Regulatory change in Western Europe', in Dyson *et al.*, op. cit., pp. 92–160.

33 K. Dyson, 'Conclusions', in Dyson *et al.*, op. cit., p. 320.

34 Ibid., p. 321.

35 E. Grande, *Vom Monopol zum Wettbewerb? Die neokonservative Reform der Telekommunikation in Grossbritannien und der Bundesrepublik Deutschland* (Opladen: Deutscher Universitaets-Verlag, 1989), pp. 140–9.

36 K. Morgan, 'Breaching the monopoly. Telecommunications and the state in Britain', University of Sussex Working Paper Series on Government–Industry Relations No. 7, Brighton, 198.

37 J. Hills, *Information Technology and Industrial Policy* (London: Croom Helm, 1984), p. 114.

38 J. Moon, J. Richardson and P. Smart, 'The privatization of British Telecom: a case

study of the extended process of legislation', *European Journal of Political Research*, no. 14 (1986) pp. 339–55.

39 N. Garnham, 'Telecommunications policy in the United Kingdom', *Media, Culture and Society*, no. 7 (1985) pp. 7–29.

40 Dyson *et al.*, op. cit., pp. 223–304.

Chapter two

The role of the International Telecommunication Union: conflict, resolution and the industrialized countries

Jean-Luc Renaud

Introduction

During the 1940s and 1950s political scientists tended to describe world politics as a Hobbesian situation in which states are locked into patterns of fundamental conflict. The academic study of international relations was therefore characterized by the use of the state as the basic unit of analysis, and the dominant school of thought was the power or 'realist' school.[1] The role of emerging actors – the international organizations – was marginalized.

The conventional analysis was undermined by decolonization. The newly independent developing countries asserted themselves as active members of the international system. The realization that international institutions might become important nodes in networks of interdependence led to the formulation of new conceptual frameworks of analysis. International organization theories emerged as part of the broader field of international relations, but distinct from conventional organizational theories.

The tremendous range of international institutions which today taps the real world in so many of its facets may provide evidence that state actors are neither the only actors nor necessarily the most important actors to be considered in an analysis of the intertwined network of world transactions.[2] Transnational interactions not controlled by central foreign-policy organs of governments are no longer ignored. On the contrary, they are regarded as often of crucial importance in the world integration process.[3]

Since the 1960s, virtually all intergovernmental organizations have been the theatre of confrontation between the north – the industrialized countries – and the south – the developing countries, as the latter grew in number. The International Telecommunication Union (ITU) is no exception. Moreover, because of its unique and increasingly central domain of jurisdiction, this international organization has been in recent years the scene of confrontation among the industrialized countries at different stages of telecommunications deregulation or liberalization.

In order to survive, an international organization, like a living organism, has to adjust to a changing environment. One might have expected that the

ITU, established in 1865 by a group of twenty European countries interested solely in co-ordinating the technical operation of their telegraph and later their telephone and radiocommunications systems, would have survived neither the new geopolitical environment caused by the newly independent nations asserting their power within international forums nor the conflicting philosophies underlying the telecommunications regulatory regime in the industrialized countries. Such was not the case, however. Not only is the ITU today the oldest international organization but, with 166 member states, it has the largest membership, larger indeed than the United Nations itself. Moreover, the technologically advanced nations have felt the necessity to maintain the instrumentality of the ITU despite their contrasting approaches to telecommunications regulation. The longevity of the ITU is unique in the annals of international organizations.

This longevity should not be taken for granted. After all, no state is forced to join an organization whose mandate they disagree with, and states can always terminate their membership as well. Not every international body is universal in scope, and some nations have actually withdrawn from existing organizations.[4]

Surprisingly, the uniqueness of the ITU has not generated the attention one might have expected from students of international organization. Is the ITU a global actor in its own right or does it merely provide an arena for the political manoeuvring of national interest? How well has the international organization done in creating for itself some degree of autonomy from member states? Is national sovereignty eroded through ITU's task expansion? Has the ITU been able to take challenges and turn them into opportunities for organizational expansion? In this chapter we attempt to find answers to these questions through an examination of the way in which the industrialized countries work out new regulatory and standardization arrangements within the ITU as they enter the telecommunications deregulation era. Thus we assess the appropriateness of the conceptual framework offered by the dominant theory of integration – functionalism – in explaining the longevity and stability of the ITU in a changing world.

Conceptual framework – functionalism[5]

McCormick has defined three major roles that international organizations can play in the operation of international politics: as an instrument of national policy, as a systemic modifier of state behaviour and as an autonomous international actor.[6]

The first role has probably been the most widely used for analysing the linkage between international organizations and international politics. In this role, international organizations are seen primarily as means that states use to obtain their self-defined goals. In this context, organizations are another tool of statecraft – along with the traditional military, economic and diplomatic tools – which nations possess. These kinds of analyses stem largely from the 'realist' tradition in the study of international relations. Political realism – which portrays international politics as fundamentally a state-to-state phenomenon – implies a limited role for international institutions. These organizations are rarely used by states, but when they are used they are only used to achieve national goals.

While such efforts have been useful in understanding the interrelationships between states and the international organizations, they are not wholly sufficient for assessing the dynamics of global politics today. As smaller or 'weaker' states increasingly appear to influence (and control) the outcomes of international institutions, we must move beyond these previous analyses to examine the activities of those states within international organizations.

In this second role, international organizations are seen as serving an intermediary role between states and seeking to moderate their conflicts and facilitate their co-operation. While the states remain the predominant actors in the international system, they are not wholly independent of the influence of international organizations and international organization processes. Unlike in the earlier concept, the thrust of research within this second orientation seeks to ascertain the impact of the organization upon state behaviour rather than to assess the effect of the states upon the international organizations. Organizations may be able to evoke systemic moderation by providing incentives and opportunities for interstate politicking and by encouraging co-operative behaviour. This outcome will be obtained by altering perceptions and norms between states which, in turn, will produce policy restraints upon the states. Assuming that this description of the role of international organizations is valid, we need some specification of the kinds or organizations that are likely to be successful in producing these moderating influences in international politics.

The third perspective emphasizes the independence of international organizations in international politics, as actors beyond the nation-state system. How well have international organizations created for themselves some degree of autonomy from the nation-states and, more generally, how far has international integration progressed? A principal way of evaluating the autonomy of international organizations has been to focus on their internal operations. Specifically, the goal has been to determine the extent to which organizational development has occurred and to ascertain how far decision-making independence has progressed. We need a greater assessment of issue areas that have been the focus of organizational independence. That is, over what kinds of issues have these international organizations gained control? And what is the degree of this control? We also need to focus on the extent to which states have complied with international organization decisions.

That the ITU not only survived numerous regional and global conflicts but prospered seems to suggest that the organization has succeeded in creating for itself a large degree of autonomy from member nations, and that it might fit in McCormick's third conceptual category. The corollary is that the ITU has been able to engineer a high degree of integration of its member states into a global network of interdependence.

The analysis of the process of integration[7] has been pioneered by Mitrany in his formulation of the theory of functionalism, which became the dominant paradigm for examining the integrative function of international organization.[8] The functionalist approach emerged after the Second World War as a major alternative to the more widely held and persuasive approach of 'political realism'. In contrast with approaches based on 'realpolitik', which elevate the nation-state to the position of supreme international actor, and which view conditions of war and peace as dependent on the distribution and nature of military capability among nations, functionalism, in its initial formulation, specified a course of developments which would eventually spell doom for the nation-state. In its conceptualization of the process which would lead to the replacement of national interest politics, the functionalist approach essentially ignored considerations that state power and political influence had any analytical significance for what was to be explained.

The essential starting point, according to Mitrany, was to concentrate in the first instance upon the particular task, problem or function, and to attempt to exclude from this analysis the 'distorting' element of ideology, dogma or philosophical system. Mitrany was convinced that it was possible to discover a kind of irreducible set of 'relations between things' which were distinguishable from relations suggested by a constitution or a dogma and which, if left to themselves, would suggest the ideal geographical extent in which the problem could be tackled and the most appropriate administrative arrangements – hence the oft-quoted functionalist dictum that 'form follows function'.

Functionalism postulates that co-operation must begin in 'low politics' issue areas which can be 'decoupled' from the more symbolically and ideologically charged 'high politics' issue areas. Co-operation in low politics issue areas could be achieved by granting to administrative experts a mandate with sufficient authority to negotiate, formulate and implement new policies. It was assumed that such low politics problem-solving processes would lead to utilitarian advantages for more and more separate segments within the states involved. This, in turn, would create cross-cutting ties and decrease the ability of the political élites of the states to mobilize all their societal resources for the purpose of adopting power politics responses to demands for changes in the environment. According to the thesis that form follows function, the political structural transformation which would result from a classical functional approach would be the creation of a global-scope cobweb of functional ties based on a perceived superiority of utilitarian advantages which would undermine the centralized coercive power available to state authorities.

Functionalism implies that the values of specialists seeking to achieve their functional purposes efficiently are compatible with the values of the consumers of their specialized activities. By confining decision making to relevant technical considerations, non-rational behaviour, i.e. decision making that seeks personal, party or other sectional gains, is reduced if not eliminated. Political decision making at any systems level would then be confined to a limited field, i.e. the allocation of resources among functional institutions operating at the particular system level.[9]

The role of the state is no longer to protect and to defend certain interests once labelled 'national interests'. It is to assist in the process of adjustment to change that is an increasingly demanding one in the modern, complex and rapidly altering world society. It is argued that the growth of functional international organizations would erode the basis for identification with the nation-state by bringing together individuals from different nations into a more neutral international context.

The major tenet of functionalism, and the one most criticized, is the distinction between political and non-political areas. It states the possibility that the experience of integration in low politics areas could release a dynamics which made integration in other areas more likely, and eventually modified high politics itself.

The International Telecommunication Union

The principal instrumentality for maintaining world order in telecommunications has been and continues to be the ITU, a specialized agency of the United National headquartered in Geneva, Switzerland. The ITU is a direct descendant of the International Telegraph Union, which was established in 1865. Historian G.A. Codding contends that the present organization 'can be considered the oldest existing intergovernmental organization and the forerunner of many of the international organizations today.[10]

By the end of the 1850s, the impediments to public telegraphic correspondence across European frontiers approached intolerable proportions. Telegraph wires from two countries would come to a common boundary and stop. The situation was ripe for international action. In 1864 the French imperial government sent invitations to all the major European countries to attend a conference in Paris to negotiate a convention that would provide a uniform international telegraph system. The International Telegraph Union was born the following year.

At the Berlin Radio Conference of 1906, a separate organization, the International Radiotelegraph Union, was formed to deal with the telegraph's wireless counterpart. The two organizations merged in 1932 to form the International Telecommunication Union. The ITU is not only the oldest international organization, but its current membership of over 160 countries exceeds that of the United Nations.

Few changes occurred in the structure and functions of the ITU from 1932 until after the Second World War. The Atlantic City Conference of 1947 has been hailed for modernizing the ITU; it made three fundamental changes in the structure of the Union. First, it created an Administrative Council of eighteen members to meet annually to take charge of the administration of the Union between plenipotentiary conferences and to provide liaison with the newly created United Nations organization. Second, it was decided to internationalize the predominantly Swiss secretariat. Third, it created the International Frequency Registration Board (IFRB). Finally, the Atlantic City Conference for the first time in the history of the ITU attempted to describe the aims and purposes of the Union for inclusion in the basic treaty. They were as follows:

- to maintain and extend international co-operation for the improvement and rational use of telecommunications of all kind;
- to promote the development of technical facilities and their most efficient operation with a view to improving the efficiency of telecommunication services, increasing their usefulness and making them so far as possible generally available to the public; and
- to harmonize the actions of nations in the attainment of those common ends.[11]

Although a number of conferences and meetings were held in the interval between the Atlantic City Conference and the Geneva Plenipotentiary Conference of 1965, there were few demands for any substantive changes in the structure and function of the ITU. Politics did arise but dealt mainly with non-technical issues. One fact about the first hundred years of the ITU should also be noted. With one exception, all the major elected officers of the ITU were citizens of Western Europe or the United States. That one exception was Andrada of Argentina, who served as the Secretary-General from 1954 to 1958.

The ITU's International Consultative Committees

Wars are, for better or worse, productive periods for technological developments. The First World War witnessed the growth of telephony, among other telecommunication systems. In the post-war era, the European capitals foresaw the benefits of all kinds that would incur from a continent-wide network. The president of the British Institute of Electrical Engineers, Frank Gill, was the first to push for standardization of operations among European telecommunications administrations. A conference was convened in Paris in 1923. Its agenda, as detailed by Codding, was as follows:

- selection of desirable characteristics for long-distance international telephone lines;
- determination of operating and maintenance methods for long-distance international telephone lines;

- drawing up of a programme of work for establishing an international telephone network capable of meeting European needs;
- constitution of a central controlling organization for the development of European international telephony.[12]

It adopted the name International Consultative Committee (CCI) on Long-distance Telephone Communications, later abbreviated to the French acronym CCIF. The Paris Conference also decided on the creation of an International Telegraph Consultative Committee (CCIT). These two bodies merged in 1947 into the International Telegraph and Telephone Consultative Committee (CCITT).

There was a great deal of opposition to the creation of the International Radio Consultative Committee (CCIR), which was eventually established in 1927. The US delegate presented the argument that since radio technology was evolving so rapidly its progress might be held back if the Committee should establish standards that were too rigid. The French were afraid that private companies would obtain the approval of the Committee and use it for commercial gain. The British registered disapproval on the grounds that, since no changes could be made to the radio regulations between conferences, the Committee would be useless.

Where should the CCIs be situated in the institutional framework of the ITU? This issue was tackled at the 1947 Plenipotentiary Conference of Atlantic City. Codding notes that 'many delegates were worried that in bringing the committees into closer relationship to the ITU they should deprive them of the characteristics, including independence, that permitted them to work effectively'.[13] He quotes the Swiss delegate, for whom the successful record of the CCIF was attributable to this body's ability to work 'with complete independence and to adapt itself, according to the various cases, to the continually changing needs created by the inevitable evolution of engineering techniques'.[14]

The most comprehensive and detailed standards are promulgated by the CCITT at its Plenary Assembly every four years. However, the establishment of a consensus within one of the CCITT study groups that meet between plenary sessions is generally sufficient to achieve *de facto* worldwide adoption of a new altered standard. The areas of standardization are as follows: (1) telegraph and telematic services; (2) telephone transmission and maintenance; (3) telephone switching, signalling and operation; (4) tariff principles; and (5) standards for protection of line facilities.

An intergovernmental organization like the ITU is not really necessary for the adoption of international technical standards. Indeed, several important private international-standard-making bodies have existed for many years. Some of the more prominent include the International Standards Organization (ISO), the International Electrotechnical Commission (IEC), the International Federation of Information Processing (IFIP) and the International

Union of Radio Science (URSI). These organizations tend to serve the needs of manufacturers for rather detailed equipment standards and for data communications standards in areas where the ITU's jurisdiction has not been strongly asserted or where its standards-making process is too slow for rapid developments in the field. There is close co-ordination between all these organizations, however, including the ITU. Their representatives attend each other's meetings, their offices are often in close proximity to one another (for example, the ISO is located across the street from the ITU) and many of the participants in the meetings of these organizations are the same.

If, at the founding of the International Telegraph Union, the national systems had been owned and operated by private corporations, it is possible that a public international organization might never have emerged. However, from the beginning, nearly all national governments asserted almost total control over communication. When governments needed to co-ordinate their communication activities, public international organizations were created for that purpose.

Standards are found in all the ITU's legislative enactments including the Convention, the Administrative Regulations and the Consultative Committee Recommendations. Thus, all the ITU bodies engaged in fashioning these instruments can be considered as standard-making bodies, and the instrument in which the standard is found is superficially indicative of the force and effect of the provision. Those that are found in the Convention enjoy the greatest stature, and those in the Recommendations the lowest. Codding notes that:

> Standards are, in the abstract, both a help and an hindrance to the development of telecommunications. By obtaining common agreement on a standard, business and government can be induced to implement new facilities and systems. On the other hand, the adoption of such a standard is usually based on existing technological assumptions which may well change. The investment of large amounts of capital in equipment based on a standard represents a significant impediment to altering that standard. In the real world of competition among the providers of telecommunication equipment and services, the adoption of standards also represents a way of creating market opportunities.[15]

The Recommendations have substantial financial implications. Local communications systems are usually designed with local conditions in mind, and consequently there are many variations between them. Connecting them can require modifications in one or more of the systems. In cases of this nature, the CCI Recommendations will determine how the burdens of making modifications will be distributed. When new technology is involved, Recommendations specifying standards may mean giving legitimacy to certain patent holders and not to others. Recommendations can obviously involve millions of dollars. Influence varies with the issue being considered, but it is almost never distributed equally. For example, it would be extremely unlikely that a Recommendation concerning telephones would be formulated which did not take into careful account the interests of the United States, which has more than a third of the telephones in service in the world.

Because of both the non-binding character of Recommendations and the substantial financial stakes involved, great efforts are made in the CCIs to achieve consensus and unanimity. Although majority voting is the formal rule in plenary assemblies, it is almost never invoked. Plenary assemblies generally accept the conclusions of study groups with little or no modifications. Since the objective of participating in the activities of the CCIs is to make it possible to communicate with others, the unequal distribution of influence in study groups seldom results in states exercising veto powers. Rather it means that all participants will compromise, but some will compromise more than others.

The recognized private operating agencies

Unique amongst the intergovernmental organizations, the ITU allows for the membership of recognized private operating agencies (RPOA), namely private telecommunications equipment manufacturers and telecommunications service providers. These entities take an active part in much of the ITU's work related to their business, such as equipment and signalling standardization. Representatives from private firms are part of the national delegations and, in recent years, largely make up the pool of ITU experts sent to developing countries on technical assistance missions.

The problem of dual loyalties has surfaced. Is the ITU's interest likely to be given priority when delegates come from private firms whose main interests are in the selling of equipment? Although condemned by the ITU Convention, the use of the ITU by private firms to foster their interests might perhaps produce benefits for the developing countries as well.

The use of the technical consultants programme of the ITU by European countries has been cited as evidence of continued European domination of the Union.[16] Unlike the United States, which has generally displayed a lukewarm commitment to international organizations, historically the European countries have maintained strong relations with the ITU. Large manufacturing concerns in Europe such as Siemens, Thomson CSF, Ericsson and Cable and Wireless Ltd send consultants to the Third World through ITU programmes. These consultants suggest programmes to build or improve telecommunications facilities. They develop personal relationships with the telecommunications administrators in these countries and as a result the nations give the consultants' corporations the long-term contracts. In view of growing recognition by Third World authorities of the importance of telecommunications to their economic development, it is probable that in the future they will become even more attractive markets for the industrialized countries.

Fearful of losing ground within the ITU, the Soviet bloc countries, with their centralized economies, have consistently criticized their Western counterparts for using the Union as a marketplace, but they have not been able to halt this trend, as recent developments show. It may be assumed that, as US firms follow the path of their Western European and Japanese counterparts, the United States will strengthen its commitment to the ITU and be less likely to threaten to withdraw and seek alternative arrangements in the case of political conflict.

The ITU Convention, by making the provision for the participation of RPOAs, has introduced into decision-making mechanisms actors whose agendas are likely to be different from those of the governments of their host countries. These private concerns are guided by economic interests rather than political priorities. Moreover, they are transnational in character and they control global markets. The ITU is not perceived by them as an autonomous actor but as a stepping stone, a means to obtaining their self-defined goals. The US government's historically lukewarm attitude towards an international forum overwhelmingly dominated by PTTs has created unique problems for US companies seeking to use the ITU as a marketplace – as many of their nationalized competitors do so effectively. However, the US government defends the interests of US private companies forcefully *vis-à-vis* proponents of regulation at the ITU.

The CCITT and CCIR provide mechanisms for efficient technical interfaces with other country and technical standards which make both international communication and international commerce possible. They perform functions which American corporations need in order to participate in international markets. Many corporations pay dues to the CCITT and/or the CCIR so that they can send delegates directly to meetings in Geneva. Technical standards are established at these meetings, and American participation ensures that the standards incorporate a wide variety of products. The countries of the Conférence Européenne des Administrations des Postes et des Télécommunications (CEPT) and their PTTS wield extensive influence over the CCIR because they sustain a pan-European telecommunications policy. The monopolistic practices of the PTTs encourage them to endorse rigid standards. US companies, which want to enhance competition, press for wider standards so that they will have wider marketing possibilities. In practice, the US private sector must contribute to the CCIs in order to trade on the world markets.

Conflict and resolution amongst the industrialized countries: WATTC-88

Drake notes that the adaptation of institutions to rapid and unpredictable changes in their operational environments is perhaps the greatest challenge in communications policy today.

The three definitive features of the emerging global information economy – the globalisation, integration and commercialization of systems and services – clearly require the rethinking of traditional roles and approaches. Past mechanisms for imposing vertical organisation on markets, such as national borders, sectoral barriers and corporate boundaries, provide less and less guidance as to effective future strategies. But while the old ordering principles are giving way, an identifiably new architecture has yet to be erected.[17]

To cope with these fluid conditions, many firms are pursuing trans-sectoral strategies of cross-entry into formerly distinct industries and are establishing new modes of remote market presence. Similarly, many governments are shifting their telecommunications administrations away from the traditional monopoly mode of provision and towards more dynamic commercially oriented postures. Traditionally, the structure of the international telecommunications environment was formed by monopoly providers on each end of a circuit who negotiated operating agreements for the provision of services. Today, the rapidly changing sectors of telecommunications and telecommunications-based services are populated by a diverse set of players who have not historically been part of that process, yet are growing in number. These entrants want a role in framing the international arena in which they operate.

The issues of interconnection are complicated enough for pure telephony. In those countries where two or more providers of international public switched telephone services have been authorized, the agreements between monopoly service providers on both sides of a circuit must be modified to take account of the existence of multiple suppliers, the need for new traffic routing and interconnection configurations, and the potential for competition among suppliers with respect to the terms and conditions for dividing revenues. Thus, there must now be new arrangements for the new services.

In the value-added and information services sector, discussions that might lead to new international agreements or other understandings are even more complex. The models being adopted by the United States, the United Kingdom, Japan and other industrialized nations for liberalized service-based competition do not coincide. Devising interconnection arrangements amongst the value-added service providers in the light of these regulatory inconsistencies or disparities will be an exceptionally important task for officials over the next several years. All these changes – the emergence of new services, new players and new industry sectors – are therefore forcing policy-makers to take a hard look at the mechanisms by which international interconnection arrangements for such new services can be worked out.

The role and utility of the ITU in such a complicated environment, marked by the cross-currents of several industry sectors, is increasingly uncertain: many of the regulatory issues raised by new interconnection relationships or by hybrid service offerings do not fit neatly within the service categories of telephony and telex, which have been the traditional subjects of ITU overseeing and regulations.

It is not clear how the CCITT Recommendations on leased-line usage will apply to new value-added service providers. The uniform global regulatory regime is being transformed into one marked by a series of bilateral relationships. In this environment, the role of the ITU is being re-examined. Furthermore, the new value-added services are often as much banking, securities or commodities transactions as they are telecommunications. Fuelled by the internationalization and globalization of financial markets, institutional trading networks and electronic markets for securities, commodities and foreign exchange are developing around the world.[18]

To treat such information or transactional services as within the ambit of telecommunications regulations is perceived by service providers and users as mischaracterizing the offerings. Although buyers and sellers can be linked together, it would be inappropriate to describe the services as message-switching activities. It is inaccurate to categorize such services as value-added – they are not communications, but financial services. However such services might be classified by national regulators, it is clear that they often have important non-telecommunications components.

The ITU's expertise, however, is in the field of telecommunications. ITU decisions are reached by engineers and telecommunications officials from the members. The ITU does not have the institutional reservoir of experience in areas such as banking, securities and commodities trading that lie wholly outside the telecommunications sector. Yet it may be necessary to develop expertise in those fields to understand whether there is a need for regulation. Thus questions are being raised as to whether the ITU is the appropriate forum for addressing the propriety of treating new services as if they involve resale, message switching or some other telecommunications functions.

Nowhere have the problems of aggregating increasingly diverse national preferences and establishing a new policy equilibrium been more evident than in the preparatory process for, and proceedings of, the World Administrative Telegraph and Telephone Conference (WATTC-88), held in Melbourne, Australia, in November 1988. Delegates found it difficult to strike a consensual balance between the expansion of market access, on the one hand, and the preservation of legitimate sovereign rights and obligations on the other.

WATTC is an outgrowth of the 1982 Nairobi Plenipotentiary Conference of the ITU, at which it was proposed that the ITU's telephone and telegraph regulations applicable to carriers should be completely overhauled. Resolution 10 of the Plenipotentiary considered it advisable to establish, to the extent necessary, 'a broad international regulatory framework for all existing and foreseen new telecommunication services'.

At the heart of the controversy over the WATTC is the question of whether the regulations should be all-encompassing or minimalist in scope. Many countries believe that it is now appropriate to develop a unified set of regulations – to create a 'level playing field' – for all carriers, value-added service providers and intra-corporate users. By contrast, the United States and the United Kingdom and other countries in the process of liberalizing take the view that regulation should not be imposed if there is no perceived need for regulation.

Moreover, the WATTC Preparatory Committee (PrepComm) Draft sought to define, for the first time, what 'telecommunication' and 'telecommunication service' are. Although historically there has been an international consensus on telephony and telex services, there is none such for 'telecommunication'.

As Drake states:

> with all aspects of the communications and information policy debate, it can be difficult to judge the true intentions and strategies of the key players. US and UK analysts in business, government and academia frequently presume that the PTT's ultimate goals are to limit the incursion of foreign competition into their once absolute domains, and to expand their powers into new areas. In contrast, many other analysts believe that the forces of liberalisation have been too aggressive in pressing for rapid change; too quick to pass judgement on diverse national policies; and too insensitive to legitimate sovereign rights and social objectives.[19]

The majority of the European PTT administrations supported a comprehensive revision of the 1973 ITU Regulations, believing that the explicit codification of new forms and rules is essential. For them, the Regulations are out of step with current conditions on several counts: they fail to deal with the growing variety of new infrastructures and services; they fail to ensure fair competition on a level playing field by applying to market participants other than PTTs and RPOAs; and they fail to ensure that norms of non-discriminatory services and tariffication are adequately served with regard to unregulated providers and offerings.

Advocates of liberalization, the US and UK governments as well as important elements of the business community, were sceptical of these rationales. They were concerned that efforts to extend regulation and public standardization into new areas could slow the rate of technical change, and thereby stifle the development of dynamic new markets. Liberalization partisans claimed that only basic telephone and telegraph services, and not the new enhanced services, really required regulatory formalization. Telecommunications is now inextricably interwoven with other economic sectors, the broad industrial and trade policy consequences of which should not be decided purely by PTT engineers.

Essentially, the debate at the preparation meetings of the WATTC turned on whether to regulate specialized networks and enhanced services or to allow them to operate outside the purview of the ITU. The Draft was at philosophical odds with the European Community (EC) Green Paper on telecommunications. The Green Paper states that it is no longer proper for the PTT administrations to embody both regulatory and operational functions. It asserts that the provision of all services over and above basic voice telephony should be opened to competition and suggests a new framework of Open Network Provision. This is a long way from the position adopted by the majority of European PTTs at the PrepComm WATTC meetings. Indeed, it raises the question of whether the EEC Treaty or the WATTC regulations would hold legal precedence if differences were to arise. There remains a gulf between the deregulators, represented by the United Kingdom and The Netherlands, and those who support a more restrictive view, represented by France and Spain.

One of the major issues with which the WATTC PrepComm had to cope concerned the scope of the Regulations. In an age of blurring boundaries, what are the inner and outer limits of the term 'telecommunications'? The answer to that question was once self-evident; today it is far from being so. Domestic and international systems are increasingly integrated, while information and value-added communications services frequently involve both enhancement and transport functions. Reporting the conference proceedings, Drake recalls that:

> For the USA, the UK and their corporate supporters, a detailed list of services to be covered by the ITU Regulations, would be counterproductive. They argue that any list that might be drawn up would quickly become obsolescent, and could raise regulatory questions about the status of future offerings which would not be included. Moreover, given their sometimes less than muted distrust of PTT ambitions, they feared that the exercise could lead to a list incorporating such items as intra-corporate services based on leased lines. Finally, such a list might compel entities other than PTTs and RPOAs to provide non-preferred services to non-preferred customers.[20]

The US and UK delegations pushed for limiting the domain of the Regulations to 'services offered to the public' to ensure that the Regulations applied only to PTTs and RPOAs. The French and Japanese delegations thought that such a limitation would be too inflexible. They were concerned with preserving the principle of non-discriminatory universal access in an increasingly multi-network environment. But this legitimate interest may have also masked a less consensual calculation. As administrations shift to more commercially oriented postures, they find themselves competing with new entrants who are not weighed down by costly social and technical objectives. They wish to avoid a situation where the PTT service providers are bound by international standards of service while private service providers would be free to ignore them.

While the Americans and British managed, in the PrepComm Draft, to restrict the domain of the Regulations to 'services offered to the public', language was added that contradicts their intent. 'Public' was defined as including 'legal bodies within the whole or part of a Member's territory'. Many transnational firms, especially those based in the United States, vigorously attacked the Regulations, advising the US government to withhold their ratification or to enter reservations. Those key players have threatened to bypass the ITU Regulations altogether.

In some quarters, a conspiracy theory has been put about to explain it. The conspirators' real objective at WATTC, it is said, was to diminish or even destroy the power of the ITU in some of or all the areas in which it operates. If WATTC fails, it is argued, it would deal a mortal blow to the ITU and affect everything it does. The most important of these areas, arguably, is the development of technical recommendations by the CCITT. Putting it plainly, it might very well be in the commercial interests of some of the more powerful players if an effective state of anarchy existed in international telecommunications. The WATTC Conference, therefore, is not merely about regulations but about the future of the ITU itself. And whilst it might be in the interests of some corporations to disrupt proceedings, would it be in the interests of those who really matter – the users? Whilst the nature of the regulations themselves does not matter as much as it might appear, the existence of an effective body to develop technical recommendations does matter.[21]

Alternative market structures based on corporate alliances or *ad hoc* mutual access agreements could emerge. If so, the ITU jurisdiction could be displaced by that of the General Agreement on Tariffs and Trade (GATT) which is now entering the field of telecommunications policy via its concern with sectors dependent on facilities and services.

Fearing a deadlock, the ITU Secretary-General, Richard Butler, proposed a compromise Draft, which was hailed by all parties as salvaging the conference. The 'Butler Compromise' defined public services as services that members 'make generally available to the public'. It also made it clear that 'specialized services' are not covered by the regulations.

The WATCC's work was characterized by a greater responsiveness to user needs and attention to commercial market-oriented issues; the integrated services digital network (ISDN) figured prominently. Businesses were now demanding more control over their networks.

The ITU distinguishes itself from other intergovernmental organizations by allowing the participation of private companies and scientific organizations. The number of such entities involved in the ITU activities has grown enormously and now totals more than 460. Most of this growth is due to increasing CCITT activities. Private companies' participation in the work of the Union has increased over the years. A total of 160 telecommunications equipment manufacturers are now members of the CCITT.

The WATTC has to a large extent accommodated the trade aspirations of new market entrants. This was reflected in Article 9 of the Final Acts:

Special arrangements may be entered into telecommunications matter which do not concern members in general. Subject to national laws, members may allow administrations or other organizations or persons to enter into special mutual arrangements with members, administrations, or other organizations or persons that are so allowed in another country for the establishment, operation, and use of special telecommunications networks, systems, and services, in order to meet specialized international telecommunications needs within and/or between the territories of the members concerned, and including, as necessary, those financial, technical, or operational conditions observed. Any such special arrangement should avoid technical harm to the operation of the telecommunications facilities of third countries.

One of the most important outcomes of WATTC was Resolution 2 which set up a mechanism for accelerated approval of new standards recommendations. Under previous arrangements, a complete 4-year study period was required for new questions to be developed into firm recommendations. In the future, when the CCITT study group develops a recommendation to the point where it is ready for approval, the group will vote on whether to put the recommendation through the accelerated procedure. If there are no votes opposing such decision, the recommendation will be circulated to all CCITT members. If the recommendation is approved by 70 per cent of those who reply, it will be adopted.

In the WATTC outcomes, private network operators escaped strict regulation, and may be exempted from all coverage through special arrangement. Telecommunications administrations – though more constrained – will continue to authorize international services offered to the public. Furthermore, CCITT recommendations were not made legally binding, as some had feared. The Final Acts of WATTC were signed by 112 countries. No delegation with proper credentials refused to sign. The compromise text meant that every country had to concede some of its ultimate objectives, but Canada, France, Japan, the United Kingdom and the USSR, amongst others, considered this a necessary price for WATTC to succeed. The United States, however, was isolated and outmanoeuvred. It wanted to water down the clause on special arrangements and remove any reference to economic harm. No other country was willing to reject the package, which would have resulted in turmoil and no WATTC 1988 regulations.

The International Telecommunications Users Group (INTUG) welcomed the conference outcome as the regulations contained considerable freedom and flexibility within the boundaries of each nation's laws.

There was a consensus amongst observers that WATTC 88 represented a victory for operators and users of private networks, and for the ITU, bringing it successfully into the 1990s.[22] The WATTC regulations recognize that there are special networks, systems and applications which do not conform to conventional telecommunications networks. While recognizing the full sovereignty of states, special mutual arrangements can be extended for specific communications needs. It also gives legitimacy to claims by trade experts that telecommunications services are indeed traded and should be governed by a trade regime now being formulated by the GATT.

The CCITT director, Theodor Irmer, had called for an overhaul of the organization, fearing that it could be overtaken by more flexible and fleet-footed standards bodies such as the US T1 committees, the Japanese TTC committee and the recently inaugurated European Telecommunications Standards Institute. In view of the WATTC results, the search for an alternative forum is not likely to happen.Too much work has already been done, and it is probably too late to consider an alternative to the present organizations. The cost of shifting to other international bodies or establishing new technical forums is increasing as time goes by.

Whereas for most of its recent history the ITU has seen a confrontation between the industrialized countries and the developing nations, WATTC was probably the first instance where a major confrontation took place among technologically advanced members. Uniquely, agreement on the Draft document brought to Melbourne was based on a majority opinion rather than the CCITT's historic consensual approach. That the Final Acts of the conference, the 'Spirit of Melbourne', was signed by all participants is a testimony that the ITU had succeeded in reassessing its centrality in a changing telecommunications environment. But what are the reasons that compelled countries with contrasting regulatory regimes to compromise?

The ITU's domain of jurisdiction[23]

In his examination of international organizations, Goodspeed attributes cooperative efforts in technical fields such as telecommunications to their physical characteristic of 'transcending purely national frontiers'.[24] Beginning with telegraphy, and then telephony, radiocommunication and digital networks born out of the marriage of the computer and telecommunications technologies, the transmission of information is trans-border in character.

For several reasons, states could hardly have confined their communications within their own boundaries. A major reason is commerce. A nation that engages in trade and seeks to enjoy the benefits of specialization needs to be able to communicate across state borders. States also have political relations with one another which can be facilitated by communications. Even adversaries can find it helpful to communicate. When communications must cross borders, however, only international collaboration can assure that they will reach their destinations.

Even the simple telegraph requires substantial co-operation. An efficient system requires at least a measure of agreement on the standardization of equipment, operating procedures and, to a lesser extent, administrative procedures, including rates for services. More complex technology requires correspondingly more elaborate agreements. The obvious benefits to be gained from international collaboration have generally been compelling, and starting with the 1849 treaty between Austria and Prussia providing for the linking of their telegraph lines, international co-operative arrangements have closely followed technological developments.

In automatic telephony, international customer dialling has been made possible in spite of seemingly formidable obstacles presented by a multitude of national dial configurations and signalling systems. For many years there was no incentive for standardizing these aspects, since telephone calls across national borders required the intervention of operators. The through connection could be handled by patching two or more separate voice circuits together. With automation, electronic signals have to do the work of routing and switching. These signals either have to be compatible all the way through or have to be machine translated from one standard to another at gateways and switching points. Data transmission emerged rapidly during the late 1950s as a field requiring standardization to keep pace with the introduction of computers. The CCITT collaboration between national operating agencies has so far been successful as pressure for expanding international trade, requiring efficient telecommunication networks, was increasing. Most of this work was accomplished in the 1960–8 period.

The need for international co-operation became even more important when wireless communications came into use. Because electromagnetic waves carrying radio messages travel through the atmosphere rather than through wires or cables, radio transmissions are not restricted by the territorial considerations that first prompted international co-ordination of wire communications.

Furthermore, even a nation's domestic radio communications can have international ramifications. The physical properties of radio make it difficult to confine transmissions within political boundaries. If the right technical and atmospheric conditions exist, radio originating in one country can be received not just in neighbouring jurisdictions but across the world. Harmful interference can be averted or minimized only through careful co-ordination of the power, direction and timing of transmissions on the same or adjacent frequencies. It is well recognized that unless users of radio as a means of national as well as international communication co-ordinate their operations, transmission will be greatly diminished and, in some circumstances, totally destroyed.[25] As the head of the International Co-operation Office of the Swedish Telecommunications Administration put it:

It is of the utmost importance that standards, as well as radio-frequency allocations, be developed in time for the emerging new services, so that interworking between installations for basic services can be safeguarded, and efficient communication between facilities for different kinds of public and specialized services can be guaranteed. Standardization is also necessary from an economic point of view, in order to reduce the need for a great variety of different techniques or for complex conversion equipment. It is of great importance to telecommunication operators and customers in both the developed and the developing world.[26]

Radiocommunication utilizes a scarce resource, the electromagnetic spectrum, whose use calls for international co-ordination.[27] Because the commercial applications of radio are quite lucrative, existing users of radio in industrialized countries are consuming more spectrum space. At the same time, demand for frequencies from the developing countries has contributed to the crowding of the spectrum, because remote or isolated areas and people can be linked together more quickly and economically with radio communication than with transportation systems or wire communication systems.

The failure or inability of any nation to conform to complex international standards will deprive it of important benefits and may impede other nations from taking full advantage of the new technology as well.

As nations become more dependent upon telecommunications, they will be less able to ignore situations that render their services unusable. Similarly, as their level of financial commitment to telecommunications facilities and services increases, nations will be less willing to risk actions that would diminish the return on investment.

Clearly, the incentives for international co-operation before conflicts arise can only be expected to become stronger. Such co-operation is most likely to exist when it is in a nation's *self-interest*. If, for example, a member nation desires international recognition and protection of its frequency assignments, it must adhere to international standards. Catering to its members' self-interests is one of the ITU's greatest strengths that distinguishes it from other international organizations. As a nation's stake in advanced telecommunications systems increases, its willingness to prevent conflict will permeate other areas of interest to the ITU community such as accommodating developing countries' requests for assistance programmes.[28]

From time to time it has been suggested that the ITU needs to become more active in the conflict-resolution process, ostensibly because the higher stakes involved in contemporary telecommunications conflicts warrant it.[29] One way to evaluate the need for such change is to examine the history of conflict resolution in the ITU, with particular emphasis on arbitration, currently the strongest available measure for settlement of disputes between ITU members. In the past, the arbitration procedures have been largely ignored, with members preferring to resolve their disputes through bilateral negotiation.[30] Most important, the reluctance of nations to resort to binding forms of conflict resolution administered by an ITU organ in the past does not appear either to have diminished the organization's effectiveness or to have adversely affected world telecommunications order.

The desire for self-preservation, and the recognition that order in the world community is essential if vital resources are to benefit all humanity, have created pressures for co-operation and mutual problem solving. Equitable and efficient management of the environment and of national resources, and the orderly development of international telecommunications systems, are vital to the national interests of all parties. The context within which international decision making occurs is therefore characterized by world tensions at one level and pressures for self-preservation and collective agreement at another.

In the final analysis, the success of any international endeavour requires the voluntary co-operation of the sovereign nations involved. Realistically, such co-operation is most likely to exist when it is in a nation's self-interest. Voluntary compliance is most likely to be attained if the organization has a worldwide domain of jurisdiction rather than the loosely defined 'international'. The ITU survives because the co-ordination of telecommunications services can only be worldwide. This situation has compelled the industrialized countries, relying heavily on communications systems, to accommodate each other's regulatory framework in an effort to maintain the resource-allocation capability of the ITU.

The ITU and functionalism

Conventional functionalist theory stressed that agencies should meet the criteria of being *technical*, *functionally specific* and *essential*.[31] An agency is technical when there is a body of sophisticated professional or scientific knowledge that is necessary to the conduct of its work. It is functionally specific when its work relates to one specialized area of public policy and it is essential when states can best organize the performance of certain tasks internationally. According to this theory, organizations with such characteristics should not be much affected by world political cleavage. The ITU, with its task of securing international agreements on the use of radio frequencies and standards for equipment, is such an organization. Indeed, the ITU's institutional structure has been affected less than others by world political cleavages. Concurring with Jacobson's own investigation,[32] the factor emerging from the present study – the ITU's domain of jurisdiction – which accounts for the centrality of the ITU partially confirms the functionalist paradigm.

The ITU was originally designed as a technical and universal organization rather than a political organization with a restricted membership. There was a strong initial notion within the ITU that technical decisions can and should be taken on technical grounds and that it will be possible for experts to agree on technical issues.

In reality, of course, the distinction between technical and non-technical issues is often far from obvious. This ambiguity is reflected in the dissatisfaction surfacing in the industrialized nations during the 1960s when the developing countries started to take the ITU to task to involve itself in technical assistance.

Much of the rationale underlying the functionalist approach is implicitly grounded in a social-psychological framework of national and international attitudes and image formation. It is argued that the integrative process engineered by international organizations is attributable to the erosion of the basis for identification with the nation-state by bringing together individuals from different nations into a more neutral international context.[33]

Functionalism assumes that people 'learn' to think in non-national terms because of a pattern of technical co-operation. At first, it is only the experts and managers who learn. They become habituated to consulting with their opposite numbers from other nations about technical problems, and eventually they come to see all problems from the perspective of humanity as a whole. Thus, the answer to maximizing the learning process lies in extending the range of participation in practical problem-solving. In the end, others besides experts, managers, and civil servants will participate in and undergo the same process, particularly by way of greatly increased work and responsibility on the part of international voluntary groups.[34]

The increasing significance of the ITU as an integrative agent in worldwide telecommunications, however, is not primarily the result of a functionalist learning process. The key factor accounting for the ITU's centrality – the domain of jurisdiction – calls for a redefinition and considerable strengthening of the concept of *essentiality*, much beyond the conventional functionalist understanding of it, if one wishes to make sense of the dynamics at work in the ITU.

The re-prioritized concept of essentiality integrates the notion of inevitability. All nations are *compelled* to work telecommunications arrangements through the ITU whether or not they 'learn' to collaborate with each other. The very nature of telecommunications makes it imperative for countries to join the ITU if they want to protect their national interests. The strength of the ITU is to cater to the self-interest of its members. In that, the ITU is unique among the other international institutions. The promotion of 'internationalism' is not the main engine to problem solving. The consensus arrived at during the WATTC-88 Conference has more to do with disaster-prevention strategies – the maintenance of the institutional status quo critical to heavy telecommunications operators – than being the result of a convergence of views.

The explanatory power of the functionalist approach is limited, as Wolf notes, by its lack of consideration of the following provisions:

International organizations vary in the degree to which their major activities are politically controversial and do not necessarily emerge 'naturally' from a consensus among members on the definition of a mutual problem.

The contexts and constituencies of international organizations vary in the amount of control which they exercise over the definition of a problem for the organization or over its activities.

International organizations vary in the extent to which their membership is composed of different types of groups having different, perhaps opposing, sets of interests.

International organizations vary by type of sociological structure, ranging in differentiation from low to high number of functional units, and in authority from hierarchical or participatory and horizontal.[35]

The ITU as a communications network

One can view the ITU according to how far it involves the effective policy-making processes of governments rather than how independent of states it has become. This view leads towards a fuller understanding of the role of international organizations in international relations, though their role does not appear to conform to the ultimate goal of functionalism.

In this perspective, international organizations are sensitive communications networks within which the power holders in world affairs have been responsive to signals from the less powerful without abandoning the control of action to them.[36] International organizations facilitate the orderly management of intergovernmental relations without significantly changing the structure of power that governs these relations, at least in the short term and somewhat beyond. Over their longer history, the greatest potential for change from international organizations may lie in the opportunity that they give the less powerful to influence the climate of opinion and the accepted values according to which action is determined.[37]

Claude's thesis is that the function of collective legitimization is one of the most significant elements in the pattern of political activity that the United Nations has evolved in response to the set of limitations and possibilities posed by the political realities of our time. Collective legitimization has been thrust upon the organization by member states. It is an answer, not to the question of what the United Nations can *do*, but to the question of how it can be *used*.

Referring to the ITU, collective legitimization suggests that it is an agency capable of bestowing politically weighty approval and disapproval upon projects and policies. One may question whether proclamations of approval or disapproval by the Union, deficient as they typically are in both formal legal significance and effective supportive power, are really important. The answer is that statesmen, by so obviously attaching importance to them, have made them important. They take collective legitimacy seriously as a factor in international politics.

Conclusion

The strength of the integration literature rests on its attempt to analyse the politics of interdependence. Its chief weaknesses derive from the strong teleological orientation. Realists in the tradition of Morgenthau have portrayed a world in which states, acting from self-interest, struggle for 'power and peace'. In such a world, the mind may safely come to rest with the proposition that the role of international institutions is a minor one limited by the rare congruence of such interests.

However, in a world of complex issues imperfectly linked, in which coalitions are formed transnationally and transgovernmentally, the potential role of international institutions is greatly increased. The role of the ITU as the central node in the global telecommunications network is a case in point. In particular, international secretariats staffed with knowledgeable individuals may have the opportunity to place themselves at the centre of crucial communications networks, and therefore to be influential as negotiators and brokers, without having significant tangible sources of power.

The interest in integration theories reflects both the persistence and the transformation of the kind of idealism that originally pervaded, guided and, at times, distorted the study of international organizations. We have come to understand that the integration of nation-states in a world system, whatever the modalities of this process, may be the most important function performed by global international organizations. Of all the international organizations, the ITU, because of its unique characteristic – its domain of jurisdiction – best exemplifies this process.

Notes

1 H.J. Morgenthau, *Politics Among Nations* (New York: Knopf, 1960).
2 There are today 300 international governmental organizations (IGOs), 3,000 international non-governmental organizations (INGOs) and a similar number of business international non-governmental organisations (BINGOs).
3 R.O. Keohane and J.S. Nye, 'International interdependence and integration', in F.I. Greenstein and N.W. Polski (eds), *International Politics, Handbook of Political Science 8*, 1978, p. 366.
4 The United States had temporarily withdrawn from the International Labour Organization (ILO) in the mid-1970s, and this country and Great Britain pulled out from the United Nations Educational, Scientific and Cultural Organization (UNESCO) in 1985.
5 For a treatment of the functioning of the ITU in the context of integration theories, see J.-L. Renaud, 'International organization and integration theories: the case of the International Telecommunication Union', *International and Intercultural Communication Annual*, vol. 14, Communicating for Peace: Diplomacy and Negotiation Across Cultures (Beverly Hills, CA: Sage, 1989).
6 J.M. McCormick, 'Alternate approaches to evaluating international organizations: some research directions', *Polity*, 14 (1982), pp. 533–5.
7 Considerable confusion continues to persist among scholars about the use of the

term 'integration'. Some scholars define it as a process, others as a terminal condition – the 'condition of being integrated' – and still others as a combination of the two. In practice, scholars often use the word interchangeably. Deutsch defines integration in terms of turning 'previously separate units into components of a coherent system'. Elsewhere, however, he stresses the condition of a secure community (K. Deutsch, *The Analysis of International Relations* (Englewood Cliffs, NJ: Prentice-Hall, 1971), p. 58). For Haas, integration is 'a process for the creation of political communities defined in institutional or attitudinal terms' (E. Haas, *Beyond the Nation-State: Functionalism and International Organization* (Stanford, CA: Stanford University Press, 1964), p. 29). Galtung defines integration as 'a process whereby two or more actors form a new actor' (J. Galtung, 'A structural theory of integration', *Journal of Peace Research*, 4 (1968), p. 39).

8 See D. Mitrany, *A Working Peace System* (Chicago, IL: Quadrangle Books, 1966); *The Functional Theory of Politics* (London: Martin Robertson, 1975).

9 J.W. Burton, 'Functionalism and the resolution of conflict', in A.J.R. Groom and P. Taylor (eds), *Functionalism: Theory and Practice in International Relations* (London: University of London Press, 1975), p. 243.

10 G.A. Codding, *The International Telecommunication Union: An Experiment in International Cooperation* (Leiden: E.J. Brill, 1952), p. 39.

11 International Telecommunication Convention, Atlantic City, 1947, Art. 3.

12 G.A. Codding and A.M. Rutkowski, *The International Telecommunication Union in a Changing World* (Dedham, MA: Artech House, 1982), p. 84.

13 Ibid., p. 88.

14 Ibid., p. 84.

15 Ibid., p. 226.

16 L. Milk and A. Weinstein, 'United States participation in the International Telecommunication Union: a study of policy alternatives', Report prepared for the US Department of State, 1984, p. 33.

17 W.J. Drake, 'WATTC-88: restructuring the International Telecommunication Regulations', *Telecommunications Policy*, 12(3) (September 1988), p. 217.

18 R.B. Bruce, J.P. Cunard and M.D. Director, *The Telecom Mosaic: Assembling the New International Structure* (London: International Institute of Communications, 1988), pp. 171–5.

19 See Drake, op. cit., p. 219.

20 Ibid., p. 221.

21 See G. Finnie, *Telecommunications* (November 1988).

22 R. Pipe, *Telecommunications* (January 1989).

23 For a further treatment of this aspect, see J.-L. Renaud, 'The ITU as agent of change', *InterMedia*, 14(4) (July–September 1986), pp. 20–5.

24 S. Goodspeed, *The Nature and Function of International Organization* (New York: Oxford University Press, 1959).

25 S. Chen, 'The theory and practice of international organization', in Goodspeed, op. cit., p. 147.

26 R. Naslund, 'ITU Conference in Nairobi: confrontation or mutual understanding?', *Telecommunications Policy* (June 1983), p. 108.

27 B. Segal, 'ITU Plenipotentiary Conference and beyond', *Telecommunications Policy*, 4 (1983), pp. 326–34.

28 D.C. Gregg, 'Capitalizing on national self-interest: the management of international telecommunication conflict by the ITU', *Law and Contemporary Problems, International Telecommunications*, 45(1) (1982), pp. 38–52.

29 D. Leive, *International Telecommunications and International Law: The Regulation of the Radio Spectrum* (Leiden: A.W. Sijthoff, 1970), pp. 313–15.

30 Of the few cases in which resort to arbitration was attempted, none involved harmful interference. The one significant reported arbitration case under the ITU procedures involved a 1935 dispute over suspension of telegraph services. See discussion of the 'Affaire de la Sociéte Radio-Orient (France v. Egypt)', Codding, op. cit., pp. 309–11.
31 Haas, op. cit.; I.L. Claude, *Swords Into Plowshares: The Problem and Progress of International Organizations*, 3rd edn (New York: Random House, 1964).
32 H.K. Jacobson, 'ITU: a potpourri of bureaucrats and industrialists', in R.W. Cox and H.K. Jacobson (eds), *The Anatomy of Influence: Decision-Making in International Organization* (London: Yale University Press, 1974).
33 P. Wolf, 'International organization and attitude change: a re-examination of the functionalist approach', *International Organization*, 27(3) (1973), pp. 368–9.
34 Haas, op. cit., p. 13.
35 Wolf, op. cit., pp. 368–9.
36 For an analysis of the ITU's responsiveness to its Third World constituency, see J.-L. Renaud, 'The ITU and development assistance: north, south, and the CCIs', *Telecommunications Policy* (June 1987), pp. 179–92.
37 I. Claude, 'Collective legitimization as a political function of the United Nations', *International Organization*, 20(3) (1966), pp. 367–79.

Chapter three

Intelsat and the debate about satellite competition

Megumi Komiya

Embodying the belief that the 'best governed are the least governed', the policy of deregulation pursued by the Reagan Administration profoundly reshaped the US telecommunications scene in the 1980s. Competitive market forces were seen by the Reagan Administration as the best guarantor of economic health. This policy represented a change of direction *vis-à-vis* the International Telecommunications Satellite Organization (Intelsat), of which the United States is a powerful member. Intelsat was exposed to the heat of this revisionist policy, raising fundamental questions about the continuing nature and role of this international organization.

Established in 1964, in the wake of the Communication Satellite Act passed by the US Congress two years earlier, Intelsat developed as an international non-profit consortium, owned and operated by 114 member countries (the 1987 figure). It was based on the principle of 'universal service'.[1] Hence its charter committed the signatories not to allow the establishment of competing international satellite systems that would do 'significant economic harm' to the organization's long-term investments and cross-subsidization policy.[2] By authorizing the launch of five private satellite systems in 1985 – a move opposed by all Intelsat signatories – the US Federal Communications Commission (FCC) was attempting to reverse a twenty-five-year history of adherence to the single global satellite system.[3]

The proponents of competition in international satellite communication contend that Intelsat is a monopoly. Their argument is based on a conventional microeconomic theory which states that traditional profit-making monopolies, by restricting output within the range where price exceeds marginal costs, charge the highest possible price in order to maximise profit. Because of the resulting resource misallocation, consumers do not realize the full potential advantages of economies of scale. This theory holds that only competition provides customers with the most efficient and lowest-cost services.

This reasoning is correct only if Intelsat's behaviour conforms to that of a private profit-making monopoly. In fact Intelsat is a member-owned nonprofit consortium. This structural feature seems to suggest that Intelsat is an international co-operative, not a monopoly. By reviewing some literature on co-operatives and borrowing elements of economic theory that discuss the uses and abuses of monopoly power, in this chapter we examine whether Intelsat's behaviour conforms to that of a private profit-making monopoly or a co-operative. The examination follows an overview of the organization and its development. It will be carried out first by presenting the principles of co-operative activity and then by discussing the concepts related to monopoly such as predatory practices, interservice subsidy, excess capacity and reaction to threat of competition. In this way it will be possible to clarify the nature of Intelsat as an international organisation and its future role.

Structure and Organization of Intelsat

The first Soviet Sputnik satellite was launched in October 1957 at a time of heightened East–West tension. As a result, the subsequent development of space technology became associated with matters of high political significance, with the United States and the Soviet Union competing for prestige and power.[4] To counter the gains made by the Soviet Union in the post-Sputnik era, the US Congress passed the Communications Satellite Act in 1962. A new private corporation – Comsat – was created, half owned by the established telecommunication carriers (they disposed of their shares a decade later) and half by the general public. Comsat was mandated by the 1962 Act to 'plan, initiate, construct, own, manage and operate itself, or in conjunction with foreign governments or business entities, a commercial communication satellite system'.

The US government and Comsat officials entered into negotiation with telecommunications bodies in Western Europe, Canada, Australia and Japan, this group accounting for 85 per cent of all international telecommunications traffic at that time. These negotiations began on a bilateral basis but, on the insistence of the West European countries, they changed to multilateral agreements.[5]

Non-US members aimed at participation in the management of the global satellite system in order to prevent what they feared would be total US control. Moreover, they wanted to benefit from the know-how and technology that direct participation would entail, the transfer of which they considered vital to the development of a domestic high technology industrial sector and essential for the creation of employment. The United States had expertise in satellite technology and rocket launching. It naturally wanted to capitalize on its leadership position and establish a system which it could control. Therefore, although the United States was willing to let other countries use the satellite system, it wanted neither shared management nor transfer of new technologies.

Although Intelsat was formally established in 1964, operational details were finalized later, after long and complex negotiations. The Permanent

Agreement was eventually ratified by eighty-three countries in 1971. Membership in the organization would be limited to entities willing to invest capital in the system. In other words, the financial burden would be shared by participating members based on their use of the system (subject to a minimum of 0.05 per cent). The charges collected are invested in the following sectors: (1) operating expenses; (2) repayment of signatories' capital (equivalent to asset depreciation); and (3) 14 per cent compensation for use of signatories' capital.[6]

At the inception of Intelsat, criteria were set so that Comsat, the United States signatory, owned approximately 61 per cent of the shares and the counterparts in Western Europe 30 per cent.[7] As other countries joined the ranks of Intelsat signatories, the control exercised by the United States and

Table 3.1 Intelsat's ten largest investment shareholders

Comsat (US)	25.64%	Australian PTT	3.15%
British Telecom	13.93%	Teleglobe (Canada)	2.68%
French PTT	4.50%	Telespazio (Italy)	2.30%
KDD (Japan)	4.41%	Saudi Arabian PTT	2.29%
German PTT	3.93%	Telefonica Nacional (Spain)	1.95%

Source: *Intelsat Annual Report*, 1986.
Note: These investment shares are annually adjusted on 1 March in proportion to each member's facility usage.

the West European countries diminished (see Table 3.1).

It should be noted that more than sixty non-member countries are currently using Intelsat's services and pay the same charges as member countries. However, they have no voice either in the Meeting of Signatories or on the Board of Governors. The latter is open to signatories which own a substantial percentage of the organization's investment shares. The Board generally takes decisions unanimously. When that is not possible, votes are weighted on the basis of investment shares.[8]

There is a requirement that utilization charges for all users are to be the same for each type of service (e.g. voice, data, video). This requirement means that Intelsat must globally average its charges for each type of service for all users in the Atlantic, Pacific and Indian Ocean regions. It must also average charges within these regions, which include small, medium and large traffic streams.[9]

Another part of the Permanent Agreement relates to the procedures associated with the introduction of non-Intelsat systems. Until the recent US private satellite applications, only domestic or regional non-Intelsat systems were allowed to operate.[10]

The ensuing debate has been concerned with the space segment of the overall Intelsat system, which is composed of sixteen geostationary telecommunication satellites, jointly owned and operated by the organization's members.[11] The earth segment includes all the uplink/downlink antennae systems (to date, more than 500 antennae located in 170 nations or territories), which are individually owned and operated by the respective national telecommunications entities.

Intelsat as a co-operative

The view has been advanced that, in terms of its structure, operation and financing, Intelsat is a co-operative, and not a monopoly as is claimed by advocates of deregulation.[12] The theoretical literature on co-operatives is scarce. Co-operatives are divided into two main categories: production co-operatives (i.e. worker-managed firms) and consumer co-operatives (i.e. buyer-managed firms). Pryor suggests a broad definition of a production co-operative:

> an organization in which productive activities are jointly carried out by the members; where the important managerial decisions reflect the desire of the members as expressed by the workers in their participation in making some of these decisions; and where the net income is divided among the members according to some formula.[13]

A consumer co-operative is

> managed by elected representatives of at least some of its customers, the latter constituting its membership. These representatives form a consumers' council that must at least ratify all basic production and pricing decisions.[14]

Intelsat is unique in that it is both a production and a consumer co-operative. As Hinchman puts it: 'Members are joint owners and users of common resources (i.e. satellite capacity)'[15] Consequently, the relevant economic indicators of Intelsat operations are neither revenues nor profits in the way that these terms are used in the case of regular profit-making activities, but rather *costs*. The organization's most relevant costs are annual costs per unit of capacity owned or used.[16] In this respect, Intelsat cannot be assimilated to a profit-maximizing monopoly or cartel.

Theories of voluntary exchange treat the budget-making process as a collective decision-making process such as takes place in a voluntary co-operative arrangement.[17] It is a political process of collective choice within which the amount of public expenditure (i.e. in the case of Intelsat, the overall investment in satellite hardware) and the distribution of the tax burden (i.e. the cost responsibilities of individual Intelsat members) are determined by *voluntary agreement* among the consumers and not through the market. Those delegated to determine policy have the task of determining the value which the consumer sets on goods and, on that basis, determining the price of those goods. When the estimated values and the prices of goods are not the same, equilibrium is restored by a reaction of a political nature.[18]

In this respect, the process of distribution of the tax burden in the Intelsat organization – the cost responsibilities of members – imposes little constraint on individual members. Whereas in other types of arrangements such as agricultural or condominium co-operatives, cost responsibilities are fixed according to the initial shares of ownership, the cost responsibilities of Intelsat members change periodically depending on their annual usage of satellite facilities.[19]

Intelsat's behaviour, examined in the light of these theoretical considerations, supports the contention that it is not a cartel. In economics, the term 'cartel' is used to refer to 'the organization and structure adopted by the firms in an oligopolistic industry in an attempt to effect a collusive (monopolistic) set of price–output decisions'.[20] In practical terms, the strength and associated harmful consequences of cartel arrangements are essentially to decrease and, at worst, eliminate the negotiating power of its clients through monopolization of the production and/or distribution of particular goods or services. This process finds its concrete expression in practices such as market allocation, price fixing, planning co-ordination and information sharing, among other collusive strategies. Two examples which illustrate best the predatory practices of cartels will be contrasted with Intelsat's behaviour.

The activities of the Hollywood majors under the umbrella of the Motion Picture Export Association (MPEA) – the international arm of the Motion Picture Association of America – is one example of a cartel. The MPEA was registered under the Webb–Pomerene Export Trade Act of 1918 which exempted the overseas operations of US firms from the provisions of the Sherman and Clayton antitrust acts regulating their domestic activities. Foreign customers, in need of film material mostly available in America, could do nothing but accept the conditions imposed on them by the US companies.[21] The news agencies cartel of the late nineteenth century is the other example. Under an 1871 agreement, Reuters, Havas and Wolff – the major international wire services at the time – allocated among themselves large areas of the world, *de facto* excluding the fledgling Associated Press (AP). As a result, AP's domestic news could only be distributed abroad by foreign news agencies, and international news distributed by the AP to its US clients could only be gathered by foreign agencies. AP seceded in 1934.[22]

In the case of Intelsat, no signatory is able to establish either a one-way or a two-way international link without the active concurrence and participation of another signatory to which such communication is desired. Therefore no single entity can dictate its regulatory framework to others. As Intelsat's former Director-General noted:

Intelsat is not a monopoly, or cartel or multinational corporation. Unlike a monopoly, Intelsat does not provide its services so as to yield the most profitable revenues, imposing its system, conditions and tariffs upon others . . . it is a public intergovernmental organization which is, in effect, a cooperative venture open to all nations and not controlled by any single member. Since all primary users of the system are its member-owners, there is no incentive for exploitation. As in a cooperative, Intelsat's services are sold at cost, and decisions regarding the system are made by all members, each with a vote proportionate to its use of the system.[23]

In effect, this arrangement means that members benefit when higher proportions of available facilities are used. The annual usage rate of Intelsat satellite facilities has increased from 35 per cent in 1984 to 57 per cent in 1986, thus reducing the costs to each member.[24]

Under a cartel, firms will produce less goods/services in order to charge higher prices than their counterparts in a competitive industry, so that greater profits can be obtained by the industry as a whole. As a result, cartels create a product scarcity. A cursory examination of its operations, however, reveals that Intelsat has built up its satellite capacity since its inception, and the annual average usage rate for the 12 years up to 1984 was around 35 per cent of available facilities.[25] In other words, there has been a large excess capacity in Intelsat operation, in contrast with the restriction of output that would characterize a cartel.

Also, there is often a tendency for some firms organized in a cartel to deviate from the established price rules which do not necessarily guarantee that a particular firm, as opposed to the industry as a whole, maximizes profits.[26] Therefore, any cartels that do not have measures to discipline member firms will be highly unstable and tend not to last long. Despite the fact that Intelsat's charter does not have any disciplinary provisions, the organization has operated more than 20 years as a co-operative.

Deregulating satellite communication

In November 1984 President Reagan gave approval to the use of private satellites for international communications; seven months later, five companies – Orion Satellite Corporation, International Satellite Inc., RCA American Communications Inc., Pan American Satellite Corporation and Cygnus Satellite Corporation – filed applications to the FCC.

In their submissions seeking permission to introduce new transatlantic satellite services, the applicants were primarily determined to meet 'public interest' criteria set by the FCC.[27] The documents were referred to the Senior Interagency Group (SIG) – consisting of representatives of the numerous agencies with an interest in international communications – since important foreign policy matters, including the status of Intelsat, were at stake. The SIG imposed two limitations on the proposed private systems in order to comply with the aforementioned Article XIV(d) of the Intelsat Permanent Agreement: (a) the systems may not carry 'public telecommunications services'[28] and (b) the US government will not grant request for connection of the systems with Intelsat unless authorization for the use of satellites between another country and the United States is given by that country's telecommunications authority (PTT).[29]

At the same time the US government put both Intelsat and foreign PTTs on notice: if Intelsat were to reject the applications of US satellite systems that met the above two conditions, the US government might authorize the system regardless of Intelsat's opposition as it will not be bound by the recommendations of the Intelsat Assembly of Parties. It argued that its action would not violate its treaty obligations, even though it would be against the will of the Intelsat.[30]

The rationale for allowing private satellite systems was articulated in the SIG's *White Paper on New International Satellite Systems* in February 1985. The White Paper acknowledged Intelsat's great success both in operational terms and in the context of US foreign policy.

> [Intelsat's success] has confined the Soviet system (Intersputnik) to a relatively small portion of the world with only five new members apart from its founding members. Intelsat has also provided developing countries with an important tool for their economic and social development and has allowed them to play a role in world affairs. . . . [T]he U.S. government is committed to ensuring the continued viability of Intelsat and to ensuring that there be no significant economic harm to the system. United States foreign policy, and international information and communications policy, required a continued strong national commitment to Intelsat as a single global system.[31]

However, the White Paper outlined Intelsat's alleged shortcomings in offering consumers the latest technological and cost benefits: (a) rates have not reflected volume efficiency in the use of communication satellites; (b) the video marketplace is not well served (few video transponders are available, and these are pre-emptible, must be reserved far in advance and are extremely expensive); (c) Intelsat does not offer customized services.[32]

The SIG made the case for allowing the new US systems, which were to provide end-users with broader service options as well as the benefit from competition among customized service providers. Last, but not least, it was thought that the new systems would force Intelsat to be more efficient and innovative. Also, SIG argued that new US international satellite carriers would permit outside financial sources to undertake high-risk speculative ventures, allowing Intelsat to concentrate its resources on extending basic services.[33]

The White Paper considered that these new benefits could be obtained without jeopardizing both the technical integrity of the Intelsat global system and its economic well-being. New entrants will be restricted to the provision of customized services that are not interconnected with public-switched networks.[34]

Perhaps the most significant fact is that, in large sections of the White Paper, the argument for competition does not revert to telecommunications economics but is couched in terms of foreign policy, trade and national security. International communications services constitute an indispensable component of international trade. Companies marketing services overseas are heavily dependent upon communications services which represent a significant part of overall costs. Therefore, the argument goes, a reduction in communications costs will greatly assist US companies to expand their business and ultimately to generate employment. Furthermore, the new satellite systems will strengthen the communications, aerospace and computer communications industries, which in turn will enable the overall US industrial sector to become more productive and competitive.

It was not unreasonable to conclude that the US administration considered the applications for new satellite systems not primarily in microeconomic terms focusing on the telecommunications industry, but in macroeconomic terms by looking at trade and economic development.

Assessing the impact of competition

Even though Intelsat is an international organization (and thus not subject to US domestic laws except in the case of the activities of Comsat) it is instructive to examine how the US courts discussed the uses and abuses of monopoly power as they were assessing whether Intelsat behaved like a monopoly. Section 2 of the Sherman Antitrust Act of 1980 states:

> Every person who shall monopolize, or attempt to monopolize, or combine or conspire with any other person or persons, to monopolize any part of the trade or commerce among the several States, or with foreign nations, shall be deemed guilty of a felony [and is similarly punishable] . . . [35]

Yet, the Act does not define how much monopoly power is considered to be excessive or what constitutes monopolization that would trigger legal actions. US courts have therefore used different approaches to measure the market power of a particular firm in an attempt to define the term 'monopolization'.

The first method is called performance tests, according to which one determines how much a firm's prices depart from its marginal cost. In general, this method is considered to be unsatisfactory because marginal cost estimates are difficult to derive. In any event, this method is irrelevant for our analysis since Intelsat is restricted to price at, or around, average cost by its charter. The second method of market power measurement focuses on competitive behaviour and examines 'the sensitivity of the particular firm's sales or output to changes in its rivals' sales and prices.[36] The present analysis of Intelsat borrows the latter method to examine the following aspects:

1 possible predatory practices;
2 interservice subsidies within the company's operation;
3 excess capacity;
4 the company's reaction to competitive threats.

Predatory practices

While no consensus has been reached on a standard definition of predatory strategies (especially predatory pricing), Ordover and Willig propose a two-fold definition that seems to capture the essential elements. First, predatory conduct is intended to ' . . . affect a rival by influencing the parameters on which his optimal decisions must rest. There must therefore be a prey.' Second, predatory conduct requires some 'intertemporal sacrifice by the predator firm'.[37] Comanor and Frech note further:

> What is required here is that the predator must sacrifice at least a portion of his profits in the short run to impose harm on his prey. The objective is to convince the rival to change its behaviour. . . . The actual carrying out of any predatory action is designed solely to make the underlying threat believed. Indeed, the optimal predatory act is a threat or commitment that is believed but never carried out.[38]

As Joskow and Klevorick, among other antitrust scholars, suggest, simple rules for detecting the presence of predatory behaviour do not seem to be workable. The shortcomings of the Areeda-Turner test (especially irrelevant in telecommunications), the marginal cost standard, as the stand-alone test demonstrate the complexity of defining 'predation'.[39] In these conditions, a detailed case-by-case analysis may be the only way to determine whether predatory practices actually take place. In the United States there are precedents.

In 1973 a company, Datran, began to offer digital transmission of computer data. Soon after, AT&T filed a tariff to provide a similar service at lower rates. Even though Datran protested over the tariff, and the FCC unanimously concluded that AT&T data service rates were cross-subsidized and predatory in intent, it took more than 10 years for the service to be suspended, because of inadequate evidence. In the meantime, Datran declared bankruptcy.[40] There are several other instances in which AT&T's pricing responses to new entrants were perceived to be predatory in intent, as in the case of the 'Hi-Lo' private line tariff, the Telpak tariff and a new tariff responding to MCI's entry into the long-distance market.[41] These events are strong reminders of how monopoly power can be abused to deter competition.

Intelsat has been accused of predatory practices as well. The first of the claims deals with the sale or lease of transponders to member countries for their own permanent domestic use. In 1985 the price structure for use of transponders was modified so that Intelsat sold single transponders at around $3 million to $5 million each, instead of the $200 million a signatory had spent on a twenty-four-transponder satellite system. Naturally, this change represented much greater operational flexibility and cost savings for signatories with light satellite traffic needs. As expected, the new satellite applicants have filed complaints with the FCC for Comsat's predatory pricing. The FCC, dismissing the charges, notes:

> Despite the efficiency benefits of Comsat [thus Intelsat] offering idle capacity at close to marginal cost, it is inevitable that potential entrants will characterize such pricing as predatory. For example, PanAmSat has recently complained to the FCC that Intelsat's plan to sell Venezuela a transponder for domestic use is predatory. . . . The Commission should treat such claims of predation with great skepticism. It would seem far better to allow the public to benefit now from low prices for transponders (or low long term lease charges) than to maintain a floor on prices in order to protect the public against possible price increases in the future.[42]

Despite the FCC's dismissal, some scholars continue to assert the predatory intent of Intelsat.[43]

The second allegation, that Intelsat (Comsat, in this case) engaged in predatory practice, was made regarding the filings of reduced rates for all services offered by the consortium, with rate reduction averaging around 13 per cent. Most notable among the changes are the discount rates of as much as 30 per cent for long-term (5-, 7- and 9-year) contracts. These filings were considered to be predatory in intent as they sought to lock-in customers before 1988 when a group of carriers led by AT&T was scheduled to begin operating highly competitive fibre-optic cables in the Atlantic and Pacific region.[44] After the investigation, the FCC ordered Comsat to lower the reduction rates.

Interservice subsidy

Analysts who claim that Intelsat operations in the Atlantic Ocean region are subsidized by the Pacific and Indian Ocean regions[45] seem to be contradicted by others, including those who favour the introduction of competition.[46] That four out of five US-proposed systems aim at serving the Atlantic Ocean region exclusively seems to indicate where profits can possibly be generated.

Intelsat claims that the new US satellite entrants will engage in 'cream-skimming', whereby the new systems chip Intelsat's profits away by luring customers with lower prices. The organization asserts that this situation will jeopardize Intelsat's cross-subsidization of the thin routes where traffic is initiated or terminated in developing countries.[47] Intelsat argues that any significant changes in its structure and operation would adversely affect the developing countries, which benefit currently not only from geographical rate averaging but also from the co-operative's development programmes aimed at assisting in the design, planning, construction and operation of earth stations. Studies have documented that access to, and use of, telecommunications infrastructure is important in the economic development of these countries.[48] In recent years, new services, such as Vista and Share, have been launched, targeted to developing countries. These efforts, Intelsat argues, will be the first to be terminated in the event of economic damage to the system.

If Intelsat is assumed to be correct, an analogy can be made with the AT&T divestiture where cross-subsidization of local calls by long-distance calls has been terminated. The fact that twelve states have had to implement some types of 'lifeline programme' (i.e. local-call subsidy for lower-income families) and another twelve states are currently considering the implementation of such a programme, seems to give some indication of the problems that developing countries might face in the future.[49] A proponent of US private systems was candid about it:

> Distributional matters are paramount in deregulatory questions. Even when economic welfare as a whole increases, the welfare of certain individual user groups (the poor, rural customers, low-volume users) [all of which can be applied to Intelsat members from developing countries] may well decline.[50]

This may be true; however, one point should be underlined with respect to details of Intelsat's operation. Many signatories utilize the Standard A earth stations which are relatively large, but other members with less traffic tend to utilize less expensive Standard B earth stations. Intelsat imposes a 50 per cent surcharge on the latter group of countries over the basic price of a leased circuit.[51] It is only natural, then, that proponents of competitive systems claim that the subsidy from the operations in the Atlantic region is cancelled out by this surcharge to the lesser-endowed countries.

Excess capacity

Intelsat has built up its satellite capacity since its inception, and the annual average usage rate for the 12 years up to 1984 was only around 35 per cent of available facilities.[52] In other words, there has been large excess capacity in Intelsat operation. If Intelsat was to take advantage of its monopolistic power, it has been argued, it would try to create a product scarcity in order to charge higher prices than its counterparts in a competitive industry. It follows that the organization is not abusing its advantageous positional, because Intelsat has excess capacity rather than product scarcity.

One can explore this argument by looking first at the process of forecasting future Intelsat traffic. At the Annual Global Traffic Meeting, pairs of countries (the two ends between which communication takes place) usually agree on the level of satellite traffic expected between them. Regional and global totals are then calculated on the basis of these figures. A common problem here is that each pair of countries tends to add a so-called 'contingency allowance' in their forecast in order to help ensure (a) that enough capacity will be available in case traffic growth is greater than expected and (b) that enough redundancy exists so that traffic can be accommodated if particular transmission links are disrupted.[53] These extra capacities for emergency will never be needed by all the member countries at the same time. Thus the forecast tends to be systematically too high.

This problem is exacerbated by the way costs are shared among Intelsat members. Any costs associated with the expansion of Intelsat's capacity are borne by all the member countries. Thus, if two countries make unreasonably large estimates for future use of satellite capacity, those two are not the only ones to share the financial burden. Without penalties, it is less pressing for any pair of member countries to make accurate forecasts than otherwise.[54] Intelsat's excess capacity seems to be attributable to this systematic upward bias in the utility forecast rather than an indication of whether the organization is abusing its monopoly power.

Threat of competition

In recent years, Intelsat has launched new services such as International Business Service (IBS) and Intelnet. Introduced in 1983, IBS is a highspeed digital telecommunications service (video, teleconferencing, high and low speed facsimile, electronic mail, packet-switching) used by businesses to link offices domestically or internationally via a network of on-premises earth stations which permit international communication that bypasses existing Intelsat gateway stations. A wide variety of communications capacity is available on an occasional, part-time or full-time basis, allowing businesses to tailor IBS networks to suit their needs. Associated with IBS is Intelnet which provides for the distribution and collection of data between a central point and multiple remote locations. It is ideal for the transmission of news and financial information to microterminal dish antennae of some 0.65 m.[55] Demand for these services took off in 1987 and has since been on the increase.

As far as service pricing is concerned, the Intelsat agreements stipulated the cross-subsidization of each service between different geographical regions. Owing to this 'universal service' concept, users in the heavy-traffic routes – large corporations in developed countries, in particular – felt they were paying excess charges. This problem has been solved in part by the introduction of the above-mentioned IBS. Intelsat can provide a particular service in one route that will not be offered in another. IBS has been offered only to signatories on heavy routes, which shows that the Intelsat structure allows for some price flexibility.[56]

In 1985, Intelsat's Board of Governors authorized the sale or lease of transponders to countries for their own permanent domestic use. For several years, Intelsat had offered transponders for individual lease, but it was difficult for users to make any long-term plans because of the 'pre-emptible' clause. The 1985 decision gave signatories full non-pre-emptible rights to transponders. The price structure for use of transponders has itself been modified. Instead of the $200 million that a signatory had spent on a twenty-four-transponder satellite system, Intelsat is now selling single transponders at around $3 million to $5 million each.

The fact that Intelsat started to be more responsive to some categories of customers by implementing more flexible strategies and introducing new services only when threatened by competitive pressures suggested to critics that the organization was acting exactly as a monopolist which perceived that the market it occupies is penetrated by potential entries. Some scholars even suggested that the satellite services market in the North Atlantic region is contestable for commercial public satellite communications.[57] Without detailed cost data (entry cost, exit cost, etc.), however, it is impossible to determine this point. Intelsat is aware that it is being challenged not only by US private satellite systems but also by other organizations.

Intermodal competition: suboceanic cables

A great deal of attention has been paid by the US telecommunications community to the five proposed US satellite systems. At the same time other changes in regulatory and technological areas, such as the introduction of transoceanic fibre-optics cable, are likely to have an even greater impact on global telecommunications development. The series of FCC regulatory changes that govern the domestic carriers offering international services, such as the Comsat, will unmistakably affect Intelsat to a considerable extent since Comsat is its largest member.

The existing US international carriers, such as AT&T, ITT and RCA, were prohibited from launching their own satellites since Comsat was given a monopoly access to Intelsat's space segment. Those carriers had to lease capacity from Intelsat via Comsat. In order to secure a competitive US environment, Comsat was banned from offering private-line services. These services should be left to existing domestic carriers.[58] This restriction made Comsat somewhat dependent on AT&T. Yet, AT&T as well as the other US international carriers may have little incentive to use international satellite facilities. Once they invest in suboceanic cable systems, the marginal cost of using additional cable circuits is zero, whereas the cost of using the equivalent satellite circuit approximates the average cost of an Intelsat circuit.

Moreover, public-switched carriers such as AT&T have a further incentive to use transoceanic cable circuits in lieu of satellite circuits because their rate of return is regulated and the investment made on cable construction can be included in the rate base. This is not the case if these carriers use satellite facilities.[59] AT&T, the largest US international carrier, is also a leading manufacturer of suboceanic cables.

In order to promote an international satellite system to which the United States has historically been committed, since 1968 the FCC has devised a series of regulations on cable–satellite proportionate loading.[60] These regulations, finalized in 1978, were called the '50/50 loading policy', whereby the number of circuits on international cable and satellite transmission facilities were to be equalized. The FCC is now attempting to remove these restrictions, which will inaugurate the beginning of a real *intermodal* competition. The impact of this move on Intelsat revenues will be very serious, much more so than the threat represented by the five US private satellite systems combined.

In line with new deregulatory moves, the FCC determined in February 1985 that the establishment of Tele Optik Limited (TOL) – aimed at providing international private communication services – was consistent with the US interests. Hence, it authorized TOL to begin construction of optical fibre suboceanic cables in the Atlantic Ocean region. In the same year, the Submarine Lightwave Cable company (SLC) was authorized to build facilities in the same region.[61]

The US administration strongly endorsed the private cable and satellite systems because it believed that the new systems would benefit US companies and the national economy in general. It did not seem to be seriously concerned with the tremendous excess capacity of international communications facilities (see Table 3.2).

Against the background of this capacity, estimated figures for service demand between the United States and Europe were 37,161 voice circuits in 1990 and 81,888 voice circuits in 1995, which include both traffic growth and new service requirements.[62] The estimated supply was 800 per cent over the estimated demand.

Fibre-optic cables and the Intelsat VI satellite will have very large capacities, and it may not be possible to size them down effectively to meet lower expected demand levels. There may thus be problems for all carriers to compete effectively. This is not to suggest that satellites will disappear at the expense of cable, or vice versa. With this magnitude of supply–demand imbalance, however, the excess capacity will introduce significant price and rate complications. It is not certain that suboceanic cables will harm Intelsat since the non-US transoceanic cable end-users are in fact Intelsat signatories: the PTTs. It is very unlikely that they will manage suboceanic telecommunications in such a way as to jeopardize their cherished property, the Intelsat space segment.

Table 3.2 Total supply of international communication capacity in the Atlantic Ocean region (equivalent voice-grade circuits)

Public-switched transoceanic cables	
TAT 8	40,000
TAT 9	40,000
Private transoceanic cables	
Tele Optik	122,000
SLC	250,000
Public-switched satellites	
Intelsat VI	120,000
Private satellites	
Orion	22,500
ISI	39,360
Cygnus	28,800
PanAmSat	33,000
RCA	29,800
Total	725,460

Source: Ronald Eward, *The Deregulation of International Telecommunications* (Dedham, MA: Artech House, 1985).

Conclusion

Is Intelsat a monopoly or a co-operative? The answer is made difficult by the complex organizational structure and conduct of Intelsat as well as the problematic definition of what constitutes predatory practices.

On the one hand, Intelsat's structure and mode of operation conform to the co-operative model. Its members, who in most cases control the earth segment, provide for themselves an efficient service at the most attractive price. Given the high economic value of the global reach of the network, members will seek any opportunity to secure the lowest operating costs.[63] Since the full potential of the earth antenna system is only realized through the use of the space segment, it can be expected that the procurement, pricing and managerial policies for the space segment will be cost efficient. As a co-operative, Intelsat becomes the most effective way of managing the common resources since it caters best for the self-interest of its members. Moreover, organized in a voluntary association, Intelsat members have built-in incentives to create the most favourable conditions for keeping investments of each partner within the organization.

At the same time, some scholars contend that Intelsat members have incentives to make profits and thus might behave like a monopoly. Jill Hills, for example, argues that 'the European PTTs have kept charges [of satellite use to the end-users] artificially high, not simply to cross-subsidize their residential markets, but also as a form of non-tariff barrier to make American companies locate in Europe'.[64] This criticism appears misdirected as it overlooks the fact that Intelsat's prime objective is to provide space segment capacity for international telecommunications services, a segment which is collectively owned. The earth segment is under the sole jurisdiction of the various national telecommunications agencies.[65] The manner in which Intelsat's space segment capacity is to be distributed and utilized within a country is not governed by the Intelsat agreements. In addition, the extent to which monopoly or competition prevails in the charges for services would seem to be exclusively within the purview of each member.[66] The Intelsat agreements leave each signatory sufficient flexibility to enter into arrangements in conformity with the domestic law of the country and to provide any degree of competition in the supply of services to end-users according to perceived national interest.

However, the gigantic size of the organization and its unique position in the market inevitably lead Intelsat into practices generally associated with a monopoly, as examined earlier. It is ultimately from the consumers' point of view that practices in the provision of satellite communications services need to be examined. Intelsat is a wholesaler, and each member country is a retailer. The high charges that end-users (residential and business customers) have to support in most countries is the result of the monopolistic practices of the individual domestic telecommunications administrations which own and operate the earth segment, as opposed to the space segment. High prices in PTT-dominated countries do not reflect Intelsat's alleged monopolistic conduct but the conduct of real domestic monopolies. As a matter of fact, 90 per cent of the cost of establishing international communications links is attributable to the earth segment.

In any event, once satellite systems are in place, pressure tends to mount to allow private earth-station ownership. This tendency has been observed in the past not only in the United States but also in Canada, the United Kingdom and West Germany where customers have operational flexibilities and unimpeded access to small and micro earth stations for both domestic and international communications services. It will thus be increasingly difficult for Intelsat to argue that it only concentrates on the space segment while the running of the earth segment is each country's business. To compete effectively with the private satellite systems which are likely to operate in the future, Intelsat has, among other things, to consider seriously changes in basic pricing mechanisms.

For the time being, at any rate, any deregulatory moves in satellite-delivered communications services are more likely to focus on breaking up the monopolistic retail end of the Intelsat system than its co-operative end.

Notes

1 In this context, 'universal service' means that international satellite transmission services are made available to everyone who desires to use them. Charges for Intelsat's various services – voice, data or picture – do not differ from one region to

the other and are proportional to the unit of use.

2 Article XIV(c) of the Agreement entered into force on 12 February 1973. TIAS No. 7532.

3 Karen Lynch, 'Intelsat opposes deregulation of international communications facilities', *Communications Week*, 24 March, 1986, p. 27.

4 See Vick Van Dyke, *Pride and Power* (Urbana, IL: University of Illinois Press, 1964).

5 See Judith Tegger Kildow, *Intelsat: Policy-Maker's Dilemma* (Lexington, MA: Lexington Books, 1973).

6 *Handbook on Intelsat* (Washington, DC: International Telecommunications Satellite Organization, 28 February 1985), p. 24.

7 It is important to note that Intelsat shares are owned by various organizations which are not necessarily government entities.

8 *Handbook on Intelsat*, op. cit., pp. 8–9.

9 Permanent Agreements, Article V(d).

10 Article XIV(c) requires that the satellite provision of domestic services be technically compatible with Intelsat's orbit–spectrum usage. In addition, international public telecommunications systems must adhere to the criteria of Article XIV(d) which seek to guarantee that the Intelsat system suffers no significant economic harm.

11 It is noteworthy that the space segment accounts for only around 10 per cent of the cost of an international link; the rest is made up of earth station charges and the charges for transmitting the message from the earth station to customers' premises.

12 In this context, a cartel is defined as a group of firms united into one monopolistic entity to effect collusive price–output decisions. See Lance E. Davis, 'Self-regulation in baseball, 1909–71', in Roger G. Noll (ed.), *Government and the Sports Business* (Washington, DC: The Brookings Institution, 1974).

13 Frederick L. Pryor, 'The economics of production cooperatives: a reader's guide', *Annals of Public and Cooperative Economy*, 54 (2) (April–June 1983), p. 135.

14 R. Carson, 'A theory of co-operatives', *Canadian Journal of Economics* (November 1977), p. 566.

15 Walter Hinchman, *The Economics of International Satellite Communications*, Report prepared by Hinchman Associates Inc., vol. II, p. II-3.

16 Ibid., vol. I, p. 3.

17 Christian Bastin, 'Theories of Voluntary Exchange in the Theory of Public Goods', *Annals of Public and Cooperative Economy*, 49 (1) (January–March 1978), pp. 8–9.

18 Ibid., pp. 5–6.

19 Hinchman, op. cit., vol. I, p. 3.

20 Davis, op. cit., p. 351.

21 Jean-Luc Renaud and Barry R. Litman, 'Changing dynamics of the overseas marketplace for TV programming: the rise of international coproduction', *Telecommunications Policy* (September 1985), pp. 247–8.

22 Kent Cooper, *Barriers Down* (New York: Farrar and Rinehart, 1942), p.128.

23 Richard Colino, *Statement of Richard R. Colino, Director General-designate, International Telecommunications Satellite Organization, before the Subcommittee on Arms Control, Oceans, International Operations and Environment, Senate Foreign Relations Committee*, 19 October 1983, p. 32.

24 Evan R. Kwerel and James E. McNally, Jr, *OPP Working Paper Series: Promoting Competition Between International Telecommunication Cables and Satellites* (Washington, DC: Federal Communications Commission, January 1986), p. 47-B.

25 Ibid., p. 47.

26 Ibid., p. 351.

27 Evan Kwerel, *Promoting Competition Piecemeal in International Telecommunications* (Washington, DC: Office of Plans and Policy, the Federal

Communications Commission, December 1984), p. 18.

28 This term is defined in Article I(k) of the Intelsat Agreements as 'Fixed or mobile telecommunications services which can be provided by satellite and which are available for use by the public, such as telephony, telegraph, telex, facsimile, data transmission, transmission of radio and television programs between approved earth stations having access to the Intelsat space segment for further transmission to the public, and leased circuits for any of these purposes.'

29 Senior Interagency Group on International Communication and Information Policy, *White Paper on New International Satellite Systems* (Washington, DC: Government Printing Office, February 1985), pp. 14–16.

30 Ibid., pp. 16–17.

31 Ibid., p. 20.

32 Ibid., p. 28.

33 Ibid., p. 18.

34 Using a 1982 Intelsat forecast, SIG argued that Intelsat traffic will be essentially telephone services and other public-switched services. Of the 15,603 satellite voice-grade circuits to eighteen European countries planned for 1988, Intelsat projected that 1,400 will be used for telephony. Thus the new entrants will be barred from 90 per cent of Intelsat's non-telephony offerings.

35 The Sherman Antitrust Act of 1890, 15 U.S.C.A., section 2.

36 Ernest Gellhorn, *Antitrust Law and Economics*, 2nd edn (St Paul, MN: West, 1982), p. 88.

37 Janusz A. Ordover and Robert D. Willig, 'An economic definition of predation: pricing and product innovation', *Yale Law Journal*, no. 91 (November 1981), pp. 9–10.

38 William S. Comanor and H.E. Frech III, 'Strategic behaviour and antitrust analysis', *American Economic Review, Papers and Proceedings*, 74 (May 1984), pp. 372–6.

39 See Paul L. Joskow and Alvin K. Klevorick, 'A framework for analyzing predatory pricing policy', *The Yale Law Journal*, 89 (2) (December 1979), pp. 213–70.

40 Gerald W. Brock, *The Telecommunication Industry: The Dynamics of Market Structure* (Cambridge, MA: Harvard University Press, 1981), p. 224.

41 For further details on these cases, see Walter G. Bolter (ed.), *Telecommunication Policy for the 1980s* (Englewood Cliffs, NJ: Prentice-Hall, 1984).

42 Cited in Kwerel and McNally, Jr, op. cit., p. 30.

43 See Harvey J. Levin, 'Emergent markets for orbit spectrum assignments: an idea whose time has come', *Telecommunications Policy*, 12 (1) (March 1988), p. 72; and Eli Noam, 'Telecommunications policy on both sides of the Atlantic: divergence and outlook', in Marcellus Snow (ed.), *Marketplace for Telecommunications: Regulation and Deregulation in Industrialized Democracies* (New York: Longman, 1986), p. 269.

44 'Comsat lowers Intelsat rates', *Telephony*, 1 June 1987, p. 14.

45 One example is Kenneth R. Dunmore, *An Analysis of the Intelsat Subsidy Issue*, a paper submitted to the International Satellite Issues, Hearings before the Subcommittee on Telecommunications, Consumer Protection, and Finance, Ninety-eighth Congress, Second Session, 13 June and 25–26 July, 1984.

46 Marcellus Snow, *International Commercial Satellite Communications: Economic and Political Issues of the First Decade of Intelsat* (New York: Praeger, 1976), pp. 87–91.

47 One-third of all Intelsat traffic originates or terminates in the developing countries.

48 For a detailed examination of the link between telecommunications and economic development, see William Pierce and Nicolas Jequier, *Telecommunications for Development* (Geneva: ITU, 1983); and Robert J. Saunders, Jeremy J. Warford and Bjorn Wellenius, *Telecommunications and Economic Development* (Baltimore, MD: Johns Hopkins University Press, 1983).

49 National Telecommunications and Information Administration, *Telephone Regulation and Competition: A Survey of the States* (Washington, DC: NTIA, 1986), pp. 26–31.
50 Marcellus Snow, 'Arguments for and against competition in international satellite facilities and services: a U.S. perspective', *Journal of Communications*, 35 (3) (Summer 1985), p. 64.
51 Dunmore, op. cit., p. 825.
52 Ibid., p. 47.
53 Leland L. Johnson, 'Excess capacity in international telecommunications', *Telecommunications Policy* (September 1987), pp. 285–6.
54 Ibid.
55 Karen Lynch, 'Intelsat proposes service letting users broadcast data bases', *Communications Week*, 8 October 1984, p. 46.
56 Karen Lynch, 'Intelsat devising lower rates for U.S.–Europe business routes', *Communications Week*, 21 October 1985, p. 25.
57 If markets dominated by a monopolist are relatively easy (inexpensive) to enter and exit, the mere threat of entry by rival firms will exert discipline on the incumbent firm to innovate and to price according to cost instead of earning monopoly profits. In order to determine whether a market is contestable or not, one needs to know how high entry and exit costs are for competitors, what assumptions the incumbent and rival firms make about each other's potential behaviour, and what the effects of both entry and the threat of entry are upon the incumbent firm. Snow, op. cit., 1985, p. 69.
58 Colino, op. cit., p. 5.
59 Kwerel and McNally, Jr, op. cit., p. 26.
60 See the proposed TAT-5 project, 11 FCC 2d 957 (1968), AT&T, ITT, RCA, 13 FCC 2d 235 (1968), Comsat, AT&T, ITT, 29 FCC 2d 252 (1971), Comsat, AT&T, ITT, 32 FCC 2d 103 (1971).
61 Tele Optik Limited, 100 FCC 2d 1033 (1985); SLC Cable Landing License No. 5241, released by the FCC on 19 June 1985.
62 Ronald Eward, *The Deregulation of International Telecommunications* (Dedham, MA: Artech House, 1985), p. 420.
63 The rationale of many proponents of the existing organization relates to the social responsibility of the industrialized countries to provide telecommunication access to their lesser endowed counterparts in the Third World. This line of reasoning is a sensible and important one, but we prefer to stay within the economics sphere.
64 Jill Hills, *Deregulating Telecoms: Competition and Control in the United States, Japan and Britain* (Westport, CT: Quorum Books, 1986), p. 167.
65 Except in the case of developing countries that do not have the managerial and technical know-how for dealing with earth stations and terrestrial signal transmission.
66 Lee McKnight, 'Comment', *Telecommunications Policy* (December 1985), p. 278. On average the earth-segment costs of any international call (i.e. earth station charges and the charge for transmitting the message from the earth station terrestrially to the customer's premises) represent as much as 90 per cent of overall charges.

Chapter four

International regime or corporate actor? The European Community in telecommunications policy

Volker Schneider and Raymund Werle

Rapid changes in technology as well as the American and Japanese challenge in telecommunications pose considerable problems for the member states of the European Community (EC). Because political and economic actors are so closely intertwined and because international organizations and regimes already exist to promote and organize transnational communication, the EC's options for involvement in this policy field seem to be particularly limited. Nevertheless, the EC's influence in this sector is increasing. In this chapter we argue that this increased influence can only be explained by viewing the EC not only as a regime but also as a corporate actor with its own power interests which have developed out of the regime.

The telecommunications policy sector represents an interesting paradox of international co-operation and integration. Although telecommunications have been dependent on international and European co-operation for many decades, not least for technical reasons, the EC as the closest form of European integration, has been intensively engaged in this sector only since the early 1980s. International co-operation was established when the earliest international correspondence and telecommunications networks came into existence.[1] As early as 1849, the first convention on telegraph connections was signed by Prussia and Austria, and in 1865 the International Telegraph Union was founded. After the Second World War the European Conference of Postal and Telecommunications Administrations (CEPT) developed into the centrepiece of European co-operation in the field of telecommunications – despite very early proposals to establish a telecommunications union within the European Economic Community. The two organizational forms of co-operation are considerably different. CEPT constitutes a forum for co-ordination or a 'regime' of the telecommunications sector that provides for the co-ordination of the respective national telecommunications systems on a transnational level. In contrast, the EC and its supranational institutions, despite also having characteristics of a regime, can be more accurately described as a 'corporate actor' that realizes its own interests and uses its own resources to occupy new fields of activity and gain new competences.

Following a brief discussion of the relevance and the basic assumption of the concepts of regime and actor in the theory of international relations, it is shown that the EC in its dynamic development cannot be adequately understood as a regime but constitutes instead a corporate actor that increasingly gains influence in new policy areas more so than in traditional ones. The telecommunications sector provides an excellent example of such an increase in activities governed by corporate self-interests.

Institutions, systems and corporate actors in international relations

Ever since its foundation, the EC has fascinated political scientists as a practical as well as a theoretical problem, inviting attention as one of the few examples of peaceful integration of nation-states and the voluntary transfer of sovereignty and loyalties to a new confederation of states. This newly developed, complex and hybrid political and institutional configuration confronted political scientists with theoretical demands of a very special nature. At first political scientists continued to apply existing and established theoretical instruments. As they were still predominantly working within the framework of a constitutional law perspective developed after the Second World War, they used traditional institutionalist concepts of constitutional and international law to understand the EC.

As political science fell under the influence of the behaviouralist revolution, functionalist thought increasingly found its way into the analysis of political phenomena in general as well as the analysis of international relations, especially the theory of West European integration. Whereas early institutionalists had attempted to explain economic and political integration by an analysis of institutions, behaviouralist and functionalist approaches aimed at discovering the real forces at work behind formal political institutions. Functionalist concepts no longer explained the stability and change of political forms by actions of political actors and institutions but in more abstract terms by reference to the problems and functional imperatives of systems. According to the functionalist dictum that 'form follows function', institutional structures represent 'effects' or adaptations that 'automatically' result from a certain process of societal development. Thus processes of political and institutional integration are more or less necessarily caused by increasing international trade, traffic and communications flows.

David Mitrany[2] and Ernest Haas[3] are the outstanding theorists along these conceptual lines. In particular, Haas's theory of European integration grew logically out of the functionalist perspective in which conflicts of interests and interest-guided action were easily neglected because of the heavy emphasis placed on problem solving.

'Neo-functionalists' reacted to criticism that pointed to the very abstract and macroprocedural automatism of functionalism by connecting functionalist and group theoretical concepts. Conflict and the freedom to decide are related to functional considerations in such a way that integration processes are the combined consequence of developmental problems and tensions and of the reactions and strategies of the nation-states involved.[4] The approaches of 'transnationalism'[5] focus on actors to an even greater degree. They view political integration almost exclusively as the product of synchronous and parallel interests and reduce institutions to mere epiphenomena. Thus Puchala[6] notes:

> The European Communities are not as supranationally authoritative as our textbooks would have us believe.... [I]t becomes clear that the national governments definitely have the final say in the operations of the common market. Putting it more bluntly, national governments will enforce Community regulations ... when they perceive their interest to be served by so doing. They will balk, delay, circumvent, or ignore Community regulations when they perceive compliance as being contrary to their interest, even when they are formally committed to compliance.

There is thus a tendency to view the EC as the sum of the interests of its members and as a set of regulative and institutional arrangements to harmonize international politics. In other words, the EC is seen 'more as a "system of actors" than as an "action system" '.[7]

The present theory of international relations employs the concept of 'regime' to interpret constellations as described above. Stanley Hoffmann[8] was the first to propose explicitly a regime perspective to analyse the EC:

> Analysing the EEC as an international regime allows one to see better what, to 'integrationalists', is a paradox or contradiction: such regimes, in exchange for curtailing the states' capacity for unilateral action, serve to preserve the nationstate as the basic unit in world affairs and actually help governments perform their domestic tasks.

The regime concept did not develop accidentally but needs to be seen in the context of changing dominant positions between competing paradigms of political science. Group and élite theoretical approaches have increasingly gained prominence in the 1980s. 'Rational choice' models which concentrate analysis on the individualistic conditions of political order and co-operation exemplify this tendency. How are political order and co-operation possible when individual actors are being guided merely by often short-term self-interests?

The theory of international relations saw the answer to this question in the regime concept. Thus regimes represent institutional and normative arrangements to facilitate co-operation and concerted action.[9] They are established by rational actors to forestall collectively undesired consequences of self-interested action and modify available options by changing the cost and benefit structure of individual action strategies on the basis of collective agreements.[10]

Whilst the regime concept provides a central perspective for analysing the 'problem of order and co-operation' in international relations, it remains one-sided. In the 1930s, Commons,[11] the founder of 'institutional economics', distinguished between two forms of collective or, as he called it, concerted action: the corporate and the regulative mode. In the corporate form, individual actors create a new corporate body entrusted with the right to act and negotiate within a specific area in the name and interests of the founders or members. Individual action is thereby excluded in that specific area. Within the regulative mode, actions are still taken by individual actors but they are committed to abide by specific rules, laws or norms that restrict their actions. Individual action is not excluded, but is limited. Obviously, regimes largely constitute a form of regulative co-ordination in which actors and decision-makers remain identical but adhere to common agreements. The corporate mode, however, transforms individual actors into corporate actors. All societal organizations, even when composed of individuals who execute all actions, represent forms of corporate action. They act *as if* the organization would be acting. The logic behind the creation of these 'new persons' in the process of social change have been analysed by Coleman.[12] In Coleman's perspective, individuals' attempts to reach common goals and realize common interests by collective action continuously face difficulties. Concerned individual actors attempt to overcome the different dilemmas of collective action by achieving a contractual combination of their interests in such a way that they remain stable and independent of situational constellations. This is achieved by transferring resources (financial means and rights) to an organizational unit which is entitled, according to a corporate constitution, to act for a certain period in an area of specific tasks and goals in the name of the organization's members. Contractual rules make it difficult to leave the collective action unit, thus increasing stability and the ability to develop and pursue certain strategies.

The institutionalization of collective action has consequences. Corporate actors do not remain mere aggregates of their members that assemble interests and transfer them to the next level of decision making. In addition to the members' interests united within the corporate actor, the corporate actor develops self-interests to preserve its existence. As soon as an action unit with authority to act and with resources is established, the possibility arises that, by its actions, the organization ignores the interests of certain members or even acts against these interests. Strategies of the organization's agents may conflict with the organization's goals set by its members. This process in which corporate actors develop an ever-increasing degree of independence from those inferior units that provide their resources has been observed in many areas of organized action (stock corporations, political parties, trade unions).

Inferior actors (members) will therefore invest their resources in corporate actors only as long as they receive benefits in return, according to a contract. They have an interest in exerting control rights that counteract the tendency of the corporate actor to increase its autonomy. 'The contract', proposed Coleman,[13]

> between the persons, the source of power, and the corporate actor, the user of power, is the constitution of the corporate actor. The constitution describes the terms of the contract, the specific rights and obligations of the persons and the corporate actor, the limitations of the corporate actor in its use of the resources, and the conditions, including voting rights and decision rules, under which the persons can exercise control over this use, by changing the officer or by giving explicit directives to the officers through a collective decision.

In contrast with traditional concepts or organizational sociology which assume an organization's identity to be based on a common goal and thereby assume that individual goals converge, Coleman's approach proposes that with the creation of a corporate actor a new reality is established that goes beyond the original common goal and is more than, or at least something different from, the sum of the particular interests and goals of the individual actors.

Thus, the concept of the corporate actor, as we understand it, encompasses the special cases of oligarchical and bureaucratic self-interest. Oligarchical tendencies or organizations can be found primarily, as shown by Michels, in democratic organizations with a large membership. The oligarchy's interest in power that is not further defined and specified can be distinguished from the often more specific interests of the bureaucracy in power. In contrast with an oligarchy, the self-interest of a bureaucratic organization is principally compatible with the members' interests but is formulated in very general terms, is rather inflexible and, as emphasized especially by Max Weber, is established to last for a duration. Therefore conflicts are always likely to appear as a result of short-term and situation-based divergences between the bureaucracy and the members' interests defined in very concrete terms.

The perspective of the corporate actor concept is not, however, limited to internal relations (institutional structure, decision-making rules, distribution of competences) but includes the actors' relations with his environment. As much as individual members tend to dislike the corporate actor's tendency to increase internal power, they usually welcome a strong position in external affairs, especially when this enables individual interests to be included in a common interest that otherwise is difficult to establish.

For an analysis of forms of international organizations such as the EC, the corporate actor concept has an advantage over the regime concept. It conceptualizes the EC from the very beginning as more than the mere sum of the interests of member states' governments which can leave the federation at minimal cost as soon as an agreement cannot be reached on central aspects. Thus the EC does not passively receive orders; rather its institutions play an active role in identifying and formulating common interests. As an actor, the EC tends to increase its areas of competence, to mobilize new resources and to achieve legitimacy to act in new policy fields. Exit barriers are constituted not only by the long-term economic and political relationships between member states as codified by contracts but also by the actor EC, its power and its instrumental benefits as a potential ally in foreign relations as well as in internal conflicts. Thus the exit barrier is increasingly less dependent on 'loyalty'.

The European Community as regime and as corporate actor

It is helpful to begin an analysis of the EC as a regime as well as a corporate actor by considering its legal foundation. A detailed legal description of the EC is not intended here. Instead, only those legal elements will be discussed that constitute the institutional framework for actions within the EC and by the EC.[14] From an institutional perspective, the legal rules may be interpreted as those elements that constitute the regime, whereas from an actor perspective they appear to form constraints on, or resources for, action.

The laws established by the member states in the form of contracts represent the fundamental legal material.[15] Next to the founding contracts of the 1950s and the fusion contract of the three federations of 1965, the primary law of the EC is constituted by several contracts establishing membership or association of a number of states. After a long period of stagnation in the development of the EC institutions, important institutional conditions for action within the EC and by the EC were greatly transformed in February 1986 when the heads of states and governments agreed the Single European Act which came into force on 1 July 1987 after protected ratification procedures in some member states.

The EC's institutions are the Assembly (Parliament), the Council, the Commission and the EC Court; they should contribute to the realization of the Community's goals and make sure that the member states and the institutions follow the EC's rules. Formally the Council, an assembly of ministers responsible for certain policy areas, is the most important EC institution that makes legally binding decisions for the Community. It is therefore understandable that analyses of the EC's policy usually focus exclusively on the Council's actions or neglected actions and the Council's framework of action. This perspective favours an understanding of the EC as a regime. Since all decisions on relevant questions have traditionally had to be made unanimously (although a qualified majority vote would be allowed), recognition of every national member state's interest is guaranteed. As a consequence, the Council's respective policies have to consist either of finding the lowest common denominator, often within the framework of a package deal, or of making very general decisions that provide those institutions that execute the programmes with considerable latitude. The Council does not seem to represent an actor with a specific European self-interest but rather an arena in which national interests collide. In this function, however, it constitutes more than a simple clearing house since all decisions are legally binding upon member states and their citizens, without further consent from national parliaments. As long as member states try to enforce self-interests within the Council and attempt to preserve national control and regulative competences, the Council can only appear to be a collective rather than a corporate actor. Collective actions exercised by the Council, without requiring further support by other EC institutions, can exhibit far-reaching consequences only if national interests massively converge. The Council develops European interests in a narrow sense, however, in the external affairs of the EC. The European idea is transformed into more than pure symbolism of formal declaration, especially in situations in which a danger to the European position in world trade is perceived. Then national concessions are made with the hope of thereby strengthened the bargaining power of the EC so that the individual states benefit.[16]

In neglecting (despite direct elections) the still very weak European Parliament, attention is focused on the Court and the Commission, two institutions that display a more EC-specific self-interest than the Council when it comes to formal competences as well as behaviour. Often, the European Court of Justice is seen as the engine of integration. The Court can be called upon by the Commission, the Council, the member states and also by national courts and by juridical or natural citizens. Among other things, the Court arbitrates violations of contracts by member states and the nullification of regulations, directives and decisions of the EC institutions. Even if judges as citizens of different member states have diverging interests in certain conflict areas, as members of an independent court they have to consider, and are able to consider, the intentions and spirit of EC law to a greater degree than politicians can in their decisions. In this role, the judges have an interest in ensuring that EC laws are established not only as an autonomous body of laws but also as superior to the laws of the individual states. Drawing on this perspective at the outset, the Court declared the EC legal order to be autonomous and to be established independently of national legal systems so as to be legally valid in all member states immediately.[17]

Naturally, the Court's interest in an absolute primacy of European law over national law is also based on the fact that its own influence depends on a strong EC and its ability to shape the Community according to the letter of the contract.[18] Thus attention is focused on enforcing the Court's decisions, especially those opposing national governments and courts. It is difficult for governments to act opportunistically and selectively accept only those decisions with which they politically agree. In fact, they are enforced to accept all decisions in order to be able to use certain decisions to legitimize their actions. This 'all-or-nothing effect'[19] is also caused by the distributive effects typical of all court decisions.[20] Those governments that profit from a decision will try to apply pressure on the governments that hesitate to act in line with the Court's decision. National courts have to be convinced primarily by juridical discourse and the practice of jurisdiction that in individual cases they should follow the decisions of the European Court.

The European Commission has to provide initiative, co-ordination and administration for a functioning and growing community. It would be premature to call the Commission the EC's government, but it does appear that its influence is often underrated. The Commission not only is supported by an apparatus with more than 10,000 employees but also is equipped with an extensive right to initiate laws and regulations. It is strong when the EC is strong. Accordingly, the broadest possible jurisdiction and the growth of its competence is in its interest. Thus the Commission is eager to portray those problems in which it is interested as being closely related to the development of the Community and of the common market in particular.

In this way, the Commission's opportunities to take initiative without anyone casting doubts on the legitimacy of the action increase. In particular, when the common market is understood not only as a customs union but also as a large 'home market' providing for 'economies of scale', it is possible to argue the legitimacy of measures designed to improve the competitive position of the Community's enterprises on the world market. Thus the Commission is able to increase its competence in the field of industrial and technology policy without meeting any marked resistance.

The Commission can be assigned direct responsibility in fields where formally it has only indirect responsibility when the Council makes only vague decisions in that specific policy field. This situation arises very frequently because of the Council's need to reach an encompassing consensus and the veto right of every member. The necessity arises in these cases to make decisions more concrete, and the Commission is ready to fulfil that task. A similar situation results when the execution of concrete decisions of the Council is explicitly assigned to the Commission without further decisions of the Council concerning the execution of its decisions.

In pursuing political goals, the Commission has a broad spectrum of instruments at its disposal. It issues statements and recommendations, makes decisions and finally issues directives or passes regulations that are legally binding. In specific cases, the question may arise of Council approval of these decisions. Frequently, the approval, if necessary at all, is a mere formality. Additionally, in a number of cases the Council may disapprove of the Commission's suggested decisions but only by unanimous vote. In comparison with the Council, the Commission has the advantage of a continuously working bureaucracy that almost exclusively deals with European questions.

In view of this broad spectrum of 'vested resources' and 'unitary action capacities', there are good reasons to prefer an actor perspective to a regime perspective in analysing the EC. The EC's Commission, the Court and, with certain qualifications, the Council as well may be identified as corporate actors that evolved out of a regime context. As corporate actors, all three institutions develop to varying degrees EC-specific self-interests aimed at a general strengthening of the Community. Since they are not only acting within the EC but also in the name of the EC, it seems legitimate to conceptualize the EC as a whole as an increasingly internally connected 'emergent' corporate actor. In external affairs in particular and more specifically in trade policy, the EC seems to represent a unitary corporate actor which follows an internally agreed, often protectionist, strategy that often has negative consequences for small European states outside, and sometimes even inside, the EC.[21] This actor has at its disposal legal and financial resources that are continuously transferred to the Community by the member states or are specifically created by them and thus provide the actor with the capacity to act and develop strategies. Since the actor does not represent a homogeneous unit, the collaboration of its elements in historical sequence as well as their strategic co-ordination is of special interest.[22] Co-operation and conflict among the EC institutions, intended or not, may be of central importance for the development of the Community, not least for the choice of policy fields in which the Community will participate.

The European Community and telecommunications policy

In the following section we show how the EC as a corporate actor succeeded in becoming involved in a new policy field, the telecommunications sector, long before it was provided with the relevant legal responsibility. This competence has not yet in fact been specifically defined in the law of the EC.[23] Important steps in this development will be presented in chronological order and the strategic moves by the EC, especially the Commission, will be analysed systematically. Basically, the analysis will remain descriptive and will use material found in libraries, archives, special documentation centres and other sources.[24]

Thwarted attempts at 'small European unification' and the founding of the CEPT

As mentioned earlier, it is surprising that the EC only recently developed a telecommunications policy in spite of the necessity for international co-operation in this field. This does not mean that the question had not arisen earlier, however. As early as the late 1940s an initiative from within the Council of Europe including the seventeen member states aimed to form a unified European postal and telegraph sector to issue common stamps. At the beginning of the 1950s, a time of a strong dynamic towards European unification, the Council of Europe's consultative assembly passed a resolution calling for a European postal and telegraph union. The Committee of Ministers, however, rejected the idea. A few years later, following the failure of the European Defence Community proposal and the reduction of the unification euphoria to a mere economic rationalism, a suggestion was made to create a European postal and telegraph union of the European Coal and Steel Community type in the summer of 1955. This proposal was discussed at several meetings between 1956 and 1958 by the six postal ministers. When the EC was founded in 1957, a permanent secretariat was established to co-ordinate the postal and telegraph policies, thus realizing the earliest institutionalized form of contacts between the six EC member states in the telecommunications sector.

A year later, in September 1958, the six met in Brussels to discuss two options for the further development of co-operation within the EC. The alternatives were to create a European postal and telegraph union either completely independent of the EC or organically integrated into the Community based on Article 235 of the Treaty of Rome. A decision in favour of the latter option was taken initially but then abandoned, in March 1959, in favour of a postal and telegraph union reaching beyond the EC area.[25] One reason for the decision was the increasing resistance of Gaullist France to further supranational competences. In addition, it was apparently felt necessary not to exclude Britain, which opposed the 'small European solution', from such a community from the outset because of its very important position within the international telecommunications sector.[26] Thus Britain as well as Switzerland sought a larger solution.[27]

The enlarged European telecommunications community was institutionalized in 1959 with the creation of the *Conférence Européenne des Administrations des Postes et des Télécommunications* (CEPT). Initially CEPT had nineteen members in Western Europe with partially separate postal and telegraph administrations. Now all West European states are members of CEPT. In contrast with the EC, CEPT does not represent a union on the level of governments (Council of Ministers) but a forum of postal and telegraph administrations. Therefore it tends to be considered as an apolitical organization. Another difference is that CEPT decisions only have the character of recommendations. CEPT thus constitutes a typical relatively soft regime whose recommendations carry only a moral normative authority. The concrete execution of its recommendations remains dependent on a consensus. In spite of a majority vote rule, all CEPT decisions are reached only after preceding discussions have concluded in unanimous agreement. Without over simplifying, CEPT can be considered as a co-operation regime that functions as long as the post and telegraph administrations (PTTs) of the different countries leave each other's domains untouched. CEPT is the institutionalized manifestation of a gentlemen's agreement according to which, as observed by Dang-Nguyen,[28] each PTT is completely free to do anything at home. On the one hand, to provide international communication, CEPT sets technical standards and announces tariff principles and other recommendations that should be taken into consideration by national PTTs; on the other hand, national monopolies are strengthened by, for example, the PTTs' renunciation of competition in delivering services. In the 1950s and 1960s, without the pressure exerted by technical innovations such as microelectronics and the information technologies, the heads of postal administrations as well as the respective ministers considered the co-ordination of national activities within a rigidly structured EC more as a limitation of their freedom to act than as a necessary alliance to secure control possibilities that were being lost within a national framework. The 'soft' co-operation regime of the CEPT was preferred to the more rigid regime of the EC.

The discovery of the relevance of the telecommunications sector to EC trade policy

Despite the concentration of European co-operation in the postal and telecommunications sector within CEPT, there were sporadic contacts within the EC on a ministerial level. The first meeting of the EC's PTT ministers took place in September 1964. The meeting's primary focus was the harmonization of postal tariffs, an area of activity which is at least indirectly legitimized by the Treaty of Rome and for which the EC has some legal resources at its disposal. Following the meeting, the Commission was asked to elicit possibilities to harmonize the telecommunications sector.

These activities have to be seen as part of more general harmonization efforts based on Article 100 of the EC Treaty. Thus, starting in 1967, within one decade more than 100 directives were approved concerning the European harmonization of technical norms and administrative rules. These measures attempted to foster trade between member states by lifting non-tariff trade barriers set up mainly by administrative action. The telecommunications sector has become a prime target of these measures as it is heavily regulated by administrative action, especially public procurement decisions. Thus in October 1968 the Commission proposed to create a postal and telecommunications committee in which such matters could be treated more intensively. At that time it could not convince the Council and in June 1973 withdrew the proposal after several years of unfruitful discussions. Another Commission report on the liberalization of public procurement in the telecommunications sector also announced that the realization of such endeavours was not considered likely in the near future.

The low priority attached at that time to the postal and telecommunications sector is exemplified by the fact that it took 13 years for the postal ministers to meet again, in September 1977. It was commonly understood that the Treaty of Rome did not provide the EC with any competences in telecommunications. Therefore the Commission and Council continued to limit their efforts to the harmonization of postal tariffs that could be legitimized on trade policy grounds. This initially led, in December 1977, to proposals for an agreement on the unification of tariffs for standard letters and finally, in May 1979, to a Council recommendation for a unitary tariff for standard letters within the EC.

It becomes obvious, in conclusion, that almost all these very timid attempts by the EC to enter the telecommunications policy arena relied on trade policy issues at that time. Legal resources existed only in this area. All early initiatives to liberalise telecommunications procurement policies and harmonize different industrial standards have to be seen against this background. But these efforts existed parallel to the still untouched position of national PTTs. They were based on an international political consensus that considered the telecommunications sector more as state infrastructure provision[29] than as an industrial policy platform for international export strategies. Telecommunications as a public infrastructure service did not have any direct relevance for trade or even industrial policy.

The discovery of telecommunications industrial policy

Since the mid-1970s a gradual change in the attitudes of the EC states towards telecommunications policy can be observed. In addition to trade policy considerations, the telecommunications sector was deemed relevant for industrial policy also. This transformation can only be understood in the context of radical economic changes in the world market. In many countries, the postwar boom ended several years before the oil crisis. Transformations of the international production structure (newly industrialized countries entering world markets) initiated crises for complete industrial sectors and thus forced European industrial countries to adapt their industrial structures. Thus more or less far-reaching state interventions in the industrial sector were initiated in almost all industrial countries. In addition, several countries launched research and technology policies in attempts to provide for structural transformations of industry.

Increasing EC activities in the area of research and technology policy have to be seen in this context. In a certain way, they parallel the debate on the technology gap that lay behind the first attempts to develop research and industrial policies in the mid-1960s.[30] Already at the beginning of the 1970s, the European Commission undertook preliminary cautious attempts to determine possibilities for an active research and development policy. These EC initiatives were still restricted to the civil aviation, shipbuilding and electronic data-processing sectors.

- In 1973 the GFS, created by EURATOM as a common research institute in 1958, undertook research projects outside the field of nuclear technologies.

- In March 1973 the Commission proposed a technology policy programme to support financially technological developments in the EC's common interest.
- In October 1974 a text was adopted by the Council of Ministers in which a common industrial policy was described as a necessity.

The expansion of fields of EC activity as well as the EC's efforts towards an active industrial policy have to be explained, as convincingly shown by Dang-Nguyen,[31] by the EC's wishes and interest to move from the negative to the positive side of integration, after the customs union had been established. The Commission perceived chances to switch gradually from merely being referee or night-watchman to becoming a stronger and more active formative force in support of the Community, in the face of member states hardly interested in further qualitative progress in the integration process. The so-called Colonna Plan was an important part of these advances. This first Commission memorandum dealing with industrial policy forcefully stated that a common industrial policy was indispensable for Europe's economic integration and technological independence. An action programme outlined five lines of action such as the removal of technical trade barriers, the harmonization of legal and tax rules and the support of European co-operation among enterprises by creating a European capital market.

The programme was intended to support the development of future growth markets but could not be carried out because the oil crisis and the consequent drastic economic slump in all EC member states forced the Commission to concentrate its efforts on the European crisis industries. Only after 1978 did attention turn to growth industries again, and somewhat later new information technologies were mentioned for the first time. The development of this technological sector as a new political theme can best be understood against the background of the general increase in importance of telecommunications. During the 1970s, telecommunications infrastructure expanded as never before in all European countries.

In parallel with these developments, the late 1970s witnessed the emerging diversification of the existing monocultural telecommunications infrastructure.[32] In the 1970s the introduction of new services – in the area of data communications – was fostered by the dominantly quasi-governmental PTTs but also by the CEPT. Indeed, in 1972 CEPT commissioned one of the first market studies in the field, the well known Eurodata study, which illuminated the perspectives of data transmission in the medium term and was continued for several years.

Several government reports as well as commissions testifying to the significance of old and new communication infrastructures also indicate the increased importance of telecommunications. In 1976 the West German Commission for the Expansion of Technical Communications Systems (Kommission für den Ausbau des technischen Kommunikationssystems) published its report. The famous French report by Nora and Minc[33] was also elaborated in that period. Additionally, several countries individually adopted specific technology policy measures:[34] in West Germany, the joint 'Programme Technical Communication' of the postal and the research ministries (1978); in France, the so-called 'Plan Télématique' (1978); whilst the British government introduced its videotext system Prestel towards the end of the 1970s and its 'teletext initiative'.[35]

EC politicians became increasingly aware of the telecommunications sector because of developments such as the growing economic importance of communications technologies and the frequent use of terms such as 'telematic' and 'information society' in discussing technological changes. The Council of Ministers generally agreed with the Commission's activities, which were still very tentative in the first half of the 1970s. Conflicts arose, however, between the EC and the CEPT, and the latter even held an extraordinary conference of its telecommunications committee in March 1974 to clarify the relationship between the EC and the CEPT. The CEPT committee concluded that the EC had initiated research efforts in fields that were overlapping with CEPT activities. The committee therefore suggested that the EC delegate CEPT to carry through studies of interest to the EC.[36] Three months after the PTT ministers had met informally, a formal meeting of the 'responsible' Council of Ministers was held in December 1977, marking the EC's first official action in telecommunications policy. In a 'tour d'horizon' the Council dealt with problems of a European telecommunications policy as well as possibilities of co-operation between the Commission and the CEPT. Based on a general willingness to co-operate, four possible areas were examined:

1 industrial policy;
2 the roles of postal administrations and the private sector in the area of telecommunications;
3 price trends for telecommunications networks and services;
4 co-ordination of research and development projects.

These first activities of the Council, to a certain degree confirming the Commission's claim to play the central role in a future European telecommunications policy, were followed in 1979 by the Commission's report which for the first time emphasized the industrial policy dimension of information and communications technologies and their closer interconnections. The report opens with the statement that Europe is in the process of becoming an information society. Here, as well as in the following sections, the report evidently adopted the well-known lines of argument that had been presented earlier by Nora and Minc: the contrast between Europe's weakness in information technology and microelectronics and its strength in the telecommunications sector was emphasized. Europe's share of the world market was estimated to be a third for telecommunications (with an annual growth rate of 7 per cent),

26 per cent for information technologies (17 per cent annual growth) and 19 per cent for semiconductors (25 per cent annual growth). Despite the existence of national programmes to strengthen these industries, Europe had not been able to improve its position in the last two industries. The strength of the United States was seen to be its large domestic market and Japan's ranking position to be its coherent industrial policy. In an obvious attempt to combine these two strengths for a European initiative, the report presented several proposals: a co-ordinated European industrial policy; an initiative to improve the qualifications of the work-force; the creation of a common European market for telematic services (e.g. integrated services digital network (ISDN)); the establishing of a European information industry; and the fostering of co-ordination and co-operation between producers and users. The Commission presented a detailed schedule for the execution of this programme.

A year later the Council announced a recommendation that was prepared by the Commission (the so-called Dublin report). In September 1980, the Commission submitted three recommendations to the Council (Com(80)422 Final) which called for efforts to harmonize the telecommunications sector, to create a common market within the EC for terminal equipment and to open public procurement telecommunications markets. These proposals were accepted, if only half heartedly, by the Council of Ministers as recommendations.[37]

The European Parliament, too, got involved in the discussion and presented a resolution in May 1981 which interestingly called on the Commission to use directives and not just recommendations in its efforts in the telecommunications sector. The resolution pointed out that an increasing number of telecommunications services had developed in Europe and helped to create the problem of international standardization. It criticized the balkanization of the European telecommunications market and stated that large development efforts were necessary to achieve continuous export successes. Markets of certain minimum sizes were required. It therefore seemed logical to request expansion in the telecommunications markets. Later these arguments were routinely used by the Commission. By the spring of 1981, despite the impetus of these early initiatives, the Commission was unable to convince the Council which took a long time to reach decisions. National egoisms represented by powerful postal administrations and telecommunications industries oriented towards home markets rendered a common telecommunications policy very difficult.[38]

The American challenge and a European counter offensive

By mid-1983 the Commission took the offensive. In June it sent a note to the Council signed by Davignon, responsible for industrial policy matters. The note once again strongly emphasized the need for a common telecommunications market. The note is seen by many as the definitive break-through of an EC telecommunications policy. In September a Commission recommendation followed, outlining six lines of action for a common telecommunications policy:

1 setting medium- and long-range goals at the EC level;
2 defining and implementing a research and development programme;
3 expanding the market for terminal equipment by mutual recognition of registration standards;
4 co-operating closely to create the future telecommunications infrastructure;
5 using fully modern telecommunications technologies in underdeveloped regions within the EC;
6 opening up hitherto protected public procurement markets.

Next, the Commission installed a group of experts to develop a common strategy in co-operation with ministers of industry, postal administrations and representatives of the telecommunications industry. In six meetings between November 1983 and March 1984, this group of experts formulated an action programme that was forwarded to the Council of Ministers in May 1984.

The question remains of how the Commission could suddenly become so active. Undoubtedly, contextual factors played an important role. On the one hand, there were institutional factors, which we shall turn to in the next section. On the other hand, there were changes in the international economy, not least in the telecommunications sector, that prompted activities in the fields of economic, trade, industrial and regulatory policy worldwide.[39]

The most important changes in a European perspective took place in the United States. One of these changes was the break-up of the private telephone monopoly AT&T. Although this divestiture weakened the company's position in the US telecommunications market, it instigated the increased worldwide engagement of AT&T. Additionally, restrictions set by the Federal Communications Commission (FCC) on the company's activities in the data-processing sector were rendered invalid by the divestiture. AT&T marked its entry into the European market by a joint venture with Philips. AT&T's efforts to enter the information technologies market were also reflected in a 40 per cent participation in Olivetti. Another factor closely related to the divestiture was increased efforts to deregulate in the United States. These actions created opportunities for Europeans to set foot in the US market. In a quasi-countermove, however, Europeans were faced with US requests to liberalize European telecommunications markets.[40]

At approximately the same time, IBM increased efforts to diversify into the telecommunications sector. It came as an alarm signal for many European states when IBM won a DM50 million contract from the West German Bundespost to build the computer centres for the new telecommunications service *Bildschirmtext* (interactive videotex), thereby beating SEL and the British GEC (in spite of interventions by the British Prime Minister). In April 1984, IBM received its hitherto largest telecommunications contract from British Telecom (BT) which was then awaiting privatization. The company was to equip 27 digital switching centres. Another (eventually abortive) agreement between IBM and BT to form a joint venture and install a text and data network was reached in July 1984.[41]

In this period, a conflict between the European PTTs and IBM developed concerning the standards for interconnections between communications networks. IBM at first did not satisfy requests to publish technical norms. The conflict became so critical that the British government intervened.[42] It annulled the agreement between BT and IBM in part because the company planned to build its data communications network on the basis of the IBM technology SNA and not the open system interconnection (OSI) standard which is producer neutral.[43] The European Commission also took advantage of the opportunity to represent common European interests in this conflict with the US company. On the grounds that IBM was abusing its dominant market position, the Commission instituted legal proceedings against the company.[44]

In general, the situation then seemed favourable for the Commission to strengthen the understanding of the member states that close European cooperation in telecommunications under the leadership of the EC was advantageous, if not necessary. To this end, dramatic pictures of AT&T's and IBM's strategies and a global industrial threat for Europe were painted. AT&T was portrayed as conquering Europe's telecommunications markets and IBM as using its market power to enforce its interconnections and communications protocols in telecommunications networks. All announcements and comments suggested the existence of an external threat or even the danger of an economic war.[45]

This series of events and the Commission's ability to use them 'rhetorically' and 'dramatically' are the main factors, according to Dang-Nguyen,[46] that explain the creation of a European telecommunication policy:

> twelve years of difficult relationships with PTTs were cancelled, thanks to what one could call a rhetoric of persuasion. The trick has been to get the political support of the heads of government, instead of the PTTs. But to get it, the Commission had to develop arguments akin to previous action in the crisis sectors. If member states could be persuaded of the likelihood of collapse, they would be induced to cooperate.

Another crisis scenario was presented by the Commission experts Caty and Ungerer[47] in an article in *Futuribles*. Telecommunications accounted for about 15 per cent of the market for information technologies; by the end of the century, 60 per cent was projected. Telecommunications would represent the 'backbone of information technology'. Technological developments would shorten innovation cycles, thereby cutting amortization periods for public transmitting technologies from 20 to 10 years. Simultaneously, development expenditures would continuously increase. For a digital transmitting station, costs would mount from US$0.5 billion to US$1 billion. A world market share of at least 8 per cent would be necessary to recover research and development costs. Since no European company would reach a market share of more than 6 per cent, however, the creation of a European telecommunications market was indispensable. As the major obstacles for such a market, the two experts identified the lack of a European network infrastructure and the fragmented and rigid regulatory frameworks.

Based on this analysis, two major strategies for common action were developed. First Caty and Ungerer called for liberalization and deregulation to open the market for new services and equipment within the EC. This did not represent the final goal but rather the means to improve the competitive position of the EC in comparison with US and Japanese industry. Second, they suggested the harmonious introduction of new telematic services within a unitary integrative digital network (ISDN). This was seen as the economic and infrastructural precondition for a European telematics and information market. The experts emphasized, thereby reflecting the interests of postal administration, that national PTTs had to invest large sums, especially for ISDN.[48]

The Commission received the Council's consent to its view that neither actions by individual states nor protectionist measures by the Community were appropriate reactions to the massive external economic threat. Instead, the challenge was to be met by a common European effort to open markets and simultaneously commit extensive investments. In May 1984, these proposals were presented to the ministers of industry (and not those responsible for the postal and telecommunications system!)[49] The ten ministers agreed on initiating an offensive to counter US and Japanese industry.[50] In particular, the French government supported the Commission since it was motivated by strong self-interests to open national telecommunications markets.[51] As a first step, the Council decided on a 10 per cent reciprocal expansion of public telecommunications markets and reciprocal recognition of certain standards of registration for terminal equipment.

Thus the Commission's and consequently the Council's activities reached a new quality. It therefore appears necessary to mention several peculiarities of the EC's actions in order to keep in mind the limited possibilities that the EC, despite its efforts, has at hand. Applying the distinction between the contents of politics and political instruments,[52] the instrumental aspect is the most interesting for analysing the EC as an actor since it draws attention to the resources of the EC for action. Financial resources and laws are the most important instruments, but persuasion in the sense of strategies to mobilize and convince may also be used instrumentally.[53]

The agricultural budget accounts for the largest part of the EC's financial resources. Considering other sectors that require large subsidies (e.g. the steel industry), it becomes evident that there is hardly any financial room left for the EC to get involved in new sectors. There are limited possibilities for the EC to mobilize more money, although its budget has increased faster than the budgets of the member states.

Given scarce financial resources, the EC's telecommunications policy remains heavily dependent on its persuasive power. This is particularly true in the inner relationship between Commission and Council. Scientifically sound reports and analyses that present clearly targeted strategic implications play a central role in the interaction between Commission and Council. The relevance of persuasion has been made clear by the development of the EC's telecommunications policy as described so far.

The instrument of law is in principle less strictly limited than financial resources. However, the whole range of legal instruments is differentiated. Contractual agreements exist that are important in particular in the EC's external affairs (e.g. with CEPT). Then there are specific legally binding decisions by the Commission or the Council, as well as by the Court, which principally address individuals. Only regulations and directives concern all governments as well as all natural or legal citizens in the EC. Directives define certain results that are to be attained and leave open the way in which this is to happen. Only regulations are legally binding in a way comparable with laws in the individual states.

As the EC's and especially the Commission's activities reached a new qualitative level in 1984, a strengthening and extension of legal instruments was required. After years of studies, opinions, appeals and moral persuasion, a basis of legitimacy was built that made more concrete action such as binding decisions and regulations possible. The Commission did not flinch from attacking those individual member states that would not or would only hesitantly follow the chosen path. When necessary, the Commission cited its mission to realize a common market and could rely on support from the European Court and its decisions upholding competition.[54] Thus the Commission's position that public postal administrations act as private enterprises if they loan terminal equipment to individuals or sell services[55] succeeded even despite powerful national telecommunications administrations such as West Germany's Bundespost. After the telecommunications sector was stirred up and the British telecommunications system was completely restructured by the privatization of BT and the admission of a competitor (Mercury) into the network, the Commission not only found itself in a sounder legal position but was also increasingly supported by political arguments and allies in the member states.[56]

As a consequence, despite resistance from the board of the Bundespost and as requested by the Commission, West Germany's federal government relinquished its monopoly for modems. Later, it also gave up its monopoly for wireless telephones. In the latter case, the postal administration was required to modify the regulation that prescribed this monopoly within only three months.

The Commission's willingness to act as well as the opportunity to make more legally binding actions in the telecommunications sector increased. In addition, the Commission accelerated its decision-making process, more detailed decisions were passed and the density of the regulatory network was intensified. The Council also followed the same course since it did not want to appear to block the integrative process. The Council assumed the initiative to reorganize the EC's telecommunications sector and now had to accept all further more detailed steps as long as the Council's consent was necessary. Thus, between November 1984 and December 1986 the Council passed eight decisions (cf. Table 4.1).

In 1984, the personnel and institutional foundation of this new policy field expanded with the establishment of a Task Force on Information and Telecommunications Technologies. A few years later, the Task Force, originally merely an *ad hoc* group of enthusiastic European professionals, was turned into an autonomous directorate general of the Commission. Simultaneously, a division of labour between the EC and CEPT, to a certain degree a competitor, was established. An agreement to co-operate, signed in June 1984, was followed by the creation of a permanent liaison secretariat (SSA, Sécretariat pour les Spécifications et les Agréments). A consensus was reached among the European standardization institutions (CEN/CENELEC) with the most important European computer companies using the OSI standardization model.[57]

Meanwhile CEPT and CEN/CENELEC established a common commission to work on standardization and to co-operate closely with the European Commission.[58] In addition, existing high-technology research programmes were integrated into the telecommunications programme (Table 4.2).

External economic threat, internal political pressure to succeed and institutional reform

As the analysis of the EC's telecommunications policy has shown, the Council, the Commission and the Court have developed an independent and dynamic policy in this area. The Commission is the driving force and follows a policy that has been dominantly guided by industrial policy concerns since the early 1970s and extends beyond the narrow boundaries of research and technology policy as defined in the Treaties. Towards that end, the Commission cites Article 235 of the EEC Treaty which includes a general clause entitling the Commission to enter policy fields for which the Treaty provides no spe-

Table 4.1 Council decisions in the field of telecommunications policy (to 1987)

Date and type of decision	Subject	Document
Recommendation 12 November 1984	Implementation of harmonization in the field of telecommunications	84/549/EEC
Recommendation 12 November 1984	First phase of opening access to public telecommunications contracts	84/550/EEC
Decision 25 July 1985	Definition phase for Community action in the field of telecommunications technologies (RACE)	86/C 160/01
Directive 24 July 1986	Initial stage of the mutual recognition of type approval for telecommunications terminal equipment	86/361/EEC
Regulation 27 October 1986	Community programme to develop specific disadvantaged regions by improving access to advanced telecommunications services (STAR)	86/3300/EEC
Directive 3 November 1986	Acceptance of common technical specifications of the MAC/packages-norm-family for direct satellite TV	86/529/EEC
Decision 22 December 1986	Norms in the field of information technologies and telecommunications	87/95/EEC
Recommendation 22 December 1986	Co-ordinated introduction of ISDN in the EC	86/659/EEC

Sources: Commission of the European Communities, Official Documents: Community Telecommunications Policy (DG XIII Telecommunications, Information Industry and Innovation), Brussels, 1986; Commission of the European Communities, 'Towards a Dynamic European economy', Green Paper on the Development of the Common Market for Telecommunications Services and Equipment, COM (87) 29 Final, Brussels, 1987; E. Lalor, Action for telecommunications development. STAR: a European community programme, in *Telecommunications Policy*, 11 (1987) 115–20; P. d'Oultremont, The RACE programme. The European route towards integrated broadband communications, in *Telecommunications Policy*, 12 (1988) 119–26.

cific legitimacy if these activities are deemed necessary for the realization of the common market. To prevent this general clause turning into a carte blanche for the Commission, Article 235 calls for the Council's unanimous consent for respective proposals by the Commission.

Initially, microelectronics and information technologies were the relevant technologies for the telecommunications sector which only gradually developed into an independent policy field in the 1970s. Commission studies and reports on the state of the EC's industry and research repeatedly evoked the threat of US and Japanese competitors. In the Commission's view, appropriate reactions would require co-ordinated actions by the Community. Accordingly, the member states' activities were to be synchronized, and the EC

Table 4.2 Old and new research programmes relevant for the telecommunications sector

COST 11	Implementation of the European Informatics Network (EIN)
Euronet/Diane	European data-transmitting network linking approximately 300 databases, Euronet since 1975, Diane since February 1980
FAST	Planning science and technology; since 1980
RACE	Research and development programme for advanced communication technologies; definition phase since 1983 Phase 1 (1987–92): development of a technological basis for integrated broadband communications
ESPRIT	10-year programme of basic research in information technologies (microelectronics, software, office technologies, production control, etc.)

Sources: H. Nasko, 'Erfahrungen, Stand und Zukunftsperspekiven der europäischen Gemeinschaftsprogramme', in W. Kaiser (ed.), *Telematica (Kongreßband) Teil 1: Integrierte Telekommunikation* (München: Fischer, 1986), pp. 15–26; M. Carpentier, 'Mit "ESPRIT" in die technologische Zukunft', in H. Afheldt, H. Schmidt, M. Carpentier, J.D. Noulton, P. Sudreau, and H. Wolff (eds), *Der Staat als Pionier?* (Stuttgart: Poller, 1987), pp. 47–61; G. Dang-Nguyen, 'A European telecommunications policy. Which instruments for which prospects', Unpublished paper, ENST, Brest, 1986, at p. 329.

had to develop its own initiatives. The co-ordination of the policies of Commission and Council as laid down by Article 235 proved to be no barrier since Commission and Council shared the perception of an external trade and industrial policy threat. In this situation of external threats, the actors are oriented more towards solving the problem than towards bargaining; the latter orientation prevails in situations when distributive effects are at stake.[59] Naturally, this outcome is also affected by the fact that the budget for the EC's industrial and technology policies did not represent a very large amount to be distributed. The Commission and the EC as a whole successfully entered a new policy field in small steps and thereby opened up additional options for action in relation to the member states.

The insight that the initial competitiveness of the EC's industries depended on the existence of a large internal market focused the Commission's attention on the structure of, and the relevant actors in, this internal market. National markets proved to be protected extensively as far as telecommunications networks, services and terminal equipment were concerned. These markets were controlled by PTTs which in fact held supply and demand monopolies. In addition, these power structures were cemented by international agreements within the International Telecommunication Union and CEPT.[60]

The strategy of the EC Commission at the end of the 1970s and at the beginning of the 1980s was therefore to make sure that the monopolies of the national PTTs would not gain additional power. This was supported by the European Court which in turn tried to expand its responsibilities continuously and enforced competitive regulations on public trade and service monopolies. These initiatives were met partly by resistance and partly by hesitant cooperation from national telecommunications administrations.[61]

Increasing activities by the Commission in the field of telecommunications and other related policy fields were accompanied by the Court's market-oriented decisions and showed the majority of the member states that European action was needed. The interests of the member states' governments in simultaneously staying in control as far as possible as well as in successfully establishing a large common market and united external representation helped to strengthen the European Council. As the forum of the respective heads of state and government, the Council exemplified the dominance of national states in shaping the EC. But it was also more dependent on political success than was the Council of Ministers.

At the beginning of the 1980s in particular, the European Council was under pressure to attain success. The widely perceived external economic threat was accompanied by a public disenchantment with a Europe that symbolized bureaucratic mismanagement much more than by a will for European unification. For leading politicians and their image at home, it seemed unpromising to meet at highly publicized summit meetings that would not produce any results. Thus they preferred to pick up Commission proposals that were not costly but promised political success. The two most important of these decisions aimed to strengthen the EC in competing on the world market and, as a precondition, to accelerate decision-making processes within the EC. These decisions involved the Council in initiating an institutional reform of the EC: the promotion of the Internal Market Programme and the Single European Act.

The Internal Market Programme originated from a meeting in Copenhagen in December 1982 at which a special Council of Ministers was established to promote the establishment of the internal market.[62] In contrast with the other Councils, this Council of Ministers was not restricted to a specific sector. Instead it was assigned an inter-sectoral task that was defined in technical rather than political terms, thus making it easier to reach agreement.[63] In 1985, the Commission proposed a schedule for the realization of the internal market by 1992; it was passed in March as a European Council decision without any problems. As early as June 1985, the Commission presented a White Paper which included very detailed plans and a list of measures necessary to reach the goal.

The Single European Act constituted an even more serious step towards institutional reform. It was passed by the European Council in February 1986 and required the member states to attempt to arrive at a common European foreign policy. In this document research and technology policy was for the first time cited explicitly as a common European task. The Single European Act proved that the European Council was able to give a fresh impetus to the further institutional development of the EC. It has to be seen as a demonstration by the member states that they are still capable of collective action to strengthen the EC, especially the Commission, as a corporate actor. In Article 145 of the EEC Treaty the Council provided the Commission with legislative powers by giving the Commission the right to regulate the execution of Council decisions. The Commission's field of activities is once again widened dynamically and legal rights of member states are drastically cut back.[64] That this was not only symbolic politics and that relevant national competences were, in fact, transferred to the EC is indicated by the slow ratification of the Single European Act by the member states.[65] It is clear, however, that the realization of the document's goals will continue to meet resistance from member governments protecting their national interests. They still remain powerful actors since it can be assumed that decisions of fundamental importance will continue to require unanimous support.[66]

In all, a strengthened Commission entered the next round of the conflict on telecommunications policy. Its strength is not, however, exclusively based on the changes in primary EC law. The Commission also achieved an important victory in the European Court. In a decision of 20 March 1985 the Court essentially confirmed the Commission's reproach of BT at the end of 1982 for abusing its monopoly power.[67]

It remains to be seen whether the national PTTs that are most severely affected by telecommunications deregulation will try to use CEPT to limit the Commission's influence when they prove to be too weak. This possibility is at least partly dependent on the opinions of the responsible ministers in the Council. The EC has a strong position in CEPT as long as the ministers support the Commission. Although the EC itself is not represented in CEPT, almost half of the twenty-six members of CEPT are from EC countries. When the ministers do not support the Commission, two different political concepts of regulating the telecommunications sector collide. On the one hand, CEPT's concept is oriented towards technical aspects of telecommunications, aims at common standards and takes the interests of the PTTs into consideration. The EC strategy, on the other hand, is guided by an industrial policy perspective and aims at setting standards quickly in order to open up markets, to unify markets and to release all potential forces to achieve economic growth. The realization of this goal necessarily requires that the telecommunications sector, especially the public sector, be completely reconstructed.

The Commission is determined at least to initiate the restructuring process, documenting this goal in the Green Paper on the development of a common market for telecommunications services and equipment published in June 1987.[68] The Green Paper represents a rather concommittal 'notification'. In contrast, a new 'Directive', aimed in a certain way 'against all member states', is much more binding. The Commission used its power to pass this Directive on 16 May 1988 without the Council's consent.[69] The Directive requires member states to cancel all monopoly rights of any 'company' (including PTTs!) in the market for terminal equipment. The ministers responsible for the telecommunications sector in the member states protested at this decision by the Commission. At an informal Council meeting in Berlin, the postal ministers had warned against such a decision. France, the United Kingdom and West Germany in particular insisted that all Directives have to be proposed to the Council of Ministers (*Handelsblatt*, 2 May 1988). Power struggles of this type are emerging between the Commission and the Council of Ministers on legal matters and between the EC and powerful PTTs on the future of telecommunications policy.

Conclusion

This analysis of the EC telecommunications policy shows that the regime and corporate actor approaches are not alternative and mutually exclusive concepts. Instead, they should be seen in combination. In contrast with other international regimes, relatively independent units were established when the institutions of the Community were created. Those institutions were able to develop into strong corporate actors. The actions of the Commission, the European Court and, as we have shown, in part the Council of Ministers suggest an interpretation of the EC as a whole as a corporate actor. These three actors are interested, beyond merely securing their existence, in strengthening their own position within the EC and thereby strengthening the EC as a whole.

The example of the telecommunications policy shows how processes of 'actor building' or 'actor strengthening' are connected to the process of regime transformation. The EC was threatened by the United States and Japan in the growth sector of information and communications. This threat was additionally dramatized by the Commission's reports and prompted the member states to accept in principle a co-ordinated European telecommunications policy under the leadership of the Commission. In a regime composed of relative equals, no single member of the regime could take on a leadership role. Given the external economic threat and worldwide economic stagnation, the telecommunications policy could only follow an industrial policy perspective. The central idea of European integration is the creation of a common market. This goal is also compatible with the idea of establishing this market as a reference market for export-oriented industry. The Commission could, therefore, hope to receive support from the European Court whose decisions are oriented towards competition and free trade on the basis of the Community's treaties.

Thus the Commission, in the end always supported by the Council, initiated a structural change in the telecommunications sector that could possibly also affect CEPT and thereby change that regime too. The rather 'soft' regime CEPT, with its more technical orientation, is characterized by national, sovereign and publicly controlled constellations of several companies in well protected markets. Essentially, its international co-operation serves to establish the technical feasibility of communicating language, images and data across borders. Established domains are respected. By contrast, the new European free-trade regime forced by the Commission results in deregulated telecommunications, in open markets for terminal equipment, services and partial networks and in international competition and co-operation among those that operate networks, offer services and produce equipment. Communication ceases to be understood as an essential social task and is seen as a commodity. A referee has only to watch that certain minimal standards are observed.

Telecommunications policy shows that the position of the EC has improved in comparison with its member states. From an actor perspective it would be incorrect, however, to isolate this policy domain. EC actors are interested in acquiring the competence to prescribe the general political guidelines not only here but also in many other policy fields that are relevant for the Community. Therefore the corporate actor EC, and especially the Commission, will continue to foster the regime transformation, not only in specific policy fields like telecommunications but for the EC as a whole.

Notes

We are grateful for valuable comments on an earlier draft to Jürgen Häusler, Beate Kohler-Koch, Renate Mayntz, Fritz W. Scharpf and Uwe Schimank. This contribution was translated from the German original by Susan Wylegala-Häusler.

1 In so far as the first integration theorists were aware of this sector, D. Mitrany (*A Working Peace System* (Chicago, IL: Quadrangle, 1966), p. 133), for example, cites the International Telegraph Union (1865) and the Universal Postal Union (1875) as prime examples of successful international co-operation. In a footnote, Mitrany proposes that Benjamin Franklin's efforts to establish a unitary postal system were more instrumental in unifying the United States than any other factor.

2 Mitrany, op. cit.

3 E.B. Haas, *Beyond the Nation-State. Functionalism and International Organization* (Stanford, CA: Stanford University Press, 1964).

4 Cf. P.C. Schmitter, 'A revised theory of regional integration', *International Organization*, 24 (1970), pp. 836–68.

5 R.O. Keohane and J.S. Nye 'Transgovernmental relations and international organizations', *World Politics*, 27 (1975), pp. 39–62; R.O. Keohane and J.S. Nye *Power and Interdependence* (Boston, MA: Little, Brown, 1977); D.J. Puchala 'Domestic politics and regional harmonization in the European communities', *World Politics*, 28 (1976), pp. 496–520.

6 Puchala, op. cit., p. 510.

7 P. Kenis and V. Schneider, 'The EEC as an international corporate actor: two case studies in economic diplomacy', *European Journal of Political Research*, 15 (1987), pp. 437–57, at p. 438.

8 S. Hoffmann 'Reflections on the nation-state in Western Europe today', *Journal of*

Common Market Studies, 21 (1982), pp. 21–37, at p. 35.

9 Cf. S.D. Krasner, 'Structural causes and regime consequences: regimes as intervening variables', *International Organization*, 36 (1982), pp. 185–205; S.D. Krasner, 'Regimes and the limits of realism: regimes as intervening variables', *International Organization*, 36 (1982), pp. 497–510.

10 Cf. A.A. Stein, 'Coordination and collaboration: regimes in an anarchic world', *International Organization*, 36 (1982), pp. 299–324, at p. 301.

11 J.R. Commons, *Institutional Economics: Its Place in Political Economy* (Madison, WI: University of Wisconsin Press, 1961), p. 342.

12 J.S. Coleman, *Power and the Structure of Society* (New York, London: Norton, 1974).

13 Ibid., p. 44.

14 Cf. L.N. Lindberg and S.A. Scheingold, *Europe's Would-Be Polity. Patterns of Change in the European Community* (Englewood Cliffs, NJ: Prentice Hall, 1970), pp. 82ff.

15 Most prominent are the contract of March 1957 establishing the European Economic Community (EEC), the contract of April 1951 establishing the European Coal and Steel Community and the contract establishing Euratom which was signed in March 1957. As early as March 1957, a contract established the Assembly, the Court and the Economic and Social Council as common institutions of the EC. But it took longer to establish a Common Council and a common Commission in the so-called Fusion Contract in 1965. Thus the federations were combined into one, the EC.

16 Kenis and Schneider, op. cit., pp. 437–57.

17 For the first time on 5 February 1963 in the case 'van Gend & Loos' (26/62) and again in July 1964 in the case 'Costa/ENEL' (6/64).

18 J. Schwarze, *The Role of the European Court of Justice in the Interpretation of Uniform Law Among the Member States of the European Communities* (Baden-Baden: Nomos, 1988).

19 J. Weiler, 'Community, member states and European integration: is the law relevant?', *Journal of Common Market Studies*, 21 (1982), pp. 39–56, at p. 53.

20 L.M. Friedman, *Total Justice* (New York: Russell Sage, 1985).

21 Cf. P.J. Katzenstein, *Small States in World Markets. Industrial Policy in Europe* (Ithaca, NY, and London: Cornell University Press, 1985), pp. 39ff.

22 Cf. R. Mayntz, 'Corporate actors in public policy. Changing perspectives in political analysis', *Norsk Statsvitenskapelig Tidsskrift*, 3 (1986), pp. 7–25.

23 Cf. T. Oppermann, P. Conlan, M. Klose and S. Völker 'Rechtsgrundlagen von Technologiepolitik (Insbesondere nach Europarecht und Grundgesetz)', *Ordo-Jahrbuch für die Ordnung von Wirtschaft und Gesellschaft*, 38 (1987), pp. 209–31.

24 We gratefully acknowledge the help of Gerda Ehrlenbruch and Günter Schröder in collecting and preparing the material.

25 A. Geerling, 'Das Post- und Fernmeldwesen in der europäischen Integration', *Jahrbuch des Postwesens*, 8 (1959), pp. 174–217.

26 Cf. C. Labarrère, *L'Europe des postes et des télécommunications* (Paris: Masson, 1985); H. Steinmetz, 'Geschichte der Deutschen Post – 1945 bis 1969', in H. Steinmetz and D. Elias (eds), *Geschichte der Deutschen Post*, vol. 4, *1945 bis 1978* (Bonn: Bundesdruckerei, 1979), pp. 14–717.

27 F. Koller, 'Die Entstehungsgeschichte der Europäischen Konferenz der Verwaltungen für Post und Fernmeldewesen', *Archiv für das Post- und Fernmeldewesen*, 12 (1960), pp. 237–75.

28 G. Dang-Nguyen, 'A European telecommunications policy. Which instruments for which prospects', Unpublished paper, ENST, Brest, 1986, at p. 329.

29 R. Mayntz, 'Zur Entwicklung technischer Infrastruktursysteme', in R. Mayntz, B. Rosewitz, U. Schimank and R. Stichweh (eds), *Differenzierung und Verselbständigung: Zur Entwicklung gesellschaftlicher Teilsysteme* (Frankfurt, New

York: Campus, 1988), pp. 233–59.

30 C. Layton, *European Advanced Technology – a Programme for Integration* (London: Allen & Unwin, 1969); J.J. Servan-Schreiber, *The American Challenge* (London: Hamilton, 1968).

31 Dang-Nguyen, op. cit., p. 181.

32 V. Schneider and R. Werle, 'The development of telecommunications in Germany after World War II: from a communications monoculture to diversification', Paper presented at the Technical University of Twente, Netherlands, February 1988.

33 S. Nora and A. Minc, 'L'informatisation de la société', Report to the President of the Republic, Paris, 1978.

34 Cf. P. Humphreys, 'Legitimating the communications revolution: governments, parties and trade unions in Britain, France and West Germany', in K. Dyson and P. Humphreys (eds), *The Politics of the Communications Revolution in Western Europe* (London: Frank Cass, 1986), pp. 165–94.

35 A. Cawson, 'The teletext initiative in Britain: the anatomy of successful neo-corporatist policy-making', Paper presented at the ECPR Joint Session of Workshops, Amsterdam, April 1987.

36 D. Elias, 'Geschichte der Deutschen Post – 1970 bis 1978', in H. Steinmetz and D. Elias (eds), *Geschichte der Deutschen Post*. vol. 4, *1945 bis 1978* (Bonn: Bundesdruckerei, 1979), pp. 719–1064, at p. 927 (our translation).

37 Dang-Nguyen, op. cit., p. 299.

38 K. Morgan and D. Webber, 'Divergent paths: political strategies for telecommunications in Britain, France and West Germany', in Dyson and Humphreys (eds), op. cit., pp. 56–79.

39 Cf. Ch. Hüttig, 'Die Reregulierung des internationalen Telekommunikationssektors', in U. Albrecht (ed.), *Technikkontrolle und internationale Politik* (Leviathan, Sonderheft 1988); Morgan and Webber, op. cit.

40 Cf. D. Schiller, *Telematics and Government* (Norwood, NJ: Ablex, 1982), pp. 149ff.; Committee on Technology and International Economic and Trade Issues, *The Competitive Status of U.S. Electronics Industry* (Washington, DC: National Academy Press, 1984), pp. 75ff.

41 Labarrère, op. cit., pp. 190f.

42 The British conservative government tried to serve its own interests here too. After deregulating the telecommunications sector and thereby attempting to create competition, the government was not now ready to substitute a private for the public monopoly.

43 Since the hardware and software architecture of SNA is adjusted down to the last detail to IBM hardware, it is practically impossible either to use different equipment in this network or interconnect this telecommunications network with others. 'Communications across the boundaries necessitates gateway processors, which will restrict intersystems communications to the lowest common denominator' (P.H.M. Vervest, 'Standardization as a governmental policy tool – West European harmonization of tele-information services', in G. Muskens and J. Gruppelaar (eds), *Global Telecommunication Networks: Strategic Considerations* (Dordrecht: Kluwer, 1988), pp. 39–56, at p. 48.

Open System Interconnection is a standard created in the international standard-setting institutions ISO and CCITT. With the OSI model, coupling of products, systems and networks from different producers should become possible (cf. L. McKnight, 'The international standardization of telecommunications services and equipment', in E.-J. Mestmäcker (ed.), *The Law and Economics of Transborder Telecommunications* (Baden-Baden: Nomos, 1987), pp. 415–36.

44 G.-F. Caty and H. Ungerer, 'Les télécommunications nouvelle frontière de l'Europe',

Futuribles, 83 (December 1984), pp. 29–50, at p. 49.

45 A good example is provided by Labarrère, op. cit., p. 199: 'Après avoir abandonné aux Japonais et aux Americains la maîtraise du marché mondial de l'informatique et des composants éléctronique, les Européens sont, sur leur sol, acculés à la défensive dans une gigantesque bataille des télécommunications. Le Vieux Continent ressemble à un camp retranché où des états-majors (les administrations des PTT) tentent de se coordonner pour faire face à l'invasion.'

46 Dang-Nguyen, op. cit., p. 322.

47 Caty and Ungerer, op. cit., p. 32.

48 Ibid., p. 40.

49 This, of course, depends on the organization of respective national governments. In France, for example, the Postal Ministry is formally subordinated to the Ministry of Industry.

50 Labarrère, op. cit., pp. 199ff.

51 In 1983, the two large French telecommunications companies (CIT-Alcatel and Thomson-Telecommunication) signed an agreement to co-operate which was initiated by the Ministry of Industry to attain a better position in the world market. Suddenly faced with a monopolistic producer, the French telecommunications administration (DGT) had an interest in a least a partial opening of national markets. The successful modernization of the French telecommunications infrastructure gave the DGT the necessary self-confidence (cf. R. Mayntz and V. Schneider, 'The dynamics of system development in a comparative perspective: interactive videotex in Germany, France and Britain', in R. Mayntz and T.P. Hughes (eds), *The Development of Large Technical Systems* (Frankfurt, New York: Campus, 1988), pp. 263–98.

52 R. Mayntz, 'Regulative Politik in der Krise', in J. Matthes (ed.), *Sozialer Wandel in Westeuropa* (Frankfurt, New York: Campus, 1979), pp. 55–81.

53 Ibid.

54 The decision on 3 October 1980 in favour of free trade is seen as epochal (decision 120/78, 'Cassis de Dijon').

55 Cf. R. Schulte-Braucks, 'Telecommunications and freedom of trade in goods and services under the EEC Treaty', in E.-J. Mestmäcker (ed.), *The Law and Economics of Transborder Telecommunications* (Baden-Baden: Nomos, 1987), pp. 295–315.

56 In Germany a government commission for a reform of the telecommunications sector was established (cf. E. Witte (ed.), 'Restructuring of the telecommunications system', *Report of the Government Commission for Telecommunications* (Heidelberg: v. Decker, 1988).

57 P. Schneider, 'Schritte zur technischen Konformität. Europäische Zulassungen von Telekommunikations-Endgeräten', *Net*, 42 (1988), pp. 134–9.

58 This was created as an alternative to CCITT's committee T1 within the ITU which was seen to be dominated by IBM and AT&T (cf. Caty and Ungerer, op. cit.). More technical regimes such as ITU or CEPT are in a critical stage because of conflicts over technical standards that are economically or politically motivated. The ITU, in particular, however, has survived several critical attempts at politicization (cf. G.A. Codding, 'Politicization of the International Telecommunication Union: Nairobi and after', in V. Mosco (ed.), *Policy Research in Telecommunications* (Norwood, NJ: Ablex, 1984), pp. 435–47).

59 Cf. F.W. Scharpf, 'Joint decision trap: lessons from German federalism and European integration', *Public Administration*, 66 (1988), pp. 239–78; F.W. Scharpf, 'Decision rules, decision styles, and policy choices', Max-Planck-Institut für Gesellschaftsforschung, Discussion Paper 88/3, Cologne, 1988.

60 Cf. J. Solomon, 'The future role of international telecommunications institutions', in

Telecommunications Policy, 8 (1984), pp. 213–22.

61 Cf. K.H. Neumann, 'Die Deutsche Bundespost vor den Herausforderungen der europäischen Telekommunikationspolitik', in J. Scherer (ed.), *Nationale und europäische Perspektiven der Telekommunikation* (Baden-Baden: Nomos, 1987), pp. 30–46, and M. Rottmann, 'Die EG und das Post- und Fernmeldewesen', in *Zeitschrift für das Post- und Fernmeldewesen*, 10 (1987), pp. 30–7, for the situation in West Germany.

62 H. Schmitt von Sydow, 'The basic strategies of the Commission's White Paper', in R. Bieber, R. Dehousse, J. Pinder and J. Weiler (eds), *1992: One European Market?* (Baden-Baden: Nomos, 1988, pp. 79–106, at p. 85.

63 R. Dehousse, 'Completing the internal market: institutional constraints and challenges', in Bieber, *et al.* (eds), op. cit., p. 318.

64 J. Falke and C. Joerges, 'Folgeprobleme der Europäisierung technischer Vorschriften und Normen für die Länder der Bundesrepublik Deutschland', in C. Joerges and K. Sieveking (eds), *Europäische Integration, Nationalstaat und regionale Politikkompetenzen*, ZERP Diskussions-Papier 2/1987, Bremen, 1987, p. 22 (our translation).

65 A referendum in favour of the EC was necessary to remove a parliamentary blockade in Denmark. Other hesitant countries awaited the Danish decision before ratifying. In West Germany, during the ratification procedure the states (*Länder*) reserved consultative rights in those cases where EC decisions concerned their competences.

66 R. Hrbek and T. Läufer, 'Die Einheitliche Europäische Akte', *Europa Archiv*, 6 (1986), pp. 173–84, at p. 176.

67 Decision in the case 'Commission vs. Italy' (British Telecom) (41/83).

68 Commission of the European Communities, 'Towards a dynamic European economy', Green Paper on the Development of the Common Market for Telecommunications Services and Equipment, COM (87) 29 Final, Brussels, 1987. Cf. also H. Ungerer, *Télécommunications en Europe* (Luxembourg: Office des publications officielles des Communautés européennes, 1988).

69 The Commission's directive of 16 May 1988 on competition in the market for telecommunications terminal equipment (88/301/EWG). The directive is formally based on Article 90, paragraph 3, of the EC Treaty, which already existed under the old law.

Chapter five

Broadcasting and the European Community: the Commission's audiovisual policy

Stylianos Papathanassopoulos

By 1992 the European Community (EC) expects to have removed all barriers to trade amongst the twelve member states and to have created a single integrated internal market. The Community's 1985 White Paper identifies the obstacles to the completion of a common market and sets out actions to be taken as well as a timetable for the removal of these obstacles.[1] Underlying this proposal is the belief that small national European markets do not have the appropriate size to benefit from the economies of scale that are needed for the development of both hardware equipment and software. Therefore the establishment of a single European market is seen as urgent: the EC, with a population of 320 million, constitutes the largest market in the industrialized world. A unified EC market would give a similar home market in terms of number of households to those available to industry in Japan and the United States. Moreover, considerable effort has been expended within the Community to explain not only the benefits but also the consequences of failure to achieve the single market target. The potential benefits of a single market, resulting from the achievement of economies of scale and removal of trade barriers, have been estimated to be an increase in the total gross domestic product of 4–7 per cent and the creation of up to 5 million new jobs in the medium term.[2]

Within this single market advanced telecommunications is seen as vital (see Chapter 4). Telecommunications will provide the electronic infrastructure, paralleling improved physical transport facilities and drawing Community countries into further economic, cultural and political interdependence, and eventually less technological dependence on American technology. In a similar way, broadcasting policy can assist not just in the cultural integration of Europe but also in the regeneration of the European programming industry as a counterweight to American programme imports and consequently the threat of American 'cultural imperialism'. These pressures for closer European integration are considerably enhanced by the technological convergence of telecommunications and broadcasting. In this chapter we focus on the European Commission's policy for the latter sector, but it will be seen that there are definite similarities between these 'converging', but still distinguishable, sectors. Just as telecommunications can no longer be seen as purely a domestic policy affair and as a distinct regulatory area, so technological advance has dissolved both national frontiers and sectoral boundaries in the field of broadcasting. Communications satellites, originally launched to carry point-to-point telecommunications signals, have become carriers of television signals across national borders. The arrival of satellite to feed cable channels has intensified the pressure for new regulation and/or co-ordination of policies with respect to the free flow of programmes throughout Europe.

Background

The European Commission has studied the future of broadcasting for some time and has come to the conclusion that, since satellite television raises a number of questions with a pan-European dimension, the Community is the appropriate body to find the necessary solutions. The Community's policy making started in March 1982 with a request from the European Parliament for a report on the legal problems raised by European broadcasting. The Commission finalized its report, 'Realities and Tendencies in European Television', in May 1983. Its main recommendation was support for the European Broadcasting Union's (EBU) plans for a European programme series.[3] On 23 May 1984 the Commission adopted a Green Paper, known as 'Television Without Frontiers', on a common market for television, with special regard to the free supply of services within the Common Market.[4] It stressed free access to television programmes across borders and invited discussion about the approximation of certain aspects of member states' broadcasting and copyright laws before formal proposals for legislation would be put to the Council of Ministers. In a Resolution adopted on 5 October 1985, the European Parliament called for a regulatory framework which would lay the foundations for an EC media policy.

The Commission published its final proposals in a Directive which it transmitted to the Council of Ministers on 16 March 1986. Its principal objective was to 'sweep away the entangled underwood of national regulatory obstacles' and to enable the free circulation of radio and television broadcasting within the EC. The aim was to establish minimum acceptable standards for all the member states, so that television viewers will be able to receive programmes from any other Community country, and to provide a liberal regulatory system to encourage the utmost freedom of broadcasting consistent with the spread of cable and satellite television.[5]

In addition, the Commission transmitted to the Council of Ministers on 12 May 1986 an 'Action Programme in favour of the EC Audiovisual Programme', which became known in January 1987 as the MEDIA Programme (Measures to Encourage the Development of the Audiovisual Industry, later renamed MEDIA 92). Its aim was to strengthen the audiovisual industries and it was based on three principles: 'pragmatism, professionalism as well as the creation of synergetic effects'.[6] In 1988 the Community and the Council of Europe launched the 'European Cinema and Television Year', a 12-month programme backed by twenty-four countries. The aim was (i) to produce a number of media events that would interest the public, (ii) to organize a number of important symposia and (iii) to create certain organizations, such as the European Academy of Cinema and Television, which would promote European cinema and television after 1988. The MEDIA 92 programme's projects and pilot schemes are summarized below.

I. DISTRIBUTION

- **European Film Distribution Office (EFDO)**
  The distribution of 'low-budget' European films, with a view to the opened market in 1992
- **European Film Club**
  European films to be broadcast by satellite television
- **Espace Vidéo Européen (EVE)**
  European video cassette films distribution network
- **Broadcasting Across the Barriers of European Language (BABEL)**
  European fund for multilingual production, proposing financial support for multilingual production, the development of subtitling and dubbing techniques, and training in jobs relating to multilingualism
- **The Independent Producers Market (EURO-AIM)**
  Setting up a promotional structure for independent productions (television, cinema, video) especially in the major European audiovisuals markets

II. PRODUCTION

- **MEDIA Investment Club**
  New techniques in audiovisual production (computer graphics, digital television, high definition television)
  Covers training, production and information
- **European SCRIPT Fund**
  Structure for the support of script development, in the means of financing script and pre-production projects, for the European Cinema and Television
- **European Association for Animation Film (CARTOON)**
  Co-operation in the area of production, distribution and training in animated films, initiated by the Association Européenne du Film d'Animation
- **Regional Development of the Audiovisual Industry**
  A project for the development of production facilities in the less favoured regions of Europe

III. TRAINING

- **Les Entrepreneurs de l'Audiovisuel Européen (EAVE)**
  Training in new management and production techniques in the audiovisual industry
- **The European Certificate for Cinema and Television Literature**
  A series of university level courses in writing scripts

IV. FINANCE

- **Media Venture / Media Guarantee**
  Setting up, at a European level, of a venture capital fund and a guarantee fund for the audiovisual industry

In its audiovisual policy the Commission has made a number of key assumptions:

1 Even though it is linked to culture, broadcasting is also an economic activity and so the Community is competent to regulate it under the EC Treaty.
2 The Community must ensure that the relevant directly applicable provisions of the EC Treaty (in particular, Articles 59, 60 and 62) should be respected, in order to suppress all discriminatory and other restrictions on broadcasting from other member states.
3 Present rules on advertising and copyright constitute obstacles to the free flow of television broadcasts between member states.
4 A limited number of measures should be adopted as a first step towards the establishment of a legal framework for a single Community.

At the European Council summit of heads of government in December 1988, it was agreed that the Community's attempts to regulate broadcasting should be consistent with the Council of Europe's draft Convention on Broadcasting, which had been negotiated in parallel with the Directive. The European Council argued that the Directive should adapt its proposals in the light of the Convention. The Directive, eventually, after a lot of political disagreement, bargaining and cross-pressures (see below), was adopted by the Council of Ministers at their meeting in Luxembourg on 3 October 1989. Typically, it will take two more years – three for Portugal and Greece – before it becomes *acquis communitaire*.[7]

The role of the European Commission

The Commission sees itself as a policy initiator pursuing incremental change, although it regards the outcomes as radical.[8] Hence it makes proposals which in reality are constantly re-adjusted. However, policy making in the Community should not be seen simply in terms of the preparation and agreement of legislative proposals. The implementation of policies provides a rich field for influence, especially where management committees and advisory committees have been established to oversee developments and to provide advice for future policy.[9] However, the absence of a clear political framework means that implementation is intrinsically an interactive and sometimes irregular process based on 'give-and-take' and 'trial-and-error'.

Apart from its traditional role as policy initiator, the Commission performs some other roles that are equally, and in some cases more, important. According to Dang Nguyen, the Commission has four options: passive or active, negative or positive involvement.[10] Active involvement is illustrated by the MEDIA programme (and by the RACE programme in the field of telecommunications), in which the Commission is an active partner and positive co-ordinator. Passive involvement refers to the stimulation given by the Commission to European projects that involve harmonization of regulations and standards, such as advertising and copyright regulations in the field of broadcasting (or standardization in the field of telecommunications).

The competence of the European Community to regulate broadcasting

One of the key characteristics of the EC lies in the scope and substance of its policy repertoire.[11] This characteristic derives from the scope of the EC Treaties which cover a broad and increasing range of external and internal policies, from trade to safety standards, from agriculture to employment, and more recently from media to some consideration of European defence. This flexibility has its roots in Article 235 of the Treaty of Rome which allows for the extension of the EC's policy agenda. In effect, Article 235 provides an *ad hoc* procedure consistent with the constantly changing situation in Europe. The dynamics of the economic process, and the fact that the objectives of the EC Treaty are gradually fulfilled, have inevitably entailed an ongoing process of development. What is different from the 1950s is that the EC now occupies itself more with common concerns than common goals. Like agriculture, broadcasting is a common concern. But just as in the area of agriculture, policy making for the field of broadcasting has proved to be a difficult process as different national attitudes to audiovisual problems have become evident.

The 'restricted' policy competence bestowed on the EC by the Treaties has not prevented it engaging in policy problems which compete and overlap with the preoccupations of national politics. However, every directive, decision or regulation must refer to the appropriate Treaty (ECSC, EC, Euratom) and to one or more articles. This formality is taken seriously in order to ensure that the Community bodies do not legislate on something that does not fall within their competence. Thus, the Commission relates its broadcasting policy to Articles 59, 60 and 62 of the EC Treaty and Article 10 of the European Convention on Human Rights, just as it relates its telecommunications policy to the goals reaffirmed by the Single European Act (as shown by Schneider and Werle). Just like telecommunications, broadcasting was seen as a purely domestic matter a few years ago but now, in the late 1980s and 1990s, is seen as a new theme for EC policy making. However, while the Community's telecommunications policy making has acquired a considerable degree of legitimacy over the last five years, and its policies are tolerated if not always welcomed, its broadcasting policy making has aroused a very considerable amount of disagreement and dissension among the interested parties and its member states, as will be seen.

In broadcasting, the Commission asserts that, since trans-frontier television does not respect frontiers, it also has a political and moral right to act because broadcasting is relevant to European integration. It justifies this particular argument by reference to Article 10 of the European Convention on Human Rights, which states that 'everyone has the right of freedom of expression. This right shall include freedom to hold opinions and to receive impartial information and ideas without interference by public authorities and regardless of frontiers'. According to the Commission, trans-frontier broadcasting will allow a closer union of the European people, safeguard and strengthen peace and freedom, create closer relationships between member states, and serve as a symbol of the fundamental liberties expressed in the Convention. Secondly, as seen, the EC asserts not only that it has responsibility under the Treaty of Rome but also that it is the appropriate common forum for action.

This view has not been widely accepted. Some commentators have argued that the existing mechanisms for regulating broadcasting are satisfactory. Some have suggested that other international bodies, such as the Council of Europe or the EBU, would be better fora for action or even that self-regulation would be preferable to the EC's legislation. For example, both the EBU, the co-ordinating body for Western European broadcasters, and the Council of Europe have a wider membership. The Council of Europe, in particular, represents the wider Europe of twenty-one member states, has been active for longer in media than the EC and has more experience of cultural and social affairs. Moreover, both the EBU and the Council have proved to be flexible enough to take account of the cultural diversity of national broadcasting organizations. Another point in support of the latter bodies is that satellite broadcasting does not respect the EC's frontiers any more than it does the frontiers of the member states. As an organization of only twelve countries, the EC is at a disadvantage. A further argument is that, since satellite technology is changing so fast, any rules are likely to be outmoded before they are adopted or have any time to take effect.[12]

But neither the EBU nor the Council of Europe are without their problems. The EBU has not been a powerful regulator in the past and has not been able to overcome the short-term self-interested goals of the larger broadcasting organizations within its membership. Similarly, the Council of Europe has never had any real power. For some, the very weaknesses of these organizations mean that they would be better regulators than the EC: they would be less likely to create medium- and long-term problems for the broadcasters. Moreover, some broadcasters have not been very happy to see the EC seek to enter into their well-protected field of action. Nevertheless, the fact that the Directive's proposals are broadly in line with those laid down by the Convention of the Council of Europe indicates that the 'turf war' between the EC and the Council of Europe may almost be at an end. Although all EC member states are also members of the Council of Europe, EC negotiators won agreement for a block EC membership of the Convention, enabling the Community to sign as a group rather than as separate countries. This move was necessary in order to give the agreement an EC legal status.

The European Court of Justice is the body at the Community level that will examine cases about satellite broadcasting and national protectionism, such as the recent case between the Dutch Advertising Society, the *Bond van Adverteerders* (BvA), and the state of The Netherlands in 1985 concerning the extent to which satellite channels can carry advertising. The outcomes of such cases are likely to affect media legislation in all EC countries and thus give an active role to the Court on the media scene. However, it is clear that the creation of a European supervisory body along the lines of the Independent Broadcasting Authority in Britain or the *Conseil Supérieur de l'Audiovisuel* in France, is likely to be vehemently opposed by those member states with a desire to maintain national state power rather than to merge their broadcasting affairs at the EC level.

Broadcasting and concepts of European integration

The Commission considers broadcasting to be relevant to European integration since it will bring closer the union of the European peoples. This view, if not driving zeal, is reminiscent of the optimism associated with integration theories. There have been three main streams of European integration theory: federalism, functionalism and neo-functionalism. All three are heavily influenced by Western liberal democratic practices and by the cultural backgrounds of their advocates.[13] These approaches are quite distinctive, however, in what they emphasize. The functionalist and neo-functionalist schools are focused primarily on the problems and procedures of co-operative policy making, whereas the federalists emphasize the formal goals of major political actors.[14]

Federalists envisage a United States of Europe and draw inspiration from existing federations, mainly from the United States. They often regard European unity as a process rather than the creation of a new constitution. In fact, federation has been viewed from two different perspectives. The first perspective regards integration as a process by which a community (consisting of a group of states) becomes integrated into a unity which will have a united external identity or personality. The second perspective considers integration as a form of government, suited to integrated communities and marked by a division of powers between central and regional action.

In contrast, functionalism and neo-functionalism in particular, stress that European union will come gradually. As regards the EC, they emphasize the flexibility of the EC Treaties which argue for further co-operation and provide a stage-by-stage process that will lead to economic integration and eventually to the transfer of political loyalties.[15] Eventually, say the functionalists, a shift will take place in the focus of economic policy making towards Brussels.[16] The traditional version of functionalism, heavily influenced by Mitrany's views, suggests that owing to the growing interdependence of the world, states have recognized that a number of technical functions might be more rationally performed through international co-operation in international bodies run by apolitical technocratic experts aiming to benefit the commonality.[17] On the other hand, neo-functionalism suggests that integration could be better promoted by the interaction or co-operation of political and economic forces seeking to benefit from this relation. Elite change provides the central dynamic of integration.

As history has shown, neither the economic nor the political assumptions of the sectoral approach to European integration were wholly correct.[18] The political outcomes of the integration process have been criticized since the expectations of the analyses have not been matched by reality. The EC institutions have been weak because they lack autonomy from the member states and also because their capacity to act is limited. It is thus questionable whether broadcasting can be considered to be a major tool for European integration. Television can hardly play the role of American films at the beginning of the film industry as a nation builder. Linguistic differences within Europe will impose the main barrier to this role. It might be argued that trans-frontier television can bring cultures together. However, this goal is also difficult to achieve because of the dominance of American programming on European channels. The potential of the smaller European countries to sell programmes to the larger ones seems very small. For example, the potential of Belgian films in the francophone market is reduced by the domination of French films even in the Belgian market.[19] The assumption that broadcasting can be employed as an instrument of integration therefore has to be seriously questioned. In the functionalist perspective of integration, European-level broadcasting policy making might provide a learning process through which citizens and policy-makers alike are gradually drawn into a co-operative ethos. Under the objective pressure of the need for co-operation in this field, citizens and policy-makers might be expected to learn to do things together and learn that they benefit from this experience. However, in practice, to what extent broadcasting will assist the achievement of a higher level of interconnectedness between the states, their policy-makers and their citizens is debatable.

Nevertheless, trans-frontier broadcasting (like the internationalization of telecommunications) confirms the paradox that exists in the unique regime of the EC. Even though the EC is a regime similar to what Keohane and Nye have called one of 'complex interdependence', the nation-state remains the basic unit within the EC and in world affairs.[20] Although the model of sovereignty as autonomy and independence is clearly impossible, the state still survives even though some of its powers have to be pooled with those of other states. In the perspective of European integration, interdependence theorists stress that there is a tendency to 'drift' towards further organized collaboration in response to the sheer density of economic transactions and of dependent relationships amongst developed economies. Indeed, trans-frontier broadcasting is an excellent example of an area of affairs where many apparently sovereign decisions are being seriously constrained or rendered ineffective by the decisions of others as well as by technological and economic trends and interests. This process can be seen, for example, in the alarmed reactions of the Spanish government to the appearance of a private Spanish-speaking channel transmitted via satellite, in the position adopted by the British delegation to the World Administrative Radio Conference in 1977 in favour of British cultural sovereignty in the face of a threatened 'invasion' of satellite transmissions from outside the country, or indeed in French fears about 'Coca-Cola' broadcasting from a Luxembourg-based satellite (see Chapter 6). Clearly, satellite broadcasting demonstrates very dramatically that states will have to adapt their policies to a new framework of interdependence. As in the telecommunications sector, this interdependence of developments and decisions in the broadcasting sector is now widely perceived.

Again, just as in the field of telecommunications, it now also appears obvious that multinational companies have gained an important role within the Community's boundaries as both political and economic actors. In the field of satellite television, both EC and non-EC multimedia conglomerates – such as those of Robert Maxwell in Britain, Robert Hersant in France, the Springer/Kirch and Bertelsmann concerns in West Germany; of Berlusconi in Italy, France and West Germany; or of the transatlantic entrepreneur Rupert Murdoch – are playing an increasingly important part in the broadcasting sector. They typically stress their role in enabling a free flow of information, programmes and advertising throughout Europe. However, as internationally mobile actors they are able to circumvent national regulatory policies, play individual state interests off against each other and exert considerable structural power in European broadcasting markets.

Hence, because purely national action can no longer be considered satisfactory, an effective system of regulation seems to require the establishment of a collective European regime. In broadcasting, in particular, individual action does not seem to promise better outcomes than does a co-ordination of domestic laws in a collective regime. This co-ordination is nothing more than a typical example of interdependence, a set of norms of behaviour and rules covering a broad range of broadcasting issues under the principle of long-term reciprocity. Such a regime, seen in the Final Directive, provides both constraints and opportunities and limits the freedom of individual member states for unilateral action in broadcasting affairs. However, the nation-state is by no means obsolete. Each nation-state has its individual calculations of self-interest and, accordingly, tries to see whether the overall balance of constraints and opportunities remains acceptable.[21] Of course, this balance is different for each state depending on the structure of the domestic political and economic systems. Such differences are very evident in the field of broadcasting. Thus the British, Dutch and Danish governments have made it clear that they would prefer the Council of Europe to promote the harmonization of television regulation. The (European) quota programming principle of the Directive has been supported by very few countries and has been opposed by, in particular, the British, Danes, Germans, Irish and Luxembourgers. The French have strongly favoured the quota provision owing to the fact that the proposed EC quotas were more aligned to French television regulation and thought of as protectionist measures for French and European programme industries. In the case of time restrictions for the scheduling of advertising, the Directive's proposal was agreed by the majority but opposed by the British, Irish and Luxembourgers.

These examples show that, even though they lose their absolute control over broadcasting policy, member states still press views aligned to domestic interests and policy. Emphasis is still given to the 'national interest'. The fact is that national governments remain the major actors in international politics because they are still the most cohesive and organized units involved. They can legitimately and effectively claim to manage the external interests of their societies. Consequently, the concept of intergovernmentalism remains central within the Community and limits the capacity of the Community institutions, and the Commission in particular, to accrue power independent from the member states. Hence, the appropriate unit of analysis remains the member state and the bargaining between it and other member states and organized interests. In the case of television, member states have served either to impede the EC's progress or to create another pole by using the Council of Europe. Paradoxically, the *acquis communitaire* has become a vital precondition of national autonomy at a time when, as in the case of television, there is a desire, at least in principle, to abolish barriers.

Ironically, the state's role has arguably been reinforced, especially in broadcasting affairs, by the fact that the liberalization of broadcasting in Europe appeared to have entailed a re-nationalization of broadcasting policies rather than an effective EC approach. In fact, so far the liberalization of broadcasting has occurred more as the result of an expansion of broadcasting usage of terrestrial frequencies (e.g. in France, West Germany and also as foreseen by the current British policy) than as the result of trans-frontier satellite transmission. This situation has also enabled states to remain largely in control of developments and to dictate their terms according to national broadcasting policies. Nevertheless, the advent of satellite television, and its undoubted future potential, does still impose an urgent necessity on states to take common action, since it amounts to a very real common concern which constitutes one of the essential characteristics of both the EC's rationale and their very complex interdependence. It is by no means certain, however, to what extent common broadcasting regulations will contribute to European integration. An impact is to be expected, but one that is likely to disappoint the optimists.

Broadcasting and Community decision making

A common feature of the EC's policies is a disproportion between effects and outcomes. Broadcasting policy has reflected this characteristic of the EC: a huge amount of political and administrative labour has so far produced meagre results. However, there is ample ground for believing that the Community will seek to speed up the policy process mainly because of the importance of the communications markets for both hardware and software. Significantly, in the field of communications, the Commission has already used Article 90 of the Treaty of Rome to attempt to bypass the more usual, and often protected, process of issuing EC Directives by consultation of the European Economic and Social Committee and the Parliament.

Helen Wallace has noted that EC policy typically consists of consultations among member states' governments on issues of common concern with the main objective of reconciling different views and the gradual alignment of national policies rather than the adoption of a comprehensive legislative programme at the EC level.[22] It constitutes a process through which a variety of agencies, groups and individuals interact to perform specific tasks and to grapple with common problems. This observation is very relevant to broadcasting policy. The procedure surrounding the production of both the Green Paper and the Directive demonstrated an obvious inclination to reconcile various views about broadcasting and an attempt to align them in a compromise. Moreover, the reluctance of many EC members to adopt the Final Directive indicates that broadcasting policy has followed this characteristic Community policy-making path. Even the latest principles of the MEDIA programme adopt the normal EC language, designed principally not to upset the heads of state.

To understand fully the Community's policy-making process it is useful to distinguish between two kinds of policy making which, to a certain extent, are elaborations of the incremental versus rational policy theories.[23] The first approach is called *re-active* policy making and is defined as an incremental process in which the solution depends on the gradual adjustment of existing policies. The objective is to alter the scope of policy instruments marginally as problems change or become more acute. By contrast, *active* policy making represents a rather ambitious attempt to establish a new set of different policies by means of a comprehensive solution.

The harmonization of broadcasting is one of the principal legal techniques which the Treaty of Rome has made available for pursuing the objective of creating and maintaining a common market amongst its member states. In broadcasting, the Commission, faced with the basic principle of the free movement of services within the EC, had two ways forward: either to produce comprehensive new legislation to harmonize every aspect of broadcasting, in order to ensure that there is no chance of the laws in any one EC country conflicting with those of another; or to propose a framework of basic rules. The first approach would require a radical and comprehensive appraisal, involving a range of specific solutions to numerous problems and in the last analysis an active policy. The second approach would involve a step-by-step reactive adjustment of policy. Indeed, the Commission chose precisely this second approach. The Commission went through the normal advisory stages over the years. It held discussions with relevant European interest groups, took opinions from advisory committees and set up working parties of government experts. In contrast, in telecommunications it seems that the Commission is attempting to pursue a rather active policy approach; the proposals in the Green Paper on telecommunications of 1987 appear to readjust domestic telecommunications regulations radically.

By 1988–9, the Community's broadcasting policy had reached its third stage and had been put before the Council of Ministers. Since the Parliament has increased its relative powers and can directly amend the Commission's proposals, it also played a part in the policy-making process. In the Directive, the Parliament made some minor amendments to the Commission's proposals. Even though they were rather rhetorical, some of them were necessary in order to clarify certain misunderstandings in the Directive. However, it was the Council of Ministers which finally approved the policy.

Nevertheless, the Commission's proposals for broadcasting have encountered considerable opposition from various groups and especially from the public-service broadcasters and countries with high programming quality. It is not difficult to see how laborious the Community's policy making is in practice. EC policy making can easily be influenced by organized interests with specialist knowledge that take advantage of the long period of time which elapses before a proposal becomes Community regulation. Thus, in most cases, a Community policy has a tendency towards compromise solutions. The Commission's broadcasting policy represents just such an approach of mutual accommodation.

Towards European television: the proposals on broadcasting

Advertising is regarded as the major contributor to the financing of broadcasting in the future. In the 1984 Green Paper, 'Television Without Frontiers', the Commission took the view that, since the EC member states had different content rules regarding advertising, unless positive steps were taken to harmonize advertising regulation broadcasters might well find it impossible to produce programmes for simultaneous transmission. It pointed out that the member states had to start looking for ways of removing legal barriers to the free movement of broadcasting services, which would also be necessary to prevent the distortion of competition. Thus the Commission proposed: (i) more air-time for television advertising; (ii) a ban on advertising tobacco and tobacco products; (iii) special rules for alcoholic advertisements; and (iv) rules to ensure that advertising-sponsored programmes are legally receivable in all member states.

As these proposals aroused immediate disagreement from various groups and governments, the subsequent Directive's eventual provisions were divided into two levels. The first deals with more restrictive regulations for domestic broadcasting along the lines of national regulations on advertising quantity and carriers (Articles 5 and 6). At the second level, the Commission establishes the free flow of advertising in trans-frontier broadcasting (Article 14) but sets a maximum threshold of 15 per cent of daily broadcast time for advertising. In addition at least one channel has to carry advertising (Articles 13 and 5). The 15 per cent quota is indicative of the compromise approach of the Commission. Most member states, and especially the Italians, had argued for a fixed percentage of 10 per cent, whereas others, and the British in particular, had argued for 20 per cent. A balance was established by the Commission in the final version of the Directive with a 15 per cent maximum per day rising to 20 per cent per hour during prime time periods.

The same approach of mutual accommodation is seen on the questions of personal rights and right-to-reply cases as well as of sponsorship. On *sponsorship*, the British Cable Authority as well as the Independent Television Association had lobbied for more flexibility to enable sponsors to become involved in the programme-making process. The Commission, however, was anxious to meet the concerns of other groups about the influences of sponsors on programmes. Ambiguity is seen on the sponsorship issue in the Directive (Article 12) which suggests that responsibility for programmes rests with the broadcaster and that the latter's editorial judgement must remain free from sponsor's influence. Yet the Directive does not even define the term sponsorship. The *right-to-reply* was discussed in some detail in the Green Paper and then disappeared in the Directive. This disappearance has to be interpreted as another compromise; it was too difficult to tackle such a matter because of the very different national approaches. For example, Britain has had no right-to-reply, although legislation is proposed in a private member's bill. The European Parliament, however, re-introduced the question of right-to-reply and asked for an independent body to enforce this right. On the *protection of children* from broadcasts that may damage their moral welfare (such as violence and pornography) the Directive is detailed because the provisions for this matter do not significantly vary between the member states. Nevertheless, the Commission does not define what would constitute common standards of protection of children, thus leaving considerable latitude to the member states about interpretation and application.

On *copyright*, the Commission's approach has produced another controversy. In the Green Paper (1984, section C, part 6) it argued for a compulsory licence for cable distribution throughout the EC countries since other alternatives such as contractual agreements or collective licensing were considered impractical. As with other issues, these proposals were strongly criticised by most interested parties. In the Directive, the question of copyright occupies Articles 17, 18, 19 and 20. In Article 17 the Commission surprisingly proposes a contractual agreement in the first instance; if that is not possible, it considers that a compulsory agreement would be necessary. At this section the Parliament proposed a major change. It suggested the formation of an arbitration body – of which membership would be determined by the member states in such a way that the copyright holders would be adequately represented – as a better way of solving this problem.

On *programming* production the proposals of the Directive (Articles 2, 3 and 4) have been heavily criticized by broadcasters. The Commission wanted to impose a minimum of 'EC-made' productions transmitted on European channels, with an initial quota of 30 per cent, rising to 60 per cent after 3 years. These programmes must not include news, sports, game shows or advertising. In Article 3, the Commission also requested broadcasters to commit 5 per cent of their budget to the purchase and transmission of work by independent producers from Community states. According to the Directive, these criteria were based on legislation in France and Italy, where, respectively, quotas of 60 per cent and 25 per cent for films were already imposed. The main aim behind these quotas was the protection of European production against foreign and especially 'Hollywood-made' programming competition as well as the stimulation of European production which will be necessary with the arrival of new channels, whether cable and satellite or terrestrial. These programming quotas, like those on advertising, aroused a large amount of criticism. Surprisingly, the Parliament proposed to make the quota stricter: instead of the proposed 30 per cent, it asked for 60 per cent immediately. On independent production it raised the initial percentage from 5 to 10 per cent.

Owing to resistance from some member states (such as Britain) to a fixed percentage quota for 'Europe-made' programmes, the EC countries decided to adopt a provision similar to that of the Convention of the Council of Europe on this issue. Thus, Article 4 of the Directive was amended, in its final version, to provide that, *'where practicable'* and by appropriate means, broadcasters should merely reserve a 'majority' proportion of their transmission time for Community works (although, following the European Parliament's amendment, Article 5 raised the quota for independent producers to 10 per cent). In terms of politics, this compromise was immediately seen as a 'victory' for the northern countries (such as Britain, West Germany, The Netherlands and Denmark) and a 'defeat' for the southern countries (such as France, Italy, Greece and Portugal). Moreover, the Americans piled on the pressure to persuade EC governments that they should not support the quota which was seen as a 'perversion' of international free trade which violated the agreements and principles of the General Agreement on Tariffs and Trade (GATT). This allegation, however, is questionable since television is not covered by GATT principles. The US reaction was motivated by fear that they will have to face a 'fortress Europe' which will jeopardize US business profits. In 1988, for example, Americal film-makers sold £393 million worth of programmes in the EC. However, the Commission sought to 'calm down' American anxiety by arguing that Europeans already produced an average of 68 per cent of all the programmes they watched, and predicted that American sales, if not market shares, would rise because the whole market would double in the next decade.[24] However, the quota issue was the one that, for some considerable time, appeared to put the whole fate of the Directive in jeopardy.

Whilst the Directive's proposals have aroused criticism, the Commission leaves the implementation as usual to the member states and they also remain in a position effectively to impose stricter rules and criteria on broadcasters under their jurisdiction (Article 3). Thus, in pursuit of its aim to 'sweep away' the obstacles that impede the freedom to broadcast across its member states, the Commission can be seen to be proceeding by means of the language of 'harmonization' as well as by reactive policy making in order to find a common acceptable denominator that might be used as a guide for the Community's regulations as a whole. It is perhaps such criticisms that caused the European Parliament to attempt to be more specific and stricter, but, if anything, its amendments strengthened rather than weakened the disagreements. The most important issue, however, is that the provisions on advertising, sponsorship and right-to-reply are bound by EC law; the provision on quotas is only a 'political commitment' by the EC countries, meaning that no EC country would be taken to the European Court for falling short of the suggested 'majority of European works'.

Towards a European policy for broadcasting: some concluding remarks

It seems that the Commission's policy for broadcasting has had one major characteristic: a market and consumer-led approach through harmonization of regulations and market unification. However, this approach seems to have encountered problems of Community-wide acceptance. In the Directive, the Commission has sought to discover a compromise amongst conflicting national broadcasting regulations, especially over advertising time and programming quotas.

In order to understand that more comprehensive alternatives to an approach of 'muddling through' will not only be unacceptable but also unrealistic, one has only to look at the various reactions not just within the Community but also within the Commission itself. There is tension, for example, between the Directorate General for the Internal Market and the Directorate General for Communications and Culture on the question of who is going to influence the Community policy on broadcasting. Moreover, the EC has seen a major debate about the social implications of the new communications technologies as well as the associated push towards liberalization within the communications sectors (including both broadcasting and telecommunications). The Commission, according to its own claims, has taken into account the social impact of its proposals and policies. Its basic argument is that citizens and consumers will benefit, as viewers, because they will have at their disposal a choice amongst a variety of services. It is not certain, however, to what extent the Commission's policy will provide all EC citizens with the benefits of the liberalization of broadcasting. It seems quite likely that the EC citizens with less purchasing power will either be excluded from these services or be offered only a basic provision.

Prior to 1992, it must be acknowledged that the Commission has at least succeeded in putting onto the European policy-making agenda the main issues about the future of European audiovisual services. The Commission has stimulated a debate about these issues. It is also clear that the Commission's proposals have had an effect, and will continue to do so, on practical policies. What is even more important is the incremental shift of the Community from its traditional policy areas to new ones, a fact that, at least, testifies to the adaptability and dynamism of this international organization. This adaptability has made the Community into a key international actor within the field of broadcasting. Even though broadcasting belongs to the new policy areas of the Community, policy was shaped by the Commission in the manner of other policies with a middle range reactive policy-making approach and with their stress on harmonization and co-ordination among the member states. In addition, in order to justify its competence in television, the Commission has approached the sector with a consumerist view which is not necessarily appropriate for this medium.

Moreover, new lines of action are required: in particular, the establishment of a coherent European position on the future development of policies for the hardware side of satellite communications in the Common Market. So far, the European Commission has proposed, and the Council of Ministers has accepted, a Directive for a common family of standards for satellite transmission, the so-called MAC-packet family.[25] In addition, in the case of high definition television (HDTV), the Commission has been spurred on by an impressive Japanese lead in this technology, which threatens the very survival of the European broadcasting equipment industry. Through its Eureka and RACE programmes, for information and telecommunications technologies respectively, the Commission has joined forces with European companies such as Thomson, Philips and Thorn-EMI to develop a broadcasting standard compatible with existing equipment. However, there remains an urgent need for action towards an open market for satellite reception antennae and other related equipment. This implies a common approach to the earth station market as well. Lastly, there is a need for a common approach to the future development of Eutelsat and the full use of the European Space Agency's potential.

Notes

1 Commission of the EC, *Completing the Internal Market*, COM(85)310, Brussels.
2 The 5 per cent calculated by the Cecchini study includes savings made by removing frontier delays and also the stimulus that would be given by new market entrants and by free play of competition. Among medium-term effects would be the advantages to be gained from the opening up of public procurement and the liberalization of financial services. In addition to boosting output, employment and living standards, cost of goods to the ordinary consumer should drop by 6 per cent. It is reckoned that the balance of public finances should benefit by the equivalent of 2.2 per cent of gross domestic product (GDP) and the Community's external position should improve by around 1 per cent of GDP. For further information, see the Cecchini report and the Information Bulletin of the EC of March 1988.
3 Interim Report on *Realities and Tendencies in European Television: Perspectives and Options*, COM(83)229 Final, European Parliament, Brussels, 25 May 1983.
4 *Television Without Frontiers, Green Paper on the establishment of the Common Market for broadcasting, especially by satellite and cable*, Communication from the Commission to the Council, COM(84)30 Final, Brussels, 14 June 1984.
5 A slight difference between Directive and the Green Paper is that the latter was addressed to television only whereas the former is addressed to both television and radio. However, most of the Directive's proposals are applicable to television only.
6 The MEDIA programme has ten main projects. In the distribution area, it aims to create a European co-operative for distributing low-budget films, a fund for multilingual productions and a means to help independent producers. The seven production projects span high definition television (HDTV), new scripts, animation, training in computer graphics and management as well as regional aid. Expenditure for the planning stage (1989) budget was to be ECU40 million.
7 *Council Directive, on the co-ordination of certain provisions laid down by law, regulation or administrative action in member states concerning the pursuit of television broadcasting activities*, 5858/89, Brussels.
8 P. Taylor, *The Limits of European Integration* (Worcester: Croom Helm, 1983); and A. Butt-Phillip, 'Pressure groups and policy making in the European Community', in J. Lodge (ed.), *Institutions and Policies of the European Communities* (London: Frances Pinter, 1983).
9 Butt-Phillip, op. cit.

10 D. Nguyen, 'Options for the European Community: arbitrator, mediator or actor', *Intermedia* (June 1988), pp. 106–8.
11 H. Wallace, 'Negotiation, conflict and compromise: the elusive pursuit of common policies', in W. Wallace *et al.* (eds), *Policies into Practice* (London: Heinemann, 1984).
12 House of Lords Select Committee on the European Communities, *Television Without Frontiers*, Session 1985–6, Fourth Report (London: HMSO, 1986).
13 J. Lodge, 'Introduction', in J. Lodge (ed.), *The European Union* (London: Macmillan, 1986).
14 C. Webb, 'Theoretical perspectives and problems', in W. Wallace *et al.* (eds), *Policy-making in the European Community* (London: Wiley, 1983).
15 Taylor, op. cit.
16 J. Pelkmans, 'Economic theories of integration revisited', *Journal of Common Market Studies*, no. 18 (June 1980), pp. 335–54.
17 See D. Mitrany, *The Functional Theory of Politics* (London: Martin Robertson, 1975).
18 C. Webb, op. cit.
19 A. Mattelart *et al.*, *International Image Markets* (London: Comedia, 1984).
20 R. Keohane and J. Nye, *Power and Interdependence* (New York: Little, Brown, 1977).
21 S. Krasner, 'Structural causes and regime consequences', *International Organisation* (Spring 1982), pp. 188–99.
22 H. Wallace, op. cit.
23 R. Mayntz and F. Scharpf, *Policy-making in the German Federal Bureaucracy* (Amsterdam: Elsevier, 1975).
24 See *Cable and Satellite Europe*, 6(19) (September 1989); *Screen Finance*, 21 September 1989; *Broadcast*, 22 September 1989.
25 Council Directive, on the adoption of common technical specifications of the MAC-packet family of standards for direct satellite television broadcasting, 5 November 1986, 86/529/EEC, Brussels.

Chapter six

Luxembourg: changing anatomy of an international broadcasting power

Kenneth Dyson

Luxembourg offers perhaps an unrivalled opportunity to study how and why broadcasting has become 'high politics' in Western Europe as well as the character of broadcasting as 'high politics'. In the case of Luxembourg public policy has sought to encourage the commercial broadcasting sector in an unparalleled manner, by building on what has been perceived as a national comparative advantage. Broadcasting seemed to be, along with banking, one of Luxembourg's two key industries of the future. The country possessed the longest experience of commercial broadcasting in Western Europe. Strategically placed to exploit the Belgian, French and West German markets, the Compagnie Luxembourgeoise de Télédiffusion (CLT) was well established as the 'grand old lady' of European broadcasting. Now, along with other sovereign states, on a basis of equality, Luxembourg had been allocated frequencies for direct broadcasting by satellite. It was also not encumbered in the pursuit of broadcasting interests by a powerful national electronics and aerospace sector. In short, a country that already had a powerful established position in European commercial broadcasting seemed well placed to enhance its role as a European broadcasting power considerably.

By analysing the development of Luxembourg's role in European commercial broadcasting in this chapter we underline the inseparability of regulation and the market in broadcasting and the complex interaction of the national and the international. The experience of Luxembourg illustrates not only how sensitive governments are to the behaviour of firms as actors in the market but also that the development of the broadcasting market has been greatly influenced by the prospects and reality of governmental actions. In the case of Luxembourg the complexity of the interaction of regulation and the market has been accentuated by the cross-national dimensions of corporate and governmental interaction, as public and private actors sought to exploit or frustrate the potential of this 'off-shore' broadcasting 'island'. Further adding to the complexity have been the factors of uncertainty and ignorance with respect to technology, consumer demand and the likely behaviour of other actors. Against this background broadcasting regulation has proved to be a

Byzantine development, and the broadcasting market has developed in unexpected ways. A chief casualty of this saga has been CLT whose ambitions have been thwarted repeatedly, notably in France and Spain. Caught up in cross-national pressures, and forced to react to new national regulatory moves in broadcasting, CLT witnessed also a deterioration in its relations with the Luxembourg government. In turn the Luxembourg government's espousal of the Coronet and then Astra satellite projects altered the balance of forces in Luxembourg broadcasting, notably by attracting Anglo-American interests. It is hardly surprising then, given the traditional concern about defending 'cultural identity' in French policy, that Coronet/Astra and CLT should form central elements on the agenda of Franco-Luxembourg relations in the 1980s. Luxembourg is, in short, a testament to the fact that 'politics matters' in broadcasting and forms an important constituent element of the comparative advantage or disadvantage that a country enjoys.

The starting point of any analysis of Luxembourg broadcasting has to be the enormous complexity of the interests involved: the French state, in all its internal complexity, Belgian financial interests and, increasingly, British and West German interests. Some of the most powerful corporate actors in Western Europe have identified Luxembourg as a central axis for their development in broadcasting: Havas, Paribas and UAP in France; Bertelsmann in West Germany; Groupe Bruxelles Lambert (GBL) and Société Générale de Belgique in Belgium; and British Telecom (BT), Robert Maxwell, W.H. Smith and Thames Television in Britain.[1] Additionally, the links of Rupert Murdoch to BT (for satellite transponder capacity for Sky Channel) and to GBL suggested, particularly to the French government, that Luxembourg could finally emerge as the Trojan horse of American-style broadcasting in Western Europe. The consequence is a quite extraordinary story of corporate and governmental manœuvring and counter-manœuvring. Policy development was governed by a heady brew of personal ambition and intrigue, of considerations of national prestige and of the clash of hard-headed commercial judgements with hard-headed political judgements. Accusations of treachery and xenophobia were traded at the highest political levels.

It is indeed all too tempting to see Luxembourg broadcasting policy as a history of acrimony and recrimination, to be best understood by teasing out the key actors, like President François Mitterrand and Albert Frère, and telling the story of their relationships.[2] In the process of outlining the complex characteristics of 'policy networks' in this way such factors as power, status and interest and the variety of inputs into policy are usefully highlighted. At the same time such a perspective underplays the fact that structure and culture are independently significant factors in policy development. A consideration of structure draws our attention to the material basis of policy, in particular to resources and technology. A vital question for broadcasting policy is the availability of companies with the resources to invest in long-term and high-risk ventures. Hence, for President Mitterrand in 1985 the choice seemed to have boiled down to 'better Sylvio Berlusconi and Robert Maxwell than Rupert Murdoch'. France's negotiating position in relationship to new media seemed substantially weakened by the absence of a powerful national media company with an international presence.[3] This weakness was all the more transparent given the cultural ambitions of French policy, not least the protection of 'European identity'. Similarly, technological change has altered the parameters of broadcasting policy dramatically during the 1980s. High-powered direct broadcasting satellites (DBSs) have lost credibility with the arrival of more cost-effective medium-powered satellites like Astra; advanced cable systems have also lost appeal to broadcasters as new terrestrial frequencies have been released, promising a more rapid market penetration for new channels.[4] Corporate strategies and regulatory policies have been forced to adjust to this situation, with destabilizing results. In addition to structural factors, policy and relationships have a normative underpinning in certain basic concepts and values.[5] Thus a part of the context of French policy under Mitterrand was the ideological concerns of his own French Socialist Party and deep-rooted cultural concerns about national independence and identity. The complex manœuvrings and counter-manœuvrings around Luxembourg broadcasting policy did not occur in a vacuum. They had historical antecedents, were based on understandings about the 'rules of the game' and were caught up in structural factors that constrained choices and forced a continuing reappraisal of decisions.

The broadcasting policy of the Luxembourg government

The broadcasting policy of the Luxembourg government bears the hallmarks of structural considerations, historical antecedent and ideology in an unmistakable manner. At the level of structure, policy was shaped by three key factors: the problems of being a small state in a fast-growing European market for broadcasting; the opportunity offered by the absence of a powerful national electronics and aerospace sector; and the constraints posed by the lack of a significant nationally-based programme production sector, as well as the financial dependence on foreign companies for investment in Luxembourg's broadcasting. Historically, Luxembourg policy was rooted in memories of attempts by French governments to use CLT to their own advantage, notably in 1965 and 1974.[6] Fear of French 'colonization' of CLT was a powerful factor. The ideological tone of broadcasting policy was very much set by the Liberal Party in the key formative period up to summer 1984. Gaston Thorn (Liberal) headed a Liberal/Socialist coalition from 1974 to 1979; and Pierre Werner (Christian Social) headed a Christian Social/Liberal coalition from 1979 to 1984. In practice the ideological underpinning of broadcasting policy did not alter radically in 1984 when Jacques Santer (Christian Social) put together a

Christian Social/Socialist coalition. Faced by powerful neighbours Luxembourg had an interest in the proposals of the European Commission's Green Paper for a 'television without frontiers'. As a small state Luxembourg stood to benefit most from a radical deregulation of European broadcasting. Accordingly, its parties could agree to support the idea of a European broadcasting market in opposition to nationalistic protectionist measures.

Luxembourg's broadcasting policy is bound up in the classic attributes of a small state – openness and dependency, and a consequent vulnerability in the face of radically altering conditions in broadcasting.[7] As a consequence, the policy process combines an acceptance of the need to work closely with an internationally oriented business community with the domestic and intensely local preoccupations of the political élite. A premium is placed on flexibility in policy, whilst the policy process displays a scarcely discernible boundary between public and private power and a notably high degree of penetration by foreign interests. Policy is constrained by the desire not to overplay its hand, and thereby invite retaliation from powerful neighbours, and occasionally impelled by frustration at disrespect for its sovereign rights. The Luxembourg government has learnt to rely on a set of techniques in dealing with larger states: emphasizing that, as a small state, it cannot be expected to be a danger to its partners; pointing to the hypocrisy of large states that ask of it what they would not ask of themselves (e.g. that Luxembourg should not make use of its right to its own DBS system); and arguing that the failure of the large states to agree harmonized European policies is to blame for its unilateral action.[8]

Traditionally, Luxembourg governments had favoured a low-profile role in broadcasting. In effect they had based policy on exploiting the one major resource at their disposal – the allocation of broadcasting frequencies. They had done so in the 1930s in a distinctive manner to create in CLT the first major commercial broadcaster in Europe. Thereafter, *de facto* CLT had come to represent Luxembourg broadcasting policy. This situation began to change after the 1977 World Administrative Radio Conference (WARC) at which Luxembourg was granted five channels for DBS and the corresponding satellite frequencies. The Luxembourg government now had a new resource at its disposal. Moreover, technological improvements to DBS soon made it clear that the footprint of these satellites would reach across frontiers. For Luxembourg this 'spillover' meant the commercial attraction of access to the French and West German markets. The government was accordingly, tempted to move from a passive to an active broadcasting policy and to become more assertive in the international arena. In the process it was forced to reconsider its traditional relationship with CLT. A further factor influencing the Luxembourg government's attitude towards CLT, and underlining the dramatic implications of its dependence, was the fate of the steel industry. Between 1975 and 1982 the Luxembourg steel industry lost 30 per cent of its workforce. In 1980–1 a governmental crisis was forced as ARBED, the Luxembourg-based multinational steel company, successfully exerted great pressure for massive public aid. The Luxembourg government came to see just how little leverage it had on the investment decisions of a company whose ownership was in the hands of Belgian and French financial interests. CLT's hesitation about the Luxembourg DBS project during the same period evoked parallels with ARBED and reinforced the government's perception of the need to give priority to the search for new sectors and partners in the modernization of the economy. The decision was taken that priority should be given to the service sector and, within that, to finance and to broadcasting.

Throughout the 1980s the Luxembourg government sought to demonstrate its resolve by arguing that broadcasting was the equivalent of the nuclear or oil industries of other states. It was a central element in tax revenue and in export earnings. CLT had demonstrated Luxembourg's potential: RTL-Television had become the leading channel in the Walloon and Brussels areas of Belgium, whilst RTL maintained its position as France's most popular radio station. With the new technologies and economic opportunities in broadcasting major new investment was needed to reinforce the role of broadcasting in the Luxembourg economy. Those actors who could deliver that investment would clearly be the chosen instruments of governmental policy. With its long experience of commercial broadcasting, and its strategic position between the French- and German-language markets, Luxembourg seemed to enjoy a comparative advantage in an expansive sector. This advantage was compounded by the apparent consistency between the international shift to deregulation and privatization in communications and the strength of economic liberalism in the governing ideology. Like Switzerland, Luxembourg was a haven of European business civilization, giving clear preference to private organization of economic adjustment. In short, Luxembourg seemed to have the sort of political structures and incentives to support an expansive broadcasting sector, with European-wide repercussions.

In practice, as we emphasize in this chapter, the attempt to realize this clear-cut vision led directly into a labyrinth of Byzantine politics, represented in particular by cross-national networks that were becoming ever more complex and difficult to manage. The overriding pattern was provided by the attempts to reassert national control and by the responses that they engendered. In its own attempt to reassert national control the Luxembourg government lost faith in CLT/RTL as its chosen instrument of policy; the latter proved too vulnerable to foreign financial and political pressures.[9] CLT/RTL sought to re-forge its strategy, structure and alliances to cope with a broadcasting environment in which there was a proliferation of regulatory initiatives at the national level in Europe, designed to safeguard a national presence in the new media. The principal casualty was the relationship of CLT/RTL to Luxembourg's broadcasting policy. At the same time CLT/RTL remained closely linked to the power structure of Luxembourg: in May 1985, for example,

Werner was elected President and Thorn Vice-President of the company. Despite often sharp conflicts public and private actors continued to see the need for co-operation. The terms of co-operation, however, had irrevocably altered.

The decisive factor for the Luxembourg government was that, just at the time when its ambitions in broadcasting were increasing, its resources for negotiation decreased in a vital aspect. Its key resource had been its capacity and willingness to allocate frequencies for commercial broadcasting. With new regulatory initiatives in Belgium, France and West Germany in the 1980s that resource was no longer unique. CLT/RTL oriented itself accordingly to new joint ventures in Belgium (TVi), in France (M6) and in West Germany (RTL-Plus and Tele 5). These ventures involved a minority role for CLT (33 per cent in TVi, 25 per cent in M6, 46 per cent in RTL-Plus and 24 per cent in Tele 5) and involved a shift in the centre of gravity of its operations away from Luxembourg. A further weakness was the lack of a strong indigenous programme production sector, reflecting the fact that Luxembourg was not a cultural magnet like Paris, London, Munich or Cologne. Broadcasting policy remained firmly anchored to transmission and hardware issues, encouraged by the resources for negotiation that Luxembourg undoubtedly possessed in its geographical position and in its lack of an important national electronics and aerospace sector. Investors could be attracted by the overspill from satellite transmission based on Luxembourg and the flexibility available to Luxembourg in purchasing satellite technology.

In the relations between the Luxembourg government and CLT the turning point took place in 1983, following years of mounting frustration. CLT had shown little interest in the WARC negotiations of 1977 and had not launched a study for a Luxembourg DBS satellite (LUX-SAT) until 1979. Hopeful signs had followed: in December 1980 CLT had reserved two satellite launches for mid-1985, showing a willingness to go it alone; and in February 1981 the Federal Association of German Newspaper Publishers (BDZV) had indicated an interest in a 25 per cent participation with CLT in LUX-SAT. However, for reasons that we shall see later, in practice the French axis within CLT won the day. As early as 1980 President Valéry Giscard d'Estaing had indicated that, with 'good behaviour', CLT could expect a role alongside Europe 1, Matra and Hachette on France's own DBS satellite TDF-1.

In November 1981 the new French Socialist Prime Minister was warning Werner personally that France saw LUX-SAT as a 'Coca-Cola' satellite that threatened European cultural values. By 1982 it was clear that the strategy of the French Socialist government was to seek to encourage Luxembourg to renounce its LUX-SAT plan by offering transponder capacity on TDF-1. Impatient, and frustrated by these machinations, the Luxembourg government issued an ultimatum to CLT in May 1982 to commit itself finally to LUX-SAT or to risk the government's choosing an alternative. In addition to these pressures from the French government, the biggest single investor in CLT, Belgium's GBL, was clearly anxious about the profitability of what it saw as fundamentally a 'prestige' Luxembourg satellite and preferred Franco-Luxembourg collaboration. The final moment of reckoning came with a resolution of the Luxembourg Parliament in February 1983, following which there was still no clear decision from CLT.

The year 1983 saw the birth of the Coronet project. In March, under instructions from the government to look for potential investors, the Luxembourg ambassador in Washington had his first meeting with Clay Whitehead, formerly head of the US Office of Telecommunications in the Nixon Administration and recently retired as general director of Hughes Communications. Hughes had developed the Galaxy system which saw in the combination of cheaper medium-powered satellites with recent advances in antenna and receiver design a way to launch a much more cost-effective satellite broadcasting system than DBS.[10] In particular, these 'second-generation' satellites could offer some 16 channels rather than the 5 on offer with DBS and a larger pan-European footprint. Both programmers and advertisers were more likely to be attracted. Primarily in the interests of promoting the export capacity of their national electronics and aerospace industries, France and West Germany had agreed at the highest levels to collaborate in DBS development, TDF-1 for France and TV-SAT for West Germany. In short, the entry of Whitehead was a challenge not just to the DBS satellite programming plans of France and West Germany but also to powerful industrial interests whose investments were being characterized as obsolescent. It was also a challenge to the role of Eutelsat in providing a 'single regional international telecommunications satellite system' in Europe. This new type of satellite could not make use of the existing frequencies allocated for DBS. It would have to be considered as a telecommunications service, using a frequency band allocated to the Fixed Satellite Service. This factor raised the issue not just of technical co-ordination with Eutelsat but also of whether 'economic harm' was being threatened to Eutelsat. The attraction for the Luxembourg government was that it could maximize its potential to broadcast by satellite by resorting to Fixed Satellite Service satellites as well as having DBS frequencies.

The GDL/Coronet project was really initiated in August 1983 when Whitehead was appointed official adviser to the Luxembourg government, which, in the same month, notified the International Telecommunication Union (ITU) of its intention to seek frequencies in the fixed satellite service band.[11] Backed by financial advice from the American investment bank Salomon Brothers and with support from Home Box Office (HBO), part of Time Inc., Whitehead toured Europe over the next 3 months to seek backers for the project. By 9 December Werner was using the occasion of a Parliamentary debate to stress Luxembourg's determination to take independent action, irrespective of CLT and negotiations with the French government, as an 'act of national sovereignty'.

The climax came early in 1984. Bolstered by the conclusion of the official report (Théry report of March 1984) commissioned by the French government that the TDF project was outdated, the Luxembourg government delivered a note to the French government on 23 April indicating its intention of pursuing the GDL/Coronet project. Both Paris and CLT were stunned. Gust Graas, the general director of CLT, was quick to express his anger in public, accusing the Luxembourg government of undermining CLT's plans and of being in breach of the concession agreement which gave CLT the exclusive right to all television transmissions from Luxembourg till 1995. Nevertheless, on 11 May the Council of State gave a positive opinion on the GDL/Coronet project, and on 25 May the Luxembourg government awarded a concession to the new Société Luxembourgeoise des Satellites (SLS) to use the new telecommunication frequencies for which the government had applied.

The drama of these events, and the legacy of bitterness, was accentuated by the context of the campaign for the Luxembourg elections on 17 June. Eutelsat's general secretary Andrea Caruso used the occasion of a meeting of the Eutelsat partners in mid-May to attack GDL/Coronet as a vehicle for the penetration of American interests and culture into Europe. The Luxembourg government of Werner was keen to emphasize that it had made a tough bargain with GDL/Coronet. Heavy taxation and royalty provisions had been imposed; an uplink tracking, telemetry and control station and a large post-production facility were to be provided in Luxembourg; whilst broadcasting regulations included that 90 per cent of shareholdings would be European (HBO was to be the only American company), that only two Americans were to work on the project (including Whitehead), that all transponders must only be leased to companies that were majority owned by Europeans, and that 65 per cent of the programming was to be of European origin.[12] These provisions were deliberately designed to accord with the ideas of the European Commission and the European Parliament. Also, significant expressions of interest were being made by the private sector, notably the Dresdner Bank and the Leo Kirch Group in West Germany and Thorn-EMI and BET in Britain. Nevertheless, their firm financial commitment was not forthcoming in the presence of clear French and West German priority to their own mutual collaboration and of Eutelsat opposition. The GLD/Coronet project foundered on these realities and on the election results which led, on 10 July, to the new Christian Social/Socialist coalition under Santer. During the election campaign the Socialist Party had pressed for a deferral of the project pending full discussions with the French. In these circumstances SLS was unable to take up its satellite option.

The new era of negotiation with the French was in fact short-lived. With the strong support of Gust Graas, Santer and Georges Fillioud, the Secretary of State in the French Prime Minister's Office with special responsibility for communications, signed a joint declaration on the development of satellite co-operation on 26 October 1984. In return for two of Luxembourg's five DBS frequencies being allocated to France, CLT would gain two channels on TDF-1, one for a French programme and the other for a German programme. There was also a non-competition clause: for a 5-year period each government agreed not to authorize an advertisement-based satellite channel in either of the two languages, and beamed directly to homes, without the consent of the other. Opposition came from the Liberal Party and from within the Christian Social Party, based on the argument that the LUX-SAT and Coronet projects were being held back for the sake of a declaration that did not even have the status of a formal intergovernmental agreement and was unlikely to be honoured.

As we shall see later, events in December 1984 (the Pomonti–Rigaud affair and Pomonti's new official mission to programme TDF-1) and January 1985 (the new Bredin mission to explore the scope for new private terrestrial television channels in France) combined to reawaken Luxembourg's suspicions about the reliability and intentions of the French government. President Mitterrand was prompted by domestic political considerations. Not least, shocked by the scale of the Paris demonstrations of June 1984 against the proposed legislation against Catholic schools, he had been persuaded by his adviser Jacques Attali that the increasingly unpopular Socialist government must realign itself with the historic theme of liberty. Also convinced by his friend Jean Riboud that private broadcasting was an inevitable consequence of new technologies, Mitterrand was determined to make a virtue out of necessity. On 16 January 1985 he publicly committed the government to the principle and reopened the whole field of negotiation.

Consequently, on 1 March 1985 the Société Européenne des Satellites (SES) was established in Luxembourg as successor to SLS. In October SES signed a contract with RCA for a medium-powered 16-transponder satellite to be called Astra. Drawing lessons from the Coronet experience, the new company emphasized its exclusively European character. The Luxembourg presence was guaranteed by a 20 per cent holding by two Luxembourg public credit institutions and holdings of over 26 per cent by three Luxembourg banks. Equally important was the commitment of Deutsche Bank, Dresdner Bank and Société Générale de Belgique (SGB) to each take an 8.9 per cent holding, and in 1986 Etienne Davignon of SGB, formerly an EC Commissioner, became chairman of the management board. Encouraged by this progress, the eleven investors agreed to double the capital of SES in February 1986, after the Luxembourg government offered a large loan guarantee to cover an additional capital increase.

For the purpose of an assessment of the impact of Luxembourg on

European satellite broadcasting, two (interrelated) aspects of SES's development are important. First, the co-ordination procedures with Eutelsat, which were began in earnest by the Luxembourg government in February 1986, involved a protracted row with its general secretary (in fact going back to August 1983). The Luxembourg government was keen to abide by the terms of the Eutelsat Convention but disagreed with Eutelsat about the kind of co-ordination required. Under the Convention 'specialized' telecommunications services' require only technical co-ordination with Eutelsat to ensure operational compatibility; 'public telecommunications services' require in addition a co-ordinate procedure with respect to avoiding 'economic harm' to Eutelsat. Eutelsat's general secretary did not accept the argument of the Luxembourg government that the proposed Astra satellite was a 'specialized telecommunications service' so that the issue of 'economic harm' was irrelevant. Eventually, in October 1987, a historic co-ordination agreement was arrived at: SES accepted the principle of economic co-ordination, whilst Eutelsat conceded that Astra did not pose 'significant economic harm' as long as no more than four of its own transponders were affected by migration of customers to Astra. Already Intelsat had indicated that Astra did not constitute a threat to its global system so that migration from its transponders had no conditions attached. This agreement was vitally important to SES and underlined the impact that the Coronet and Astra projects had had on Eutelsat. Eutelsat had had to accept the principle of a competitive service, to learn to introduce a stronger marketing dimension into its business policy and to accept that medium-powered satellites were the vehicle of the future. This development owed something to the active lobbying by Davignon, a credible and highly respected 'Europeanist', but even more to the role of BT International.

BT International's role reflected just how important the British axis had become in the Astra project and therefore in Luxembourg's broadcasting policy. A strong British presence was welcomed by the Luxembourg government as a counterweight to France in political and economic terms, as a source of broadcasting expertise and as a means of accessing a major television market in which a 'general entertainment' alternative to public-service broadcasting might prove popular. With its stronger commercial orientation as a privatized company BT was keen to acquire a strategic position in European satellite television and to serve existing and potential customers by finding a more cost-effective means of distributing programmes. Eutelsat was, in its judgement, too slow to see the potential of medium-powered satellites. Following some 15 months of negotiation, which involved the Luxembourg government, SES and BT International agreed a joint venture in March 1987. They were jointly to market up to eleven Astra transponders to British programmers, with BT building an up-link facility at London Teleport. BT also agreed to use its leverage as Eutelsat's biggest customer to ensure a successful co-ordination with Eutelsat. Further confirmation of the leading British role in Astra came with the decision of Thames Television in January 1987 to take a 5 per cent shareholding; of Rupert Murdoch's News International in June 1988 to relaunch Sky Channel as Sky Television from Astra, with four channels (Sky One, Sky Television News, Sky Movies and Eurosport) and plans for an additional two; of W.H. Smith to relaunch two channels from Astra (Screen Sport and Lifestyle); and of Robert Maxwell to transfer the pop channel MTV (Europe) to Astra. Thames Television's shareholding was soon complemented by those of two other British independent television (ITV) companies. ITV companies were in part motivated by the desire to find an alternative in case they lost their franchises in the auction of terrestrial franchises planned by the British government in 1991. In fact, in the interest of retaining credibility as a European satellite SES was actually turning away potential English-language customers. The emphasis turned to attracting West German broadcasters, again attractive to the Luxembourg government as a counterweight to France. West German interest was not least motivated by the failure of West German TV-SAT after its launch in November 1987.

Following the successful launch of Astra in December 1988, confidence mounted in its capacity to emerge as the 'hot bird' of European broadcasting. With the lease of eleven of the sixteen transponders (including two ScanSat channels directed at the Scandinavian market), SES was already breaking even. By February 1989 it had agreed to launch a second satellite in October 1990, giving SES a thirty-two-channel capacity. Thames quickly took an option on two channels on the new satellite. The key question remained unanswered, however, in the short run: would there be a sufficient demand for satellite television for the programmers to recover their start-up costs and early large losses and begin to make a profit? On the answer to that question depended the whole credibility of the Luxembourg government's policy. Politics and policy mattered, but ultimately they could not defy the consumer. By August 1989 Murdoch was still losing nearly £2 million per week on Sky Television, against the background of an expected operating cost of £170 million in the first year. Faced by the daunting economics of satellite broadcasting, key shareholders in the British DBS venture, British Satellite Broadcasting (BSB), whose programme launch had been rescheduled to 1990, were considering merger plans with Sky Television.

At the heart of the Coronet/Astra projects lay a continuing preoccupation of the policy of the Luxembourg government with hardware, with exploiting the commercial potential of teledistribution by means of medium-powered satellite. It sought also to affirm its identify as a 'good European' by remaining close to the European Commission's proposals for satellite broadcasting. The additional concern was to find a more effective instrument for Luxembourg's national interests than CLT. As we shall see, CLT was more interested in exploiting the new terrestrial frequencies in Belgium, France and West Germany and, for this purpose, in developing its programming capability. The

Achilles' heel of the policy of the Luxembourg government remained programming. In this respect it continued to depend on CLT and to seek to encourage its investment in Luxembourg. It hoped further that CLT would play an active role in the Astra satellite as a programmer by leasing three transponders. These hopes remained largely unfulfilled, however (although in April 1987 CLT took an option on one Astra transponder under pressure from the Luxembourg government). In this key respect the policy of the Luxembourg government remained incomplete. It also remained constrained by the basic fact that CLT continued to remain so important a source of revenue to the government.

CLT: theory and practice of a 'European vocation'

An analysis of the role of CLT in Luxembourg broadcasting policy must be rooted in a recognition of the powerful effect of certain basic ideological and structural factors on its development in the 1980s, as well as of historical events and experiences. The dramatic events and encounters of these years, involving leading personalities in Belgium, France and Luxembourg, can only be properly understood in this context.

Ideologically, from its very inception CLT has been a commercial broadcasting company, financed solely by advertising and pledged to entertainment programming; a company whose professional management is deeply pledged to the principle of independence of reporting; and a European and Luxembourg company, a factor that is reflected in its shareholding. In this respect cultural tensions are built deep into its heart. At the apex of CLT, in its administrative council (*conseil d'administration*), there has to be a majority of Luxembourg nationals and residents; the president and the director general must also be of Luxembourg nationality. Additionally, the Luxembourg government nominates a commissioner who is to safeguard the interests of the state and ensure respect for its charter. He is assisted by a technical commission and an artistic commission, on which CLT and Luxembourg representatives form a majority. On the other hand, the dominant shareholders have traditionally been French and since 1946, and especially since 1974, Belgian. Their power is expressed in the management board (*comité de direction*), half of which comprises shareholder representatives and half management. The senior official responsible to this board (the *administrateur-délégué*) is traditionally French.

In this sense a tension between a Luxembourg identity and a European identity is built into the very structure of CLT. The consequence is a highly complex structure which is hardly understood internally, let alone externally. This structure provided a site where the contradictory ambitions and interests of Belgian, French and Luxembourg actors, notably GBL of Belgium and Havas and Schlumberger of France, came into confrontation. The Luxembourg government was in effect limited to a strategy of 'divide and rule'. As events gathered pace in the 1980s, CLT found itself without the necessary leadership to compete effectively with such media entrepreneurs as Sylvio Berlusconi and Murdoch. No less importantly, CLT had problems of scale. In an interview with *Le Monde* on 7 August 1985 about the French market Berlusconi commented: 'Award two channels to CLT? This small regional television?' By 1985 the combined television audience for RTL-Television in Luxembourg, France (Lorraine) and French-speaking Belgium and for RTL Plus in West Germany was a mere 5 million. It had in fact taken 20 years for its television service to show a profit, and by 1985 80 per cent of profits was still generated by radio. French-language commercial radio was the traditional main axis of CLT's activities. Also, for the purpose of expansion in television, CLT was severely undercapitalized. The company's operations were highly profitable, and key shareholders had traditionally preferred to take a high dividend rather than invest. Its turnover put it on a different scale from other companies: in 1986 $0.35 billion compared with Maxwell ($1), Hersant ($1.3), Murdoch ($2.6), Havas ($3.5), Bertelsmann ($4.4) and Berlusconi ($5). Finally, in addition to problems of scale, CLT had to adjust to the regulatory initiatives of powerful neighbouring states. These states were concerned to protect the position of national media interests. These three major structural factors disposed CLT towards a cautious strategy of working with different partners in different countries and of diversifying its activities in programme production. The 'grand old lady' of European broadcasting lacked the physique and drive of its competitors.

CLT's tumultuous history had also left an accumulation of frustrated ambitions and resentments, expressing themselves in an unstable coalition politics at the heart of the company. CLT was caught up in complex manœuvrings within the French state and by the Belgian holding companies, notably GBL. As we shall see, these involved not least bitter disputes amongst French shareholders. The policy of the Luxembourg government had been, from the very beginning, to encourage dynamic foreign investors like Havas in CLT whilst seeking to balance shareholdings, particularly to avoid French dominance. Its approach was deeply influenced, however, by the Franco-Luxembourg crisis of 1965 when Werner was head of government. This crisis was precipitated by the attempt of SOFIRAD, the French holding company controlling the interests of the French state in broadcasting, to acquire CSF's 13 per cent shareholding in CLT. Combined with the 15 per cent shareholding by Havas, also controlled by the French state, this move was seen in Luxembourg as an attempt to punish RTL radio for its independent reporting during the Algerian crisis by bringing it into line with other 'peripheral' stations like Radio Monte Carlo. Backed by a strongly worded Parliamentary resolution, Werner threatened to nationalize the company's installations. SOFIRAD backed away. When CLT's franchise was renewed in 1973, the Luxembourg government sought to learn the lesson by taking reserve powers to control share issues and transfers. Even so, the highest-level interventions by the French government reappeared. From September 1978 to December 1979, following the resignation of Christian Chavanon as *administrateur-délégué*, this post remained vacant as French nominations were blocked. Notably, Thorn, as head of the Luxembourg government, greatly angered President Valéry Giscard d'Estaing by blocking his personal nominee, Philippe Grumbach. Eventually, following mediation by Jean Riboud, a French diplomat, Jacques Rigaud, was appointed. The events of 1965 and 1978–9 left deep impressions on Werner and Thorn and formed an important part of the context of the Coronet project.

The legacy of the events of 1972–4 also left a deep imprint on CLT. This period saw four interrelated developments: the attempt by Riboud (president of Schlumberger and owner of the Compagnie des Compteurs), in conjunction with Jacques de Fouchier (Paribas), to extend their combined 20 per cent holding to gain a majority in CLT; the creation of the Bruxelles Lambert company, whose shareholding in CLT was transferred to a new Luxembourg company, Audiofina; the strengthening of Audiofina to become CLT's principal shareholder, a development welcomed by the Luxembourg government as means of securing a more stable majority in CLT; and finally the intervention by President Georges Pompidou, through his Finance Minister (Giscard d'Estaing), who supervised Havas, to block the moves of Riboud, an old and close friend of the opposition candidate Mitterrand. The context was the failing health of Pompidou, the French Left's success in the National Assembly elections of 1973 and the prospect of a Presidential election. The French government sought to insulate RTL radio from the French Left by backing Audiofina; Havas sought to benefit by securing its own nominee as *administrateur-délégué*. Consequently, in March 1974 Havas joined Audiofina, which then had a 53.56 per cent holding in CLT. This French intervention was fraught with paradox. The Luxembourg government welcomed the move by Havas which was seen as a dynamic resourceful company, keen to develop its role in media and naturally close to RTL radio in the selling of whose advertising it had had a monopoly since 1930. As part of the informal pact governing the relations of Bruxelles Lambert and Havas it was agreed that Havas would maintain a veto power within Audiofina and also would have the right to nominate the *administrateur-délégué* (its president Chavanon succeeded to this post). However, most importantly of all, for the first time the informal French majority in CLT had ended, and Riboud awaited his opportunity to redress the defeat of 1974. By the end of 1974 CLT represented the largest shareholding by Bruxelles Lambert.

These historical, structural and ideological factors impinged deeply on CLT's consideration of its strategy in response to the new technological opportunities that emerged from the 1970s onwards – cable, satellite and new terrestrial frequencies. Although RTL maintained its position as the leading

French radio station, the story was one of repeated humiliations in France. By contrast, the successes, in terms of market growth, were in Belgium and West Germany. In 1970 RTL-Television was introduced on Belgian cable; a microwave link between Luxembourg and Brussels enabled RTL to offer, from September 1983, news programmes aimed specifically at Belgian audiences; in July 1984 the decision was taken to divide French from Belgian programmes on RTL-Television (thereby also doubling the audience in Lorraine); and in September 1987 RTL-TVi was launched as the first Belgian commercial television channel in Wallonia. In the process RTL surpassed the Belgian public-service broadcaster RTB-F in Wallonia and Brussels. CLT combined with Bertelsmann to launch a German-language commercial television channel, RTL-Plus, off-air in January 1984 and from the ECS1 satellite in August. RTL-Plus was also successful in being awarded new terrestrial frequencies in West Germany, notably in North-Rhine Westphalia and in Hamburg, although it remained in second place to SAT 1. Political factors were central in shaping these stories of market failure and success. In Belgium three factors were important: the Belgian prominence within CLT through Audiofina; the major decentralization reforms since 1980; and the formation of a Social Christian/Liberal coalition in 1981. In West Germany the new Christian Democratic/Liberal coalition in Bonn after 1982, and its partner governments in various states (*Länder*), were determined to break the monopoly of public-service broadcasting. In Bertelsmann CLT had a powerful and prestigious partner, albeit one more sympathetically received in Social Democratic states. In France, however, the story was very different.

CLT's development in the 1980s is inseparably connected with ideological changes and political manœuvrings within the French state. The key episodes were the election of a Socialist President, François Mitterrand, in 1981, followed by a huge parliamentary majority for the Socialist Party; the manœuvrings of Mitterrand to limit the expected large Socialist losses in the National Assembly elections of March 1986; and the legacy of the period of *cohabitation* from 1986 to 1988, when Mitterrand had to coexist with a centre-right government under Jacques Chirac pledged to liberalization and privatization in broadcasting. Both Mitterrand and Chirac took a deep personal interest in broadcasting, elevating it to the status of high politics, particularly during the period 1985–7 when CLT was deeply affected.

Two of Mitterrand's closest and oldest collaborators were intimately linked with CLT: Jean Riboud, a friend from Resistance days, had a 12.3 per cent holding through Schlumberger and long-standing and, as we have seen, frustrated ambitions in the media field; and Andre Rousselet, who had been head of Mitterrand's ministerial cabinet in the 1950s, was soon to move from being head of the new President's cabinet in the Elysée to become head of Havas. In addition to its 30 per cent holding in Audiofina, Havas enjoyed through its subsidiary Information et Publicité (IP) the lucrative monopoly of RTL advertising. Havas was also to be the key shareholder in France's first commercial television channel, Canal Plus; Rousselet became its president. Rousselet's ambition was for Havas to become a 'cultural Ariane', whilst continuing to act as a 'guardian of the peace' in the communications sector. The interests and ambitions of Riboud and Rousselet were to play on Mitterrand and influence his moves, particularly in response to the emergence of Albert Frère, the Belgian industrialist, as head of GBL in 1982–3 and to the Coronet project.[13] In autumn 1981, through the activities of his Swiss holding company Pargesa, Frère was seen by the French Socialists as a central figure in the attempt to free Paribas Suisse and Paribas Belgique (Copeba) from Paribas' control as the bank was being nationalized. Riboud in particular sensitized the President to the need to combat Frère's influence within CLT, whilst Rousselet was more disposed to moderation in the interests of maintaining Havas's privileges under the Audiofina pact and the advertising monopoly on RTL. Also, both Rousselet and Riboud were disappointed by Rigaud, who in summer 1982 resisted pressures from the Elysée (conveyed by Rousselet) to have the RTL reporter Philippe Alexandre removed to Washington.

A series of events in 1984–5 convinced Riboud that CLT was Frère's puppet and precipitated Mitterrand's active entry into broadcasting policy. In May 1984 Riboud was rebuffed in his attempt to persuade the administrative council of CLT to invest in new media rather than distribute profits. He found himself opposed by Rousselet as well as Frère, causing a rift with Rousselet. The Pomonti affair of November–December 1984, however, was the real turning point for Franco-Luxembourg relations, undermining the joint declaration of October. Mitterrand determined on replacing Rigaud as *administrateur-délégué* by Jacques Pomonti, head of the Institut national audiovisuel (INA); Rousselet negotiated the agreement of Frere in return for Thorn's being elected president of CLT in May 1985. However, determined that a prestigious Liberal opposition politician should not gain such an office, the Luxembourg government blocked the nomination of Pomonti and Thorn to the administrative council in December. Mitterrand was furious; Pomonti was a disappointed man; and two weeks later the French Prime Minister, Laurent Fabius, entrusted to Pomonti the mission of assembling a programming consortium for the TDF-1 satellite. The co-option of Pomonti and Thorn to CLT's administrative council in January 1985 was interpreted as a gesture to Paris but as signifying little of substance. Pomonti focused his mission on talks with Maxwell and Berlusconi, not with CLT, and in April 1985 Mitterrand had his first meeting with Berlusconi, following initial contact through Riboud. When Pomonti reported in June, the possibility of a CLT channel was left open, but the emphasis had changed to a concept of Europeanizing' TDF-1 by establishing an operating company with holdings of 34 per cent by the French state, 16 per cent by French investors and 50 per cent by overseas investors like Maxwell and Berlusconi. By then, on 21 May 1985, the big blow to French pride had been delivered. After France and Luxembourg had seemed to be agreed in opposing Thorn, the administrative council of CLT simultaneously elected Werner (the originator of Coronet) as President and Thorn as Vice-President (in May 1987 Thorn replaced Werner as president). Frère interpreted this move as an attempt to strengthen leadership in CLT as a condition of injecting further capital; Paris saw it as the promotion of a strong man against French interests. In July Rousselet sought to restore an equilibrium of interests to suit France better by an explicit reinforcement of Rigaud's role as 'managing director', assisted by Graas (programmes), Thorn (external relations and finance) and Jean-Pierre de Launoit (as head of the *comité de direction*). By contrast, Riboud was now fully convinced about the unreliability of CLT and even of Rousselet. His attempt to evolve a broadcasting strategy for Schlumberger independently of CLT was apparent when he established his own mission under Bernard Miyet, formerly president of SO-FIRAD.

President Mitterrand's famous press conference of 21 November 1985 took place against the background of memories of Frère's role in 1981, of the Pomonti affair (which Frère himself believed was the decisive influence) and of the recent death of his old friend Riboud (in October). Whilst these factors were not mentioned by Mitterrand, they were referred to by those adversely affected as evidence of revenge. Mitterrand drew attention, somewhat inaccurately, to the 'company with a Luxembourg majority, with a driving force, a stage manager, which is a Belgian bank . . . associated with an American . . . Mr. Murdoch'. It was also clear that the joint venture (Media International) announced by GBL and Murdoch in the previous September was seen as a further provocation by the French government. Both had agreed to explore the development of satellite and terrestrial broadcasting jointly. CLT had become subsumed in the French Socialists' perception that, with the National Assembly imminent in March 1986, Frere had hostile intentions. Hence Mitterrand confirmed that the main recommendations of the Bredin report of May 1985 had been accepted. There were to be two new national commercial channels which would also be carried on TDF-1 to maximize their coverage: however, their operating conditions were to be very much more relaxed than Bredin had wanted, and his concern about franchising procedures was completely overlooked. Mitterrand was combining *raison d'état* with partisan pre-emptive action in awarding the fifth general entertainment channel to a consortium principally comprising Jerome Seydoux (52 per cent), socialist millionaire, an heir to the Schlumberger family fortune and head of Chargeurs SA, Christophe Riboud (8 per cent) (son of Jean Riboud) and Berlusconi (40 per cent). He was also honouring his dead friend. Faced with only the much less attractive possibility of the sixth music channel (which it was not awarded anyway). Rigaud appealed the franchising procedures to the Council of State on the basis of a 'misuse of power'. CLT, and the Luxembourg government, felt betrayed; Frère spoke of French xenophobia. The final insult came just before the National Assembly elections, on 11 March 1986, when Fillioud's announcement of a European Consortium for Commercial Television to programme the two other channels on TDF-1 killed CLT's remaining hopes: La Cinque, Berlusconi, Maxwell and Leo Kirch were preferred to CLT. Also, the critical judgement of the Council of State did not include a cancellation of the contracts.

The emergence of a centre-right government under Chirac at the end of March 1986, however, did open up a new opportunity to CLT. Franchising decisions were to be given to a new regulatory body, the Commission Nationale de la Communication et des Libertés (CNCL). The prevailing climate of liberalization was confirmed in May when the new Minister of Culture and Communications, François Leotard, announced the impending privatization of TF-1. In August Chirac finally revoked the licences of La Cinque and TV6 and cancelled the concession to the European Consortium. CLT's seriousness about its bid was apparent from a number of moves: in February RTL-Television moved a quarter of its personnel to Paris as a sign of the seriousness of its ambitions; on 20 May the administrative council of CLT agreed to increase its capital by LFr1 billion to a total of LFr3.8 billion by the end of 1987, especially to buy programmes for the French channel; in June Thorn announced the establishment of International Film Productions (IFP) between CLT and American interests to develop co-productions as European projects; and Santer put presentation of CLT's case high on the agenda of his first meeting with Chirac. By June Havas and CLT were claiming to be joint candidates for La Cinque.

With three franchises (TF-1, La Cinque and the sixth channel) to be awarded, corporate manœuvring and political lobbying became so intense that the independence of the CNCL was soon seen as little more than symbolic. With a Presidential election due in 1988, Chirac was keen to construct a friendly broadcasting environment as quickly as possible. The press baron Robert Hersant was a central part of such a strategy. For CLT and Havas the decisive moment was Hersant's announcement that he would bid for La Cinque and not for TF-1. Havas saw a Hersant–Havas link as impossible because of Havas's commercial links to other competitive press interests. Despite commercial doubts about the price (which finally led it to withdraw completely from the bidding), Havas decided to join Hachette in bidding for TF-1. CLT was stunned, not least by the rupturing of its traditionally most important French link at so sensitive a time (January 1987). Havas encouraged negotiations for a CLT-Hersant bid (abortive) and then sought to encourage CLT to bid with it for TF-1 (no answer was received). Confused and bitter towards Havas, CLT eventually decided, with reluctance, to bid for the sixth channel as part of the Métropole TV consortium: whilst the sixth channel was now to be a general channel, it lacked the territorial coverage and hence audience penetration available to La Cinque. Indicative of the politicized character of the bidding, Métropole TV was headed by Jerome Monod, formerly general secretary of Chirac's RPR party (Rassemblement pour la République). By the new French broadcasting regulations CLT was limited as a foreign company to a 25 per cent holding (the same holding was taken up by Monod's Lyonnaise des Eaux), but other smaller shareholders – Paribas, Parfinance (a subsidiary of GBL) and the Union des Assurances de Paris (UAP) – had, or would soon develop, close links to CLT. More disconcertingly, the CNCL awarded the franchise to Métropole TV with the slenderest of majorities: it then refused to allow the consortium to use 'RTL 6' as the name of the channel (it would confuse the audience). In short, the Chirac government was a disappointing and bruising experience for CLT, not least in relation to Havas. Havas paid in the sense that IP was not given the monopoly of advertising on M6 (the name of the new channel).

CLT was also deeply affected by the privatization programme of the Chirac government, particularly as it affected Havas and Paribas, and by the consequences of the withdrawal of the Schlumberger and Moet Hennessy shareholdings in CLT. These changes gave a more solid and stable structure to French interests in CLT and strengthened the linkages to Chirac in particular. In July 1987 Paribas took up the Schlumberger shares in CLT (13.4 per cent) to become the second largest shareholder (with 24.6 per cent) after Audiofina. In September UAP, France's largest insurance company, acquired the old Moet Hennessy shareholding (8.8 per cent) from Parfinance (which had been temporarily holding the shares since April). These acquisitions were complemented by the consequences of the French government's method of privatization by selecting a *noyau dur* (hard kernel or nucleus) of investors for each company. Ostensibly, the *noyaux durs* were designed to protect the newly privatized companies from hostile take-over bids. In practice they were used to ensure control by business friends and allies of the Gaullist RPR party. The UAP became part of the *noyau dur* of Paribas, and Paribas part of the *noyau dur* of Havas. Also, a factor in common between Jean Dromer (head of the UAP), Michel François Poncet (head of Paribas) and Pierre Dauzier (the new head of Havas) was their friendship with Chirac. Paribas was close to Frère and therefore seen as both highly acceptable to Belgian interests and a means of promoting closer co-operation of GBL and Havas at the heart of CLT. A factor that made these changes acceptable to the Luxembourg government was the huge investment needs of CLT, notably for M6. Havas, the key French actor earlier, was no longer seen as big enough to rival Berlusconi, Bertelsmann, Murdoch or Maxwell, particularly after its withdrawal from the bidding for TF-1 because of the cost (Maxwell became part of the TF-1 consortium). In this sense such powerful financial giants as Paribas and the UAP were welcome. At the same time CLT was inexorably drawn into the 'closed-circuit' privatization programme in France. For instance, GBL was part of the *noyau dur* of Paribas; its partner in M6, Lyonnaise des Eaux, was part of the *noyau dur* of Havas. Above all, however, the CLT seemed to have been given *de facto* its own *noyau dur*.

The re-election of President Mitterrand in May 1988 and, following National Assembly elections, the formation of a centre-left government under the Socialist Prime Minister Michel Rocard could not be expected to improve CLT's position. However, more so than in 1986, the emphasis was on continuity. Heading a minority government Rocard was keen to seek allies in the centre. Rocard and Mitterrand spoke of political *ouverture* and a new consensual approach. The President pledged to inaugurate a new era of 'state impartiality', involving an end to the nationalization–privatization debate and a non-interventionist approach to business. Examples of the new approach were the abolition of the device of the *noyau dur*, opening up new possibilities for hostile bidding, and the creation of a new and more independent regulatory body for broadcasting, the Conseil Supérieur de l'Audiovisuel (CSA), in January 1989. In practice, the peculiarly incestuous character of French capitalism proved difficult to dislodge, based as it is on the historic prestige of the *grands corps* whose networks span the public–private divide.[14] The *'tours de table'* continued to operate, with informal syndicates of principal shareholders shaping the process of friendly or hostile deals. Within this context the Rocard government proved unable to refrain from intervention, in particular by a series of personnel decisions (the chairman of the UAP state insurance group was replaced) and by giving support to manœuvres to unsettle the Gaullist *noyaux durs* through open market operations. In the case of Havas Rousselet, its former chairman, succeeded in counterbalancing the Gaullist *noyau dur* by negotiating the entry of a new club of institutional shareholders favourable to the Socialist government. However, the controversy aroused by the French government's role in the raid on Société Générale in November 1988 the Socialist government became more reluctant to pursue this policy.

Rousselet was also the victor in the CSA's first major programming decisions, on the allocation of the five channels on TDF-1 in April 1989; Canal Plus was the only existing channel chosen, and in addition had a major role on two other channels (one being Canal Plus Allemagne, in collaboration with Bertelsmann). Whilst TDF-1 was launched in October 1988, CLT had already seen, in November 1987, the failure of the West German TV-SAT from which RTL-Plus was to have been transmitted. It was now forced to wait for TV-SAT 2, and meanwhile had to carry losses on RTL-Plus. CLT was also desperate to extend the territorial coverage of M6 but had been concerned about the high rental costs of TDF-1 (compared with TV-SAT). As far as M6 was concerned, its options were narrowing down to Astra, and Astra was unpopular with the French government. Failure was succeeded by dilemma.

Despite the intense political and corporate manœuvrings surrounding it, and in large part conditioned by these manœuvrings, CLT management had developed by 1984 a clear-cut European strategy that continued to support a quiet success story. Its main elements included the development of co-production arrangements, notably with France and Belgium, and its film archive; organization of programming specifically for each country (as apparent for TVi, M6 and RTL-Plus); forging links to the local and regional press in order to build relevance and appeal into programmes (notably with TVi and RTL-Plus); and developing local 'windows' in programming. The unfulfilled part of the strategy was the combination of these separate programmes into a European network by means of satellite. Perhaps the most successful aspect remained the diversification policy which had been strengthened considerably as early as 1973. Its success has been apparent in the performance and reputation of its subsidiaries such as Hamster Productions, DIC (Diffusion Information Communication), Pandora and VCI (Video Centre International). In practice, CLT's 'European vocation' was reducible to two main elements: attainment of synergy amongst its numerous and diversifying activities across Europe, as it adapted to being French in France, Belgian in Belgium and German in West Germany; and development of its programme production and distribution capacity for this purpose. It had identified the new terrestrial franchises of Belgium, France, West Germany and Spain as its priority rather than satellite transmission. Above all, it recognized that the newly re-regulated national broadcasting markets were unleashing centrifugal pressures to which the company had to adapt. In seeking out new opportunities and alliances in this way, CLT was forced to reconsider its traditional relationships: with the Luxembourg government, to which it began to feel that it was paying exorbitant taxes now that its monopoly position was gone with the Astra project and that it needed to present a set of national identities rather than a Luxembourg identity; and to France where its development had been so frustrated. Both market and political realities suggested that CLT would have to define its 'European vocation' to embrace a greater role for West German interests in its affairs. Here Bertelsmann was a key player. In addition to the collaboration in RTL-Plus, in 1986 Bertelsmann bought a small shareholding in Fratel (which had a stake of 27.6 per cent in CLT); by 1988 this holding was 14.3 per cent. With the 24 per cent participation in the Munich private television company Tele 5 CLT had almost reached the upper limit allowed by the West German broadcasting state treaty to companies that already had a shareholding in another private television channel. CLT was not without future cards to play against the Luxembourg and French governments.

Conclusions

This case study of Luxembourg broadcasting has highlighted a paradox. On the one hand, the domestic regulatory policies of Luxembourg's powerful neighbours have had powerful effects on CLT's strategy and its relations with the Luxembourg government. A centrifugal development of CLT has underlined the dependence and vulnerability of an international operator to domestic policies. It has also revealed an element of fantasy in the policy of the Luxembourg government with respect to CLT. On the other hand, the international impact of the Coronet and Astra initiatives of the Luxembourg government has propelled changes in Eutelsat and constrained the domestic policy choices of other national governments. In this complex interaction of the national and international dimensions of policy Luxembourg has been able to act as a major catalyst for change in European broadcasting, with hardware as well as software implications. It remains to be seen whether it can maintain a central position in this process of change, or whether the Astra project will prove no easier to control than CLT.

Luxembourg also illuminates the complex relationship of politics and markets in broadcasting policy. On the one hand, the impersonal market does not seem to represent a central overriding logic that politics is powerless to influence; on the other, states cannot detach themselves from firms as actors in the market. In this chapter we have emphasized the importance of history, ideology and structure in forging the context of the complex interactions in and surrounding the Coronet/Astra projects and CLT. These factors shape the resources of negotiation available to actors. The development of Luxembourg broadcasting reflects the complex changes in the distribution of these resources brought about by new technologies, new regulatory initiatives and the entry of new international media companies and entrepreneurs. It also reveals that broadcasting policy could not be made autonomously. For instance, the events surrounding the nationalization of Paribas by the French Socialists and later the privatization programme of the Chirac government had deep effects on CLT. A whole new pattern of incentives and constraints was created as a consequence, apparent for instance in the revised strategies of the Luxembourg government and of CLT. In this new climate of great risk and uncertainty both governments and corporate actors were involved in a common but seemingly fruitless search to re-establish a measure of stability on 'favourable terms'. Of course, whilst this aim was shared by the Luxembourg government, the CLT, the French government and Belgian and French corporate interests, their judgement of what constituted 'favourable terms' differed significantly. Politics remained, accordingly, pre-eminent.

Notes

This chapter was greatly assisted by a grant from the Nuffield Foundation. My thanks are also due to Bernard Guillou and to Mario Hirsch, as well as to academics, journalists, officials and broadcasters in Belgium, Britain, France, Luxembourg and West Germany too numerous to mention.

1 For details of the interlocking nature of Belgian capital see E. Lentzen and A. Vincent, 'La concentration économique et les groupes Société générale de Belgique,

Copeba, Bruxelles Lambert et Frere-Bourgeois en 1981–82', *Courrier Hebdomadaire, no. 993–994* (Brussels: CRISP, 1983).

2 Such a personality-based approach is adopted in J.-M. Quatrepoint *et al.*, *Histoire Secrète des Dossiers Noirs de la Gauche* (Paris: Alain Moreau, 1987).

3 For an analysis of the French media companies see B. Guillou, *Les Stratégies Multimédias des Groupes de Communications* (Paris: La Documentation Française, 1985).

4 For details see chapter 1 of K. Dyson and P. Humphreys, *Broadcasting and New Media Policies in Western Europe* (London: Routledge, 1988).

5 For a classic study of the importance of culture in public policy see D. Vogel, *National Styles of Regulation: Environmental Policy in Great Britain and the United States* (Ithaca, NY: Cornell University Press, 1986).

6 See E. Lentzen, 'Compagnie Luxembourgeoise de Télédiffusion "CLT" ', *Courrier Hebdomadaire, no. 1066* (Brussels: CRISP, 1985).

7 See P. Katzenstein, *Small States in World Markets: Industrial Policy in Europe* (Ithaca, NY: Cornell University Press, 1985).

8 A useful insight into these attitudes is presented by a former adviser to Thorn and former spokesman for the Coronet project in M. Hirsch, 'Who is in charge of the destinies of small states? The case of Luxembourg', in O. Hoell (ed.), *Small States in Europe and Dependence* (Braumuller, The Laxenburg Papers, 1983.

9 For a good example of Luxembourg views of CLT (from the perspective of the Liberal opposition) see M. Hirsch, 'La CLT serait-elle ingouvernable?', *Communication et Langages*, no. 67 (1986), pp. 71–88.

10 See M. Hirsch, 'The doldrums of Europe's TV landscape: Coronet as catalyst', in D. Demac (ed.), *Tracing New Orbits: Cooperation and Competition in Global Satellite Development* (New York: Columbia University Press, 1986).

11 Das Hindernisrennen des Unternehmens Coronet', *Neue Medien*, no. 2 (1985).

12 S. Koltai, 'New media developments in Western Europe', Paper for the Centre for Telecommunications and Information Studies, Columbia University, New York, May 1986. Koltai worked on the Coronet project.

13 For an analysis of Frere's potential international media power, based on the Swiss holding company Pargesa, see A. Lange, 'Skizze eines ersten weltweiten Fernseh-Networks', *Media Perspektiven*, no. 2 (1986), pp. 81–9.

14 On the role of the *grands corps* in France see E. Suleiman, *Elites in French Society* (Princeton, NJ: Princeton University Press, 1978).

Chapter seven

British television in an age of change

Ralph Negrine

Introduction

The Government's 1988 White Paper on broadcasting, *Broadcasting in the 1990s: Competition, Choice and Quality*,[1] (the main lines of which have since been adopted as a Broadcasting Bill – editors' note) prepared the way for probably the most radical transformation of the structures of British broadcasting ever contemplated by a British administration. By contrast with the more incrementalist and gradual processes of change favoured by governments in the past – an extra channel here, a bit of liberalization there – the approach adopted in the White Paper challenges all established assumptions about the value of the existing duopoly, their practices and their underlying operating philosophies.

The main objective of the White Paper is to alter the existing structures and the practices of the broadcasting institutions in such a way as to make them more responsive to the marketplace, to consumer demand, to the new media and to new relationships between international media.

Not surprisingly, the government's critics see these objectives in a different light. Apart from decrying some of the more 'fanciful' ideas contained in the document, they see the government's intended action as one of throwing away 'the baby with the bathwater', i.e. of abandoning everything that is worthwhile in British broadcasting in pursuit of a political ideology.

This difference of opinion over the way in which British broadcasting ought to develop in the future is itself mirrored in the background and contents of the White Paper (reviewed more fully below). After all, it is the culmination of a long drawn out and sometimes acrimonious consultation process. Not only does it bring together the fruits of a number of inquiries undertaken in the 1980s into various aspects of British broadcasting but it also treads a careful path between Prime Ministerial desire for radical change and Ministerial and Departmental (Home Office versus Trade and Industry) disputes about the direction and the precise nature of that change. Given the difficulty of reconciling so many political and policy positions, it is not particularly astonishing to note that the Paper's publication was delayed for a considerable time.

In spite of its difficult conception – and an extensive leaking of its contents – the document's formal public appearance in November 1988 marked the beginning of a crucial debate about the future of British broadcasting. It contained a set of proposals which, if adopted in their entirely, would completely restructure the British broadcasting scene.

The aim in this chapter will be to identify not only the proposals for change but also their points of origin. Part One will thus focus on 'the road to reform' and it provides a review of the White Paper as well as a discussion of its main proposals. Part Two offers a broader analysis of the White Paper and it situates the proposals within the changing nature of television. Such changes include a growing internationalization of television production and trade, a considerable amount of trans-frontier broadcasting, the transfer of ownership and/or control to non-nationals (including non-European Community nationals) and the development and impact of a European legislative framework for broadcast regulation (see Chapter 5). However, one of the main arguments which will be pursued in this chapter is that the White Paper, and British media *policy* more generally, is a peculiarly domestic concern and so fails to address the vast international changes which are beginning to have an impact on domestic broadcasters.

Part one

The road to reform

The 1980s have been marked by a series of important reports on, and reforms of, British broadcasting. The 1982 Information Technology Advisory Panel report, 'Cable Systems',[2] and the 1986 Peacock Committee report, 'The Financing of the BBC',[3] are perhaps the most public manifestations of a sea change in thinking about broadcasting. But there are other reports, for example Charles Jonscher's report *Subscription Television*,[4] published in 1987, which have also contributed to the gradual erosion of the legitimacy of the existing structures.

So long as there was a general agreement on the worth of the duopoly, there was always the possibility of substantial resistance to change. But these reports put a radically different interpretation on the very nature of the duopoly. It was no longer a benevolent public servant. The 'reality' of the matter was quite different: it comprised institutions which had tremendous control over an industry and over access to culture, entertainment and advertising revenue. It was precisely this stranglehold which these reports, in their various ways, attempted to loosen.

Though each of the reports explored different parts of the broadcasting and communications industry, they were informed by the need for some sort of governmental action in three broad and interrelated areas.

1 The independent television (ITV) companies are currently operating under franchises which run until 1992–3. The British Broadcasting Corporation (BBC), by contrast, has had its licence renewed until 1996. Decisions thus need to be taken very shortly in order to allow for both sets of institutions to plan ahead. The more radical the contemplated change, the more urgent the decision since it would not be reasonable for current operators to be dismissed pre-emptorily. One major focus of enquiry was therefore the very nature of the duopoly itself, in the present and in the 1990s and beyond.

2 By the early 1990s, the 'new' media will have ceased to be 'new'. Their precise, and long-term, relationships with the reformed commercial and public-service broadcasting sectors will need to be determined (possibly in advance). For example, if the new media are absolved of all public-service broadcasting requirements, should not a similar policy be adopted for the terrestrial commercial television companies?

3 Strategic decisions about the communications infrastructure (and therefore also the superstructure) of the future are also pending. Currently, both British Telecom (BT) and Mercury – strong players in 'communications *and* culture' – are operating under rules which have to be reviewed by 1990. If, for instance, cable systems are to play an important part in the future of British television, decisions about Mercury and BT will impact on cultural questions.

All three areas called for some fundamental thinking about the whole nature of Britain's communications structure and, perhaps more importantly, the nature of the relationships which ought to exist between sectors within that overall structure. Although the many reports produced did contribute to those particular tasks, they have somehow failed to address both the European and the international dimensions of television. No official study has yet dealt properly with the implications of the internal European market from 1992, the role of the EC in setting a new media agenda or the internationalization of television flows and productions.

In this respect, British policy making continues to be dominated by mainly internal domestic considerations and interests. Unlike nations which have aggressive media neighbours, Britain's cultural and linguistic isolation in Europe has allowed it to develop its broadcasting structures to suit its own needs. Rarely has it had to consider infringements of its cultural barriers and its consequent strength as a programming centre has enabled it to move outwards, so exploiting the demand for high quality English-language television content.

The White Paper continues this tradition of relative insularity. Despite its references to the new satellite-delivered services, its overall tone is peculiarly *domestic*. There is nothing in it which could remotely be constructed as a concern for the implications of 'Coca-Colanization'. Unlike their French neighbours, the British have long accepted a significant presence of American content and philosophies in the broadcasting system. The 14 per cent quota on foreign programmes which applies to the BBC and ITV companies, for instance, is a global quota and so does not adequately detail the concentration of foreign programming during the peak viewing hours.

Broadly speaking, then, the White Paper is about the future of *British* broadcasting; it stops short of any analysis of the growing internationalization of media productions and structures which are gradually sucking British broadcasting into the international arena. This omission has resulted in a curious paradox: whilst existing British broadcasters have moved outwards in their strategies for survival *in anticipation of* the proposals in the White Paper, the White Paper has moved in the opposite direction and has continued to treat the major players as domestic ones (see Part Two).

There are countless other gaps in the White Paper but it is abundantly clear that, even if the government pursues only a few of its many proposals, British broadcasting will undergo tremendous change. Many of these proposals relate to technological change and, without doubt, new technologies – as well as 'old' technologies freed from regulatory control – allow for new developments. The government therefore intends to facilitate the introduction of new services using new means of video signal delivery. But underlying this desire for increasing 'consumer choice' there is a political will to move broadcasting (*and* communications technologies) into the marketplace and so remove them from under the regulatory umbrella which, many claim, has allowed for the creation of 'the least worst television' in the world.

This free market and *laissez-faire* ideology has re-drawn the British political, social and economic map. It is an approach which is best, if crudely, characterized as a desire to move away from state control and state direction of industrial sectors and towards competition and market regulation, and it has given rise to policies of privatization (e.g. of BT), of competition across many sectors (e.g. Mercury in telecommunications) and of deregulation (e.g. in relation to cable systems). Moreover it is an approach that has been applied across a wide spectrum of activities, and as far as this government is concerned there is no rationale for excluding broadcasting from this more 'invigorating' regime. Broadcasting, so the argument goes, should also 'benefit' from the competitive and enterprise spirit which the government has willed into other sectors.

The White Paper then is the mechanism by which a new environment will be allowed to develop. By proposing the licensing of a fifth commercial channel (and eventually a sixth) and commercial direct broadcasting satellite (DBS) services, by proposing a system of auctioning for commercial television franchises, by suggesting that the BBC become a subscription-funded service and by giving the go-ahead for the full use of microwave transmissions

(MVDS or MMDS) to provide extra television services, the government is effectively abandoning the regulated duopoly and leaving it to find a new role within a competitive environment. The government's intention then is to parallel the American experience of 'deregulation [which seeks] to protect the public interest by *commercial* competition, rather than by regulatory defense of the "public interest"'.[5]

The effects of this shift in emphasis in a sector which has economic as well as cultural properties is of great concern to many since it opens up the 'culture industry' to the full force of the marketplace. One immediate result of this is to transform broadcasting content from a cultural product which reflects and draws upon a community's interests and desires into an economic and international tradeable commodity. As Tunstall observed,

> The thrust of deregulation is to strip public service/public utility/regulated industries of their special status and to put them back into the mainstream of the economy.[6]

And as so often within the 'economy' there is no room for uneconomic and unprofitable cultural products, for public-service obligations. A prominent ITV executive recently declared that

> The duopoly allowed for certain types of programmes and, when ITV faces competition, it will have to be very different. That's all there is to it. . . . We are being forced to face up to what is in our commercial interests . . .[7]

The government's belief in, and desire for, competition also underlines its reluctance to intervene and to direct. In its current proposals for the future development of cable systems and in its general thinking about the communications infrastructure of tomorrow, it has now adopted a 'technology neutral' approach namely, an approach which emphasizes the need for markets and for consumer demand to determine the nature of technological change. The significance of this approach is that it rejects any hints that governments can have a part to play in the construction of national systems, be they of communications, water or health. Its implications for the concept of the 'wired nation' are discussed more fully below.

There is one other crucial dimension to the government's approach which occasionally becomes very visible, and that is its desire to reduce the bargaining (and other) powers of labour both through legislative acts but also by forcing capital to reassess its (mainly labour) costs of production. As the printing unions found out to their cost following their dispute with Rupert Murdoch, recent labour legislation has weakened the power of the trade union movement and has allowed a new managerial style to confront and undo established union practices and conditions. That very same process is now taking place in the field of broadcasting; commercial television – according to Thatcher – was, after all, 'the last bastion of restrictive practices'.

It would be wrong, however, to characterize the Thatcherite zeal for whole-sale reform of broadcasting as a total commitment to the marketplace for it is tempered by a paternalist concern over media content. The belief in competi-tion and the free market in broadcasting stops well short of complete support for all-out liberalization. The government has not, for example, 'abandoned' completely either the BBC or its commercial rivals, nor has it found the pol-itical muscle to even think the unthinkable, namely selling off the BBC. Like the Peacock Committee's deliberations (see below), the Thatcherite free-market liberal ideal also favours large doses of regulation to limit the excesses of the marketplace. Thus, whilst applauding the increased choice which the new media bring, the Thatcher Government established a Broadcasting Standards Council (1988) to oversee content.

The strong strain of paternalism in Thatcher's position is perhaps also evi-dence of a lack of clarity in the overall direction of developments. For a start, the paternalist streak runs counter to the liberal ideology which the govern-ment allegedly espouses. More importantly, it ignores the 'reality' of British broadcasting. As many have readily pointed out, the broadcasting duopoly is not *without* standards. Broadcasters have long exercised a public duty *vis-à-vis* taste and decency. They have also been extremely careful about violent or sex-ually explicit material.

The zeal to oversee 'sex and violence' therefore ignores the multiplicity of existing mechanisms which make the likelihood of such content being broad-cast either terrestrially or via satellite minimal. Broadcasters and DBS pro-grammers are currently constrained by the terms of their licences and by their regulatory bodies, e.g. the Independent Broadcasting Authority (IBA). Those who run cable systems are constrained by such things as the obscenity laws and the regulatory duties of the Cable Authority. In spite of claims to the contrary, even satellite broadcasters are restrained. The terms of the agreement be-tween would-be satellite programme providers and Astra effectively prohibit 'undesirable' programming. Not only is programming 'regulated' by the Duchy of Luxembourg – the body licensing Astra for the Société Européenne des Satellites (SES) – but programme providers have to abide by terms and conditions set out in their own agreements with SES Astra.[8] These emphasize standards of taste, decency, fairness and morality and not some form of un-regulated and totally exploitative television.

Reviewing the scene as a whole, one can see that the government has been able to effect radical change in the terms of the debate about 'communications and culture'. However, much of the initial intellectual groundwork for intro-ducing change was carried out by the Peacock Committee in its assessment of the prospects of television in the 1990s and beyond. It is this influential report which is examined in the next section.

Report of the Committee on Financing the BBC and the White Paper on Broadcasting

Over four years after the Peacock Committee was published in 1986, the broadcasting scene in Britain has, as yet, undergone surprisingly little visible change. However, it now stands on the threshold of very major change, as the result of the adoption of the 1988 White Paper's main recommendations by the Broadcasting Bill of 1989 (see editor's note above). In fact, the Peacock Committee was a major step in this process. Although the Committee's report itself had failed to produce the momentous change in government policy that its main authors had hoped for, it legitimated a 'radical' re-think of the true nature and duties of broadcasting in Britain. In this respect, its importance lies as much in the manner in which it shifted the intellectual paradigm as in the sorts of changes which were eventually incorporated into the White Paper (and the subsequent Bill). Like the 'Cable Systems' report, it provides an important historical landmark.

Although the Committee was charged with the duty of assessing the effects of different methods of funding broadcasting services in the future, it produced a document which took a much broader view of the issues that confronted British broadcasting. The result of this change of emphasis – from a narrow conception of the problem to a much wider one – was a report which undertook an extensive analysis of every facet of the 'comfortable duopoly' on the grounds that changing circumstances and changing technologies necessitated such a fundamental review of existing principles. And within these changed circumstances and explosion of channels, the key question was

> how can British broadcasting be financed in such a way as to bring the greatest enjoyment and pleasure to as many viewers and listeners as possible while at the same time fulfilling the public service obligation?[9]

This libertarian perspective was to set the pattern for the many recommendations which were made by the Committee.

Three major sources of funding were examined by the Committee: the BBC's licence fee, advertising revenue and subscription payments for television. By and large, the Committee took the view that under present conditions of television scarcity the present methods of funding broadcasting were satisfactory. Although there were many real problems with the licence fee as a method of funding broadcasting, for example it could never be raised to a level which would create financial parity with the commercial sector, these problems were minor by comparison with those which would follow from the introduction of advertising on the BBC as a means of supplementing its income (as the government had wished). The impact of advertising on the BBC would be a negative one, it would probably reduce the revenue of the ITV companies, it would affect the potential revenues of the embryonic 'new media' services and it would generally not be in the interests of viewers and listeners.

The only beneficiaries of such a move would be the advertising lobby which would gain from the reduced costs of advertising rates which competition for the same source of funds would bring.

The real issues were not so much how to devise funding structures for the future but how one could marry the explosion in television with the desire 'to bring the greatest enjoyment and pleasure to many viewers and listeners'. As the Committee saw it, the proliferation of broadcasting systems, of television channels and of payment methods for television would sweep away the existing funding structures based, as they were, on the fact of scarcity. With proliferation of channels, it would no longer be possible *or desirable* to retain the licence fee. One could move instead to a situation where a market in broadcasting would be encouraged; where, in other words, viewers would act as consumers, choosing and paying for what they watched.

For the Committee, then, the central objective for the future was to re-create broadcasting as a market of consumers and producers and so to transform the existing relationship between the producers of television content and the viewers/consumer. Viewers would pay for what they watched. Such a system of financing broadcasting would ensure that the public exercised a choice over what they watched and expressed their preferences through direct payments. No longer would a viewer pay for what he or she did not watch or for a service which he or she did not use.

Such a transformation of broadcasting and of long-established relationships would be neither easy nor immediate. For these reasons, the Committee envisaged three stages in the future development of British broadcasting and these would eventually lead towards 'a sophisticated market [in broadcasting] based on consumer sovereignty'.[10]

In the first stage (the present and the very near future) the duopoly would remain dominant in a slowly changing scene. In the second stage there would be a proliferation of systems, services and payment methods. Consequently, subscription would begin to replace the main part of the licence fee. The final stage was the most radical for it foresaw an indefinite number of channels and therefore a 'multiplicity of choice leading to [the] full broadcasting market'[11] where

- there was freedom of entry for all programme makers,
- viewers could register their preferences directly through payment schemes such as pay-per-view,
- there was no monopolistic concentration among either channellers or producers and
- common carrier obligations were imposed upon owners of transmission equipment.[12]

The shift from one type of system to another required both technological change *and* political will. Technological change eased the transition but the responsibility for signalling the point of transition lay with government. It was up to government to call for the 'almost immediate introduction' of television sets with 'a peritelevision socket'[13] and to signal, for example, the point of changeover to subscription or encryption services and so on. In this way, governments had a positive role to play in transforming broadcasting.

However, there was one way by which all these developments could be speeded up. The Committee's Recommendation 15 described how the construction of a national fibre-optic grid as a common carrier would allow for both a multiplicity of services and a competitive structure provided that competition between services was encouraged and maintained. In this way there would continue to be competition between service suppliers rather than between networks. This would 'lay the foundation of a system giving multiplicity of choice even before Stage 1 is complete'.[14]

The rationale behind all these scenarios could hardly be faulted. As far as the Committee was concerned, technological change made new arrangements in the field of television possible and so it took the view that, because it was no longer feasible or desirable to remain wedded permanently to the status quo, it was necessary to re-think fundamental relationships in broadcasting. In this respect, the report is a coherent intellectual exercise in the re-definition of the aims of broadcasting and its re-creation as a market to serve the consumer better.

Even its desire to 'safeguard public-service broadcasting' by creating a structure for nurturing the production of the non-profitable programme genres, e.g. arts programmes, was justified in terms of providing for greater consumer choice.[15] It was not the Achilles' heel in the libertarian argument, as the report's critics would have it.

In addition to this long-term strategy towards broadcasting, the Committee made many recommendations which prepared the scene for greater competition amongst producers and channels. Three such recommendations were particularly important.

1 The Committee recommended that commercial television companies should in future take part in a 'competitive tender' for franchises. As long as the IBA's minimum requirements were met, the highest bidder for each franchise would be awarded that franchise. In exceptional circumstances, the IBA could award the franchise for a lower price but it would then have to justify its decision publicly.
2 The Committee also recommended that Channel 4, which is currently owned by the IBA and is funded by the ITV companies in return for selling its air-time, should be given a full and autonomous financial existence. Not only should it have the right to sell its own air-time but it should cease to be a subsidiary of the IBA. Such a change would leave Channel 4 in open competition with the commercial channels, in contrast with the present cosier arrangements, and it could lead the channel to abandon its remit to serve minority interests.

3 Finally, the Committee recommended that both BBC and ITV 'should be required to increase to not less than 40 per cent the proportion of programmes supplied by independent producers'. As with the recommendations discussed above, the long-term effects of this would be widespread. On the one hand, it would increase the importance of the independent production sector and so loosen the stranglehold that commercial television companies had over the industry but, on the other hand, it would also act as a 'check on costs' since independents were able to produce 'some programmes of comparable standard and content but at lower cost than the BBC or ITV could achieve in-house'.[16]

Although the government has proposed a lower limit of 25 per cent the effects of this are not dissimilar: existing companies would have to divest themselves of their consequent over-capacity and to plan for productions based on reduced costs so as to match the competition from independents. The knock-on effects of these moves to restructure the industry are significant and include the shedding of labour, slimming down operations and generally the introduction of more flexible working arrangements.

When published, the report was severely criticized but it soon became clear that its general themes of greater consumer choice and deregulation were being considered seriously by the government. It came as no surprise then to find these ideas in the government's own proposals for the future of broadcasting. As the White Paper observed,

The Government places the viewer and listener at the centre of broadcasting policy. Because of technological, international and other developments change is inevitable. It is also desirable: only through change will the individual be able to exercise the much wider choice which will soon become possible. . . . The Government is also clear that there need be no contradiction between the desire to increase competition and widen choice and concern that programme standards on good taste and decency should be maintained.[17]

The government proposes three major sets of changes.

1 A major reform of the duopoly and the introduction of greater choice via new video delivery systems, e.g. the introduction of a Channel 5, possibly a Channel 6, releasing the remaining two DBS channels, and the introduction of local and other television services via microwave distribution systems (MVDS).

2 A reform of the present methods of funding broadcasting services. Such reforms would allow for greater competition for advertising revenue and for any revenues which can be obtained directly from consumers, e.g. via subscription payments. For example, the BBC will be permitted to introduce

subscription services during the night hours and, in the long term, will also be encouraged to replace the licence fee by subscription revenue.

3 The general loosening up of the regulatory framework of commercial broadcasting. The existing commercial television companies will be re-formed into a Channel 3 structure and integrated into an expanded commercial television sector which will include a fifth, and possibly a sixth, terrestrial channel as well as satellite and microwave delivered (MVDS) television services. These will all be 'lightly regulated' by a new body, the Independent Television Commission (ITC), which will replace the IBA and the Cable Authority.

Other examples of the new commercial and liberalized spirit include the reform of Channel 4, the proposal that commercial television franchises be auctioned, the 25 per cent quota for independent productions – all proposals which can be found in the Peacock Committee report – and, most critically, the proposal that commercial television companies should no longer be protected from commercial take-overs. This last proposal emphasizes the new commercial characteristics of tomorrow's television companies.

If the general theme of introducing more competition by allowing for the full exploitation of available technologies *and sources of funding* is in keeping with the spirit of the Peacock report, the White Paper parts company with it, or with reports inspired by it, at two crucial stages. First, it does not endorse Recommendation 15 and the development of a national fibre-optic grid and, second, it proposes a much more radical change in broadcasting than either Peacock or the Home Office study into subscription television considered possible. The implications of both rejections are significant.

Recommendation 15

Recommendation 15 addressed the impasse which characterized the UK telecommunications scene. Having promised the 'wired nation' competition in telecommunications and consumer choice, the government had actually delivered little. Cable had not progressed, BT was still dominant and consumers were stuck without much choice.

When the government had granted Mercury a telecommunications licence in 1981, it also put into effect 'the duopoly policy' which permitted only BT and Mercury to provide national network facilities and basic telecommunications services until the early 1990s. One rationale for this policy was to permit a period of stability; another was to allow Mercury, and BT, to adjust to the reality of competition. So the desire to stimulate competition has been constrained by a series of policies that fell short of full liberalization. Similarly, government regulations of the relationship between BT and Mercury *and* the embryonic cable companies favoured separateness and competition. Thus, cable operators were able to offer voice telephony services in conjunction with BT or Mercury – the latter provide an overlay case for telephony – but BT and

Mercury were not permitted to use their basic telecommunications systems to transmit cable (entertainment) services.

Although these barriers to a fully competitive environment were justified in terms of the need to protect industrial sectors in their infancy (in the face of a large and dominant BT) the Peacock Committee 'took the view that current Government policy was failing to stimulate the desired development of high grade networks'.[18] It felt that the key to overcoming this lay in the idea of common carriers and that the current restrictions on cable systems, on BT and on Mercury would not lead to the creation of a sophisticated broadband telecommunications system in the near future, if ever.

Recommendation 15 therefore put forward the view that 'national telecommunications services (BT, Mercury or future others) [could] act as common carriers with a view to the provision of a full range of services', including television. In this way, one could take full advantage of BT's and Mercury's installation of their fibre-optic networks. Moreover, Peacock was persuaded that if BT were freed from the existing restrictions on its provision of services it would be willing and ready to establish a fibre-optic grid as part of its replacement programme for the ageing telephone network. However, if BT were to continue to be restricted to telephony and data transmissions then it would 'be necessary only to patch up existing local circuits.'[19]

The Department of Trade and Industry's consultant's report identified the major flaw in the Recommendation, namely, that it reversed government policy on competition in both services *and* networks; it encouraged competition 'in the provision of services *at the expense of competition on the network side*'.[20] It also smacked too much of interventionism.

This position was further reinforced by two subsequent reports. The first pointed out that there were so many players and potential players in the telecommunications field that government policies need to be constructed around the particular objectives that the government wants to pursue, and those objectives – 'the oversight of fair competition, only intervening in market operations to restrict any unfair use of market power by dominant players'[21] – are extensions of current policies rather than reversals or major amendments. The second report endorsed this position under the heading of a 'technology neutral' approach to change, an approach which was based on the view that, since technologies were evolving rapidly, it was difficult

> to convince ourselves that it was sensible for government to pin its colours solely on one particular option [such as the national grid]. Furthermore we could not see how such an approach was compatible with the twin desires . . . that user needs should determine the pace of development . . . and that competition should be a powerful influence in the market place.[22]

One (policy) consequence of this was that the White Paper proposed that cable system operators should no longer be required to construct sophisticated broadband systems. Thus, existing policies were completely abandoned in favour of a different liberalized regime. Operators, in future, would 'be free to decide upon the best mix of technologies' as between cable, MVDS or a combination of both.

> The extent to which they lay down cable facilities physically capable of functioning as a fully interactive telecommunications network will be a matter for their judgement; not one for Government or regulators.[23]

An equally dramatic reversal of policy which derives from the technology neutral approach is the proposal that the 'monopoly rights' which cable operators were granted over 'both the delivery and retailing of services' should be removed. In future, the task of delivery of services, i.e. the construction of the network, will be separated from the retailing of the services on the network so that the former does not preclude competition in the latter. Furthermore, the ITC retained the power to award more than one franchise for any one local area.

These proposals have caused much anguish amongst existing cable operators for numerous, and very obvious, reasons. They either risk losing control over their complete operation beyond the life of their current licence or they have to divest themselves of their control over 'retailing' on the network and become common carriers. Neither option is particularly attractive and both have implications for prospective operators. (One should also add that few have been convinced by the view that on local networks the delivery of services can in reality be distinguished from retailing of services.)

What is clear from these, and related, proposals is that although they follow through the logic of the government's new-found faith in 'technology-neutrality' they reverse existing policies in favour of a market-led strategy. Competition is the key word for the future. But, unlike the Peacock report, that competition does not represent one facet of a coherent approach to the creation of a sophisticated broadcasting market – it is competition for its own sake with no particular predetermined objective. In this respect, the White Paper lacks the coherence and the well thought out aims which are continuously articulated in the Peacock study.

Subscription television

The other major departure concerns the introduction of subscription television. Peacock's suggestions were explored in detail by Charles Jonscher's report, *Subscription Television*, for the Home Office. The report favoured a rather gradual approach to the reform of British broadcasting. In place of wholesale change, it proposed that the government introduce another terrestrial broadcasting service (Channel 5) as a subscription service but that otherwise the existing duopoly should be retained.

These conclusions were based on three main considerations. First, the report suggested that the present duopoly could not survive a complete transfer to subscription funding. There would be insufficient demand for these services *as currently constituted* to attract sufficient subscription funding. To succeed, pay television channels had to offer 60–70 per cent 'premium services and no information programmes at all'.[24] Such an economic requirement would necessarily impact on the existing services and their current wide-ranging offerings.

Second, there was no guarantee that services which did not offer such a large measure of premium material could rely on additional funds from advertising. Advertising revenue could fluctuate with increased competition between services. Indeed, increased competition for advertising revenue could, in fact, lead to lower rates and therefore a stagnant pool of revenue to satisfy more players.

Finally, and perhaps most critically, in view of the uncertainty over 'how the content and the financing of television channels will develop over the next decade', the options adopted in the report – use of night-time broadcasting for subscription and/or the introduction of a fifth and sixth national terrestrial channel – 'avoid introducing major disruptive changes in the broadcasting mechanisms or the mechanisms by which they are funded'.[25]

In other words, one could increase the viewer's choice and introduce new funding mechanisms through judicious incrementalist measures. This rather cautious approach is completely overturned in the White Paper. Its own proposals recommend the creation of an unlimited number of channels – local, national and international – to be funded from advertising revenue and/or subscription payments. This would also apply to the BBC which will be encouraged to abandon the licence fee in favour of subscription in the near future.

In view of the uncertainties which the Jonscher report so clearly identified, it would seem that these current proposals will almost certainly create havoc in order to please the gods of competition and 'technology-neutrality'.

The White Paper has had one other crucial effect. It has focused attention on the domestic broadcasting scene. This is hardly surprising since its cumulative effects would be to redesign the British broadcasting scene. Although it is significant in the long term, the international media scene is still, at present, of secondary importance. We are in Peacock's Phase One for the foreseeable future despite the proliferation of satellite services.

These are important considerations and go a long way towards explaining current developments on the British scene. Commercial television companies, for example, are now primarily concerned with the implications of the White Paper rather than future and as yet undetermined changes. Many risk losing their franchises and so the plans which they have put into effect are plans to ensure their continued survival and profitability once the broadcasting reforms are implemented. If those strategies for change also place the companies in a strong international position then they have additional merits.

Part two

Television in an age of change

The White Paper's proposals directly challenge the existing structures of the independent television companies. It does not present the BBC with a similar set of problems; the BBC will have until the late 1990s to adjust to a new regime whilst the ITV companies will face challenges to their franchises well before 1992. In view of these challenges, the ITV companies have put into motion plans for reform. Some have restructured their operations, others have diversified and all have become aware of the need to prepare for a growing internationalization of the television market.

The restructuring and diversification of operations

Margaret Thatcher's comments about independent television companies (see p. 152) painfully exposed one (alleged) facet of their operations, namely, their inefficient and costly structures. But television companies had started to deal with these costly practices well before the Prime Minister had uttered her now famous remarks. Thames Television, for example, was involved in a dispute with the broadcasting unions in 1984 over the specific issue of working practices. Since then, the commercial television companies have moved rapidly ahead with major plans to reorganize themselves in order to reduce their costs and the size of their operations. London Weekend Television, for instance, announced the reduction of its permanent staff by some 20 per cent by the end of the 1988 financial year.[26]

Such restructuring falls in line with the recommendations of the 1988 National Economic Research Associates report for the ITV companies which forcibly warned that production costs would have to be radically reduced if the companies wished to survive the next round of franchise applications. Its *least* worst scenario suggested that 'unless ITV takes positive action to reduce costs or increase revenue it could be losing up to £550 million a year by the end of the century . . .'. As other factors are added to this scenario – a fifth channel, separation of Channel 4 from ITV and so on – the consequences become more severe.[27]

One reason for the severity of this warning has been the success of the independent television production sector and its statutory insertion into the broadcasting scene. The government's pursuit of a 25 per cent quota for independents has forced the commercial television companies to confront the logic of their own operations. Unlike independents, companies usually have large numbers of permanent staff working to strict union guidelines and practices. Consequently their costs are far in excess of those of independents who work without permanent staff and on contracts. It was the nature of the latter's operation which had attracted the Peacock Committee and the Committee was well aware of the implications of a move to a quota for independents (see p. 157). The companies will have to meet the production costs of independents if their own operations are to be competitive domestically and internationally. Additionally, as commercial television companies acquire more and more of their content from independents, they will have to reduce the size of their own operations: the greater the proportion of their acquisitions from independents, the lesser the need for a large in-house production facility.

Another compelling reason for cost cutting can be found in the economic forecasts of the new satellite delivered channels which became available both via SES Astra and via the DBS venture of British Satellite Broadcasting (BSB). Though both represent potentially lucrative markets for the existing programme suppliers, their ability to exploit those markets will depend on their success in meeting the strict cost requirements of the new media. Rupert Murdoch's Sky Channel reputedly spends some £2,500 per show for old episodic series and its own variety and chat shows are produced at about one-tenth of the cost of the lowest production costs in British television on Channel 4. Even BSB's larger budget spent on programmes is only a small proportion of the total BBC and ITV annual expenditure on programmes: BSB's breakdown includes £12 million per annum for 8 hours of domestic and international news material, £8 million per annum for 5 hours of women/lifestyle material and £15 million for 5 hours of sport.[28]

The same pattern is also true for the news services promised by BSB and others. BSB's NOW news channel baulked at the prospect of paying ITN some £20 million per annum for about 8 hours of news material per day. Its most recent proposal was to pay no more than £12 million for that service. By comparison, ITN's contract with Channel 4 to provide 1 hour of news material per day was negotiated at just under £10 million in 1987–8. (Brooks, *Observer*, 31 January 1988). Similarly Super Channel's half-hour news programme in mid-1988 was provided by ITN at a cost of £1.5 million per annum. (The original contract between ITN and Super Channel was costed at £3 million per annum but it was renegotiated in early 1988 at less than 50 per cent because of pressure from Super Channel to reduce costs.) The implications are clear; as the Chairman of London Weekend Television was quick to point out, there would be severe strains and pressures which would become apparent both in the short term and the long term if a single production company such as ITN were to produce news for one operator (BSB) at a much cheaper rate than it charges another (ITV).[29]

What also needs to be borne in mind is that the increase in the number of domestic television channels will lead to further competition for revenue and that, unless there is a commensurate and proportional increase in national and international advertising and subscription revenues, there will be less money available for television productions.

These processes of restructuring have acquired a different sort of urgency in the light of the White Paper's proposal that ITV franchises be auctioned to the highest bidder. The current method for allocating franchises comprises a series of submissions to, and interviews with, the IBA. It was never a popular process but it was at least less of a lottery than the current proposals. These give no guarantees to incumbents and put an undue emphasis on high bids. In other words, current proposals are likely to put all the existing companies at risk and in danger of extinction in 1992 when the bidding process is in full swing.

In view of these proposals, commercial television companies, not unnaturally, have taken precautions to protect themselves. As noted above, many have restructured themselves so as to increase their profitability in the short term (and prior to 1992). Others have been more adventurous. Thus,

> Several ITV companies have taken the precaution of isolating the TV franchise from other activities, creating separate profit centres out of production, sales and distribution. These could have an after-life should the contract be lost.[30]

HTV, the Welsh commercial television company, has recently announced a large-scale reorganization aimed at providing at least half of its profits from non-ITV sources by the time it has to re-apply for its franchise in 1993. Similarly, TVS has recently acquired the American MTM TV company (Hill St Blues, St Elsewhere, etc.) with a view to exploiting its national and international library potential in the 1990s. This is also true for Thames Television, one of the largest television contractors. Other examples of diversification include the ITV companies' investment in DBS and initially in Super Channel.

Clearly, not all companies have followed this particular route and some have moved back into the heartland of their original business in television programme productions but even here there are renewed efforts to exploit the growing international demand for television products.

The international trade in television

The trade in television programmes is not a new phenomenon and like other trades there are regulations and obstacles – in this case linguistic, political and cultural – which appear to work against the ideal of a free trading market. Nevertheless, the trade's importance for British broadcasters cannot be underestimated. Imported programmes provide a ready supply of relatively cheap and popular programmes, whilst television exports not only provide Britain with a vital source of foreign revenue but also establish its reputation as the second most powerful television trading nation.[31]

At present, both the BBC and ITV companies operate a voluntary 14 per cent quota on foreign programming. The quota therefore prevents schedulers from inundating viewers with imported programmes and it continues to remind broadcasters of their own primary duties and responsibilities to serve their domestic markets with culturally relevant material. But it also represents a real obstacle to the full exploitation of imports and the enormous savings which could accrue if the quota did not exist. Whether a policy of wholesale importation would enable programmers to reach more viewers more often is an issue which is tackled more fully below. As will be argued, cultural and linguistic barriers do exist and may themselves act as a brake to the hopes of a pan-European television trade and market.

It remains the case though that there are cost savings to be made through the importation of programming. Although the whole question of the economics of television production is dogged by different accounting procedures across different organizations, recent figures give a good indication of the relative cheapness of imported compared with home-produced television content. A popular American drama such as Dallas may cost some £0.8 million an hour to produce but it was acquired by the BBC for a mere £40,000 per episode – 'less than one fifth of the costs of a UK production of the same type of programme'. With other American episodic series costing British buyers only £20,000–£30,000 an hour, 'it is not surprising that popular US imports accounted for 15 per cent of BBC air-time in 1983'.[32]

If the American market is the most important source of programme imports and the most powerful media nation, it is also the most important market for British exports. This is not a new development; the North American market is the key market for television trade and both the BBC and ITV have long supplied it with programmes and formats. In more recent years, as the drive to increase programme sales as a source of revenue has grown in importance, so too has the volume of trade. BBC Enterprises, 'the world's largest exporter of television programming, selling more than 12,000 hours . . . to over 100 countries',[33] still mainly exports to the two major single English-language markets – American and Australia principally – with Europe *as a whole* an important close rival. Even so the net contribution of all this activity to the BBC's revenue amounts to only about 1 per cent of its total revenue. For commercial television, the £47.3 million gross value of programme exports (in 1984) is also a very small proportion of its total revenue. The point is not so much that the British programme makers have not taken up the challenge of marketing their products abroad but that they have so far failed to make significant inroads into *the* major market for television, the American networks. As long as they remain at the fringes of that system – on PBS or cable channels – they are unlikely to make the profits that repeat sales guarantee for programme makers. The European market, by contrast, does not at present offer the same financial gains that success in the United States guarantees.

There are other means by which British (and other) broadcasters can ease their financial burdens and so produce high quality, high cost dramatic productions. These include co-production and pre-production deals where the costs are shared amongst a number of major producers such as American, Australian or Canadians. Such deals are now fairly common and illustrate how the cost of television has forced co-operation between partners. But that co-operation is not always benign: foreign partners may impose their own re-quirements on the production with respect to, say, casting, funding and even decision making. More importantly, that co-operation continues to reinforce the existing pattern of trade: namely, a healthy trade across the world, particu-larly the English-speaking parts of it, but imports mainly from the United States. Whether the creation of an open European market from 1992 onwards will significantly shift the attention of British programmers is thus a critical question.

But it is a question which cannot be detached from its cultural and legisla-tive dimensions. Enabling the free flow of television programmes from, say, France to Britain will neither increase their preponderance on British screens nor their ratings. Similarly, the worth of the open European market will de-pend greatly on the enabling frameworks which are at present being con-sidered in Europe. Both the European Commission and the Council of Europe have been actively pursuing a policy to Europeanize – as opposed to Americanize – television in Europe. The European programme quota and the availability of state funds for co-productions as well as European productions are all designed to redress a situation where 'only 40 per cent of drama one-offs, series and TV films now shown in Europe are European originated'.[34]

The proposals for a 60 per cent quota of European-originated programmes across all television services – including private commercial satellite services – will *if adopted* undoubtedly increase the size of the market for European products and, more particularly, British products. But if a quota is not adopted by Britain – and British policy has been consistently against a quota – then the European market will strengthen the positions of both the United States and Britain as media producers without any major reciprocal benefits for European producers.

Indeed, British policy to date has been fairly supportive of opening up the trade in television as long as British interests are not adversely affected. This has been the position with respect to advertising, European programming on domestically regulated services such as DBS and broadcasting standards. The British government has accepted the European position precisely because none of the rules involve major modifications to British television practices. Similarly, although the requirement that nationally regulated media be owned by EC nationals has been retained – in the face of considerable opposition from the cable industry – it has not acted as a major obstacle to American involvement in cable. In fact, American interest in British cable is anything but on the wane.

Despite these few agreements, there are many doubts about the British government's desire to intervene, even via the EC, in the broader aspects of the television market. One such area of doubt concerns existing (and future) satellite channels such as Sky or Screen Sport. At present these are lightly regulated and they have to comply with a few, very general, obligations regarding impartiality, taste, decency and so on. As long as these are fulfilled they can transmit whatever they, and their viewers, want. Many therefore carry substantial proportions of American programme imports.

What is not yet clear is whether the British government will accept EC Directives to impose a European origination quota on these services. The White Paper provides no clear answers; it distinguishes between these services and DBS services and it proposes a quota for the latter but not for the former. The key to this apparent anomaly lies in several opaque statements in the White Paper concerning the EC Directive. These refer to the need for legislation which is 'satisfactory from the viewpoint of UK interests'[35] and, more strongly, to the fact that there

> should be no question of UK broadcasting interests being denied access to other European markets because of any absence of agreement on international regulation.[36]

But what precisely are UK interests and how would the Commission interpret this? Is a BSB/BBC film channel showing mainly American films a UK interest and would it fall foul of European proposals? Is the criterion one of ownership or content or a combination of both? Does this effectively mean that CNN will be at risk – it falls down on both criteria – or that there can never be a Disney Channel in Europe?

The obvious danger is that rules and regulations will be created to deal with very complex situations involving international trade and capital. More than this, the rules may establish criteria which do not allow for cultural diversity and preferences: why should one choose between Berlusconi (European and therefore permissible) and Murdoch (American and therefore not permissible)? Such rules would be empty of any proper analysis of culture in the international context.

Needless to say, such rules would also come into conflict with this government's desire to create a framework which would allow 'increased opportunities for broadcasters *and* viewers'[37] since 'increased opportunities' must include permission for satellite operators to use imports and to develop as the market demands. One effect of this liberal interpretation of trends in broadcasting is to create a powerful Anglo-American force in Europe. The already strong American presence in cable and satellite broadcasting will in the near future and with British co-operation move into newer areas of programming. The American company United Cable plans to bring The Discovery Channel into Britain (and hence Europe) via Astra and Murdoch has already signed deals with The Disney Channel for a channel also on Astra; both Sky and BSB have completed extensive film deals with American film producers and the other markets such as sports, music and children's television continue to be dominated by Anglo-American interests.

The explosion in television and the growing internationalization of programme production will increase the opportunities for trade but this should not be taken as a signal for the demise of the present domestic broadcasters. There is a view, albeit supported by some rather sketchy evidence, which suggests that the strength of the domestic broadcasters will continue to be a characteristic of television in the age of trans-frontier broadcasting.

At present, satellite services are locked into a domestic or a common linguistic market, be it Anglophone, Francophone or Germanophone. Such linguistic and cultural barriers may be real obstacles to the internationalization, perhaps even the Europeanization, of television. (Incidentally, advertisers – who will have to fund many of these new services – have long been aware of the difficulty of creating advertisements which successfully cross cultural boundaries. The full implications of this have not yet been fully analysed.) A recent Pan European Television Audience Research (PETAR) report starkly highlighted the failure of English-language services to penetrate the West German market – a principal reason for Sky's withdrawal from that country's cable market. By contrast, in Scandinavia where Sky was once a strong player the advent of Scansat has had an adverse effect on Sky's market and led to a significant decline in its share of viewing.[38] British cable viewers, however, completely ignore non-English channels.[39] If this pattern persists – and it is worth noting that Astra and BSB will be primarily aimed at the British market – then the prospect of a pan-European or even international service dims rapidly.

Another way of supporting the thesis that internationalization is still a long way off is to examine viewing preferences. Although American television productions are generally popular, their popularity is not universal. In the case of the UK market – which shares a common language with the United States – domestic productions consistently dominate the top twenty-five most viewed programmes. Evidence from other countries also tends to confirm the consistent popularity of domestic output. A survey in the West German magazine *Stern*

found a general dissatisfaction among the viewing public for imported US TV series – the staples of private stations. Only 20 per cent of those questioned professed to liking the American series shown on German television.[40]

This has led some critics to suggest that

the strengths of national cultures along with the power of language and tradition, have been grossly underestimated by those who have sought to establish pan-European markets.[41]

This is not to say that new services will not be watched nor that those who watch them will not find them popular. The point is that of the total universe of viewers those who express a consistent preference for non-domestic productions are a very small minority. Cable households, for example, still account for less than one-fifth of all homes passed: is this a sign of consumer resistance to indifferent programming on the new media?

Admittedly, the 'new' media are still in their infancy and direct-to-home satellite services only became a reality in Britain from February 1989 when dishes – and services – became readily available at reasonable prices. If they succeed in penetrating the market then the above comment may still turn out to be premature but it does nevertheless provide a salutary warning to those who believe that the route to success lies in the provision of cheap, mainly American, imports.

Conclusion

There are many influences currently shaping the future of British broadcasting. The most critical ones, as we have argued in this chapter, flow from the recent White Paper. The proposals which this document contains will have a considerable impact on broadcasting and if they come into force British broadcasting as early as 1992 will be very different from what it is now. By the mid-1990s when the proposals start to impact on the BBC the change will be even greater. There will be more channels, different players, larger groupings of commercial companies, different menus, alternative payment systems and so on. On top of this massive internal change will come the changes from the sky – by 1991 Britain will have an extra eleven (minimum) channels. Clearly not all of these will be able to survive financially and this will also be true of those new channels available terrestrially.

In these times of radical change, the European and the international dimensions are important but secondary considerations. Britain is a dominant media player, second to the United States, and it will continue to play a significant part in the international trade in television but, at the moment, its attentions are on domestic affairs. Such key players on the international scene as the BBC and Thames Television will need to survive in their domestic markets in the next few years of change in order to have a presence abroad. They are national broadcasters first, international players second.

Notes

1 *Broadcasting in the 1990s: Competition, Choice and Quality. The Government's Plans for Broadcasting Legislation*, November 1988 – henceforth the White Paper.
2 Information Technology Advisory Panel, *Cable Systems*, March 1982.
3 *Report of the Committee on Financing the BBC*, Chairman: Professor A. Peacock, Cmnd. 9824 (London: HMSO, July 1986) henceforth the Peacock report.

4 C. Jonscher, *Subscription Television: A Study for the Home Office* (London: HMSO, May 1987).
5 J. Tunstall, *Communications Deregulation* (Oxford: Basil Blackwell, 1986), p. 3, emphasis added.
6 Tunstall, op. cit., p. 33.
7 D. Elstein, quoted in *Broadcast*, London, 7 October, 1988.
8 House of Commons, Home Affairs Committee, Minutes of Evidence, HMSO, 17 February 1988, pp. 117–19.
9 The Peacock report, p. 2, para. 7.
10 Ibid., p. 133, para. 592.
11 Ibid., p. 136, para. 608.
12 Ibid., p. 150, para. 701.
13 Ibid., p. 136, para. 611.
14 Ibid., p. 145, para. 666.
15 Ibid., pp. 148–9, paras 682–9.
16 Ibid., p. 142, para 647.
17 The White Paper, p. 1, para. 1.2.
18 Department of Trade and Industry, *The Development of UK Communications Systems* (London: DTI, 9 April 1987), p. 5, para. 2.3.
19 The Peacock report, p. 115, para. 493.
20 *The Development of UK Communications Systems*, p. 10, para. 4.3.
21 Department of Trade and Industry, *Evolution of the United Kingdom Communications Infrastructure*, Phase 1 Discussion Paper, written by PA Consulting Group, London, September, 1987, p. 12.
22 Communications Steering Group Report, Department of Trade and Industry, *The Infrastructure for Tomorrow* (London: HMSO, December 1988), p. iii, para. 2.
23 The White Paper, p. 27, para. 6.33.
24 Jonscher, op. cit., p. 159.
25 Ibid., p. 167–8.
26 *The Guardian*, London, 22 October 1988.
27 National Economic Research Associates, Quoted in *Broadcast*, 11 March 1988.
28 *Broadcast*, 20 May 1988, p. 6.
29 *Broadcast*, 4 March 1988.
30 *Broadcast*, 14 October 1988, p. 66.
31 For a recent discussion of these issues see R. Collins, G. Garnham and G. Locksley, *The Economics of Television* (London: Sage, 1988). Also J. Tunstall, *The Media are American*, Constable, 1978.
32 Jonscher, op. cit., p. 105.
33 Ibid., p. 100.
34 *Broadcast*, 1 October 1988, p. 5.
35 The White Paper, p. 43, para. 11.9.
36 Ibid., p. 43, para. 11.10.
37 Ibid., p. 43, para. 11.9.
38 *New Media Markets*, London, 14 October 1988.
39 R. Negrine and A. Goodfriend, 'Public perceptions of the new media: a survey of British attitudes', *Media, Culture and Society*, 10 (3) (July 1988).
40 *Broadcast*, 14 October 1988.
41 M. Tracey, 'Europe's TV audiences: what will they really watch', *Columbia Journal of World Business*, 22 (3) (Fall 1987), p. 82. See also M. Tracey, *A Taste of Money: Popular Culture and the Economics of Global Television* (London: Broadcasting Research Unit, 1987).

Chapter eight

New media in West Germany: the politics of legitimation

Wolfgang Hoffmann-Riem

On 24 June 1983, unnoticed by the West German public, a short debate took place in the West German federal parliament (the Bundestag).[1] It concerned the concluding report of the Commission of Inquiry into Information and Communications Technologies (the *Enquete-Kommission Informations-und Kommunikationstechniken*, EK-IuK).[2] Established by the Bundestag, this commission of inquiry had had the task of preparing policy decisions about the new forms of electronic communication such as videotex (*Bildschirmtext*), teletext (*Video-text*) and cable and satellite broadcasting. In the short debate ten minutes to address the house were allocated to each of the four parliamentary groups – the governing parties of the 'Union' (CDU/CSU) and the Liberals (FDP) and the opposition parties, the Social Democrat Party (SPD) and the Green Party. The report was referred to five specialist committees. Since that time there has been almost no further news of the work of the commission. The debate in the Bundestag appears to have been a 'pauper's burial', attended by not a single mourner.

The date of 24 June 1983 – in the middle of World Communications Year – symbolized the burial too, for the time being at least, of numerous earlier controversies about the development of telecommunications. The absence of public interest was a clear indication that the new information and communications technologies were no longer seen as a 'hot subject', and that the majority of the Bundestag saw no further need for policy preparation. This situation stood in strong contrast with the controversies that had been bitterly fought out in the Federal Republic over preceding years. The main directions of future policy development had been determined in the intervening period and public protest had been extensively deflated. From this time onwards the policy process was able to dispense with any further forums of public debate and conflict resolution – in short, any further process of legitimation of the new media, involving the absorption of conflict and promotion of acceptance. In this chapter we aim to describe and analyse some significant milestones along the way to this state of affairs and also several subsequent events.

On the requirement of legitimation

Nearly all experts are agreed that innovations in the field of information and communications technologies will fundamentally influence and transform modern societies. These experts talk about a 'mega-technology' with a very great economic significance. It will affect almost every field of occupational and leisure activity. This technology has the potential to alter economic and political power structures irrevocably, from the level of the individual firm to that of the entire body politic. It will be able to penetrate into the deepest recesses of the individual's private sphere. Comparison has often been drawn with the industrial revolution of the nineteenth century.

The possible consequences of these technologies for state, society and individual cannot be safely predicted. Yet it would be quite feasible to make forecasts within the parameters of a technology assessment programme, to rehearse alternative scenarios and to determine likely positive and negative effects.[3] It may be difficult but does not seem impossible to envisage a rational policy approach that makes every effort to engage in such a technology assessment programme and to take decisions in the light of academic and scientific expertise. However, in the real world of policy this type of approach seldom occurs. Typically, policy is a matter of acute conflicts involving the interplay of powerful interests. Against this background policy-makers adopt strategies of muddling through in an incremental manner. Far-reaching and long-term analyses are disturbing – at any rate, when they show negative consequences or indicate alternatives that would conflict with the aims of powerful interests. Thus it cannot be a matter of surprise that decisions about the introduction of the new information and communications technologies have not been based upon any such technology assessment programme.

In the 1970s and to some extent in the 1980s some relatively open and important questions were requiring answers. Should the West German telephone network be digitized? Should a broadband distribution network (one-way) or a broadband interactive (two-way) network be built? Should the new information and communications technologies be used primarily for social purposes or should the aim be private commercial usage? Should the broadcasting system be opened up to private commercial operators with the help of cable and satellite? Only a small circle of experts were competent in such matters. By the end of the 1970s, however, the interest of sections of the German general public had been aroused. In the foreground of public debate stood the question of the broadcasting system – or, to be precise, the question of its privatization and commercialization. In particular, concern focused on the question of whether publishers and the press should also be allowed to operate as broadcasters.[4] Other questions, such as the potential offered by the new technologies for the rationalization of work, other kinds of transformation at the work-place (i.e. de-skilling) and even impact on unemployment, were also discussed to some extent. The possibilities that the new technologies opened for supervision and surveillance, by the firm or the state, appeared threatening. There was apprehension about changes in the power relations within both individual enterprises and the wider political sphere.[5]

Conversely, there were also many hopes placed in the new technologies. The Federal Republic is not well-endowed in raw materials and energy. It lives from its exports. The competitiveness of German industry in international markets seemed to depend on the development and utilization of the new information and communications technologies. This economic argument became a significant factor, particularly at the beginning of the 1980s, as the Federal Republic searched for a way out of economic crisis. The modernization of the national economy was widely recommended as a recipe for combating the crisis and reducing unemployment.[6]

The Bundespost – the West German PTT, a federal public institution directed by a minister – is the largest economic concern in the Federal Republic. A broad section of the information and communications industry depends on it. Correspondingly, the business policy of the Bundespost has great significance for the development of economic policy generally. The Bundespost maintains very close contact indeed with many private firms, in particular Siemens.[7] It is to a very considerable extent the Bundespost that these firms have to thank for their economic position domestically and indirectly also in international markets. In turn, they are directly interested in the outcome of the Bundespost's policies. Accordingly, the interests of both the Bundespost and the telecommunications industry were important factors in the development of new media policy.[8]

It was not simply a matter of the economic exploitation of the new information and communication technologies, however; it was also a question of media policy and of the distribution of power between the federal authority (*Bund*) and the federal states (*Bundesländer*). On the one hand, the confrontation about the introduction of private commercial broadcasting was a dispute between the political parties, in particular the CDU/CSU and the SPD. On the other hand, it was an argument about where the competences lay for regulatory policy. As far as the mass media are concerned, legislative competence is vested mainly in the states. By contrast, the federation is responsible for telecommunications policy. However, the demarcation between these two areas is a controversial matter. The federation is also responsible for decisions about the technology, particularly the transmission and relay systems. The network is installed and operated by the Bundespost. Yet, decisions taken about the telecommunications network can prejudice the possibilities open to the broadcasting system. Conflicts between the Bundespost and the states were, accordingly, almost unavoidable.

In all political camps there was uncertainty over the future course of action. On no side was any comprehensive concept to be discovered. All sides bemoaned the great difficulties of understanding the current state of technological and economic development and of anticipating future developments correctly. These substantive and conceptual uncertainties impeded practical policy making. In the absence of any clear direction it was impossible to develop formulae for reacting to public protest and dissent. In periods of such uncertainty, commissions are most useful and universally applied expedients.[9] Commissions can be useful in the identification of the range of possible conflicts; they can postpone active decision making; they can elaborate workable compromises; and they can clear the ground for the actual execution of decisions.

Commissions can relieve the government of the burden of sole responsibility for decisions. Yet since their observations and recommendations are non-binding, the option of disregarding their advice remains available. Even in the latter instances their work can be highly useful: they are testimony to the attempt to bring the available state-of-the-art expertise to bear on the subject. Commissions are particularly well suited to the absorption of conflict, notably so if it is possible to bring together important political actors and representatives of interests. If it is further possible to involve independent experts – particularly academics and scientists – in the commission's work, then the results are very difficult to attack politically.

Correspondingly, commissions were established in the Federal Republic in order to supply legitimation for the introduction of the new technologies. They always comprised representatives of diverse political forces, industry and science. However, they never reflected the complete spectrum of social and political interests. Opponents of the new technologies were considered to be inadmissible – scientists and experts who held fundamentally sceptical views.

The preparation of the public for the introduction of the new information and communication technologies: the case of the KtK

The first important commission was the Commission for the Development of the Technical Communications System (*Kommission für den Ausbau des technischen Kommunikationssystems*, KtK). The KtK was established in 1974 at the instigation of the Federal Minister for Research and Technology, Horst Ehmke (SPD). It presented its report at the beginning of 1976.[10] Its work was very closely associated with both of the ministries that were (at that time) jointly directed by Ehmke, namely the Ministry for Research and Technology (Bundesministerium für Forschung und Technologie, BMFT) and the Bundespost Ministry. With respect to its composition, the KtK was 'pluralistic' in its membership, i.e. it contained representatives of the political parties, industrial firms, trade unions, publishers, broadcasting institutions and scientists, among others. In its concrete activities the commission was serviced by further experts, among whom specialists from the telecommunications industry and the state administration were especially active.[11]

The KtK worked in an atmosphere of momentous anticipation: it was a matter of opening up German society to new technologies, which until then were hardly known and uncontroversial. Supported by the negotiating skill of its chairman, Professor Witte, the commission was able to deliver a unanimous report. It recommended in a cautious manner an opening towards the new technologies, but only in such a way that the interest of the Bundespost and the telecommunications industry – especially Siemens – in exploiting their previous investments would not be threatened.[12] The commission concentrated upon 'narrowband' telecommunications. It decided (for the time being) against integrated broadband telecommunications networks and instead in favour of developing a number of different networks for the various kinds of telecommunications services.[13] This pragmatic decision was thoroughly consistent with the production plans of Siemens. Moreover, it did not collide with the interests of the federal states: crucial decisions determining the future course of broadcasting were not recommended. The decision about the future of broadcasting was already becoming lively at this time. However, growing conflict was absorbed by a compromise formula: the report recommended the establishment of pilot projects to test out the new modes of finance, organizational forms and content of mass communication.[14]

Social and political implications of the new technologies were ignored. The report confined itself to making observations and recommendations about technical possibilities and applications, without analysing more closely the possible social consequences. Instead, the criterion for the further development of policy became the so-called 'need' (*Bedarf*) – in the sense of 'economic demand'. In short, the criterion for the introduction of the new services was whether they could be turned to profitable account in the market.[15]

At the same time, the KtK report prepared the general public for the first time in a broad manner for the new media.[16] Despite all the cautious recommendations, it aided the political break-through of the new technologies. The unanimity of its conclusions suggested the existence of a consensus and thereby gave succour to the (problematic) idea of the neutrality of the technology itself. Only insiders recognized that this 'consensus' was bought at the expense of facing up to the politically controversial questions about both the social consequences and the impact on broadcasting of the new technologies. Furthermore, 'consensus' was pre-programmed by the very composition of the commission; technological optimists abounded among its entire membership. Since no conflicts had become visible, the impression was easily awakened that the political decisions now placed on the agenda could be safely left to the experts. Because of its studious avoidance of difficult social and political questions, the report did not stimulate a public debate of the pros and cons of the new technologies.

In the wake of the KtK report, political debate turned to the broadcasting question. The KtK suggested pilot projects to test different modes of organization and finance for cable networks. This recommendation meant that, in fact, for the first time in the history of the Federal Republic, private commercially financed broadcasters would be permitted. In this respect, though, the federal states remained responsible for decision making. The party political conflict over private broadcasting now broke out in the form of a confrontation over the pilot projects. It lasted well into the 1980s. Not until January 1984 did the first of the pilot projects finally open (Ludwigshafen).[17] The recommendation in favour of pilot projects was a skilful ploy on the part of the KtK. It smoothed away the political stigma with which until then the protagonists of private commercial broadcasting had had to reckon. Unanimously, an official commission had recommended experimentation with private commercial broadcasting.

However, since the decisions about implementation of the recommendations lay with the federal states, the commission did not directly carry the responsibility for the actual introduction of private broadcasting. In so far as there was any criticism of private broadcasting it had to be aimed at those (CDU/CSU-governed) federal states that wanted to introduce it. These federal states – Schleswig-Holstein, Lower Saxony, Rhineland-Palatinate, Baden-Württemberg and Bavaria – were quite prepared to withstand criticism. To this extent the KtK had given renewed stimulus to the debate over private broadcasting.[18] The discussion came to focus now upon questions about the multiplication of broadcasting channels, the access of the publishing houses (largely of the press) to the electronic media, the significance of commercial broadcasting for the 'diversity' of programmes, the effects of an increased consumption of television on children and family, and so on. Such questions are more amenable to political discussion than difficult questions about the structure of the network, digitization, the convergence of telecommunications and computing, etc. Discussion of these questions and the effects of modern telecommunications beyond the specific field of broadcasting was thus averted. The social and political consequences of private commercial broadcasting are (presumably) secondary concerns compared with those of an 'information revolution'.[19] Emphasis on these secondary concerns made it easier, however, for the Bundespost and for industry to make their policy decisions about the new information and communications technologies without having to put up with public controversy.

This 'depoliticization' of the introduction of the new technologies was again a – presumably 'unintentional' – outcome of the establishment of the KtK. In future, the Bundespost could begin to change its strategy for the development of its communications networks fundamentally. It was even able to depart from the recommendations of the KtK, without causing any great comment, at the end of the 1970s.[20] From now on, the Bundespost set itself the goal of the digitization of the telephone network and the development of an integrated services digital network (ISDN), although the latter was to be a narrowband national system accompanied by certain broadband experiments (called the BIGFON project). The transition to integrated networks and to fibre-optic cable systems has very considerable consequences for the kinds of service possible.[21] However, a public discussion about this transition and its consequences failed to materialize.

The transition to broadband communications: the EKM

Instead of a wide-ranging public debate a new commission was established in 1980: the Experts' Commission for New Media (*Experten-Kommission Neue Medien*, EKM) in Baden-Württemberg.[22] This commission contributed still further to the process of focusing attention on the expansion of the broadcasting system. At that time neither a commission of all the federal states nor a joint commission of federation and federal states was politically possible. Both media policy (*medienpolitisch*) controversies among the federal states and political disagreements between federation and the states were too great. In place of any such joint commission, the state of Baden-Württemberg now seized the initiative. Baden-Württemberg is the heartland of the West German electronics industry. This state saw the opportunity to improve its economic position still further by a rapid development of the new information and communications technologies. Once again, a 'pluralistically' composed commission was established. The large political parties and important associations were involved, but only in such a way that the protagonists of a speedy development of the new technologies clearly predominated. As regards the subject matter of the commission's work, the social and political affects of the new media could not be excluded from the agenda this time. However, it was predictable – in view of the interests of Baden-Württemberg, the intervening developments and the commission's composition – that a recommendation for embarking on the era of broadband communication was imminent. The commission occupied itself with the whole spectrum of new media but concentrated – like public debate at that time – on the broadcasting system. The report was presented in February 1981 and had been approved unanimously with several abstentions. However, this outcome did not indicate unanimity about matters of real substance. For one thing, in certain sections – such as those concerning organizational questions – alternative recommendations were merely juxtaposed, without any clear preference expressed. Moreover, in many places in the report it can be noticed that conflicts had not been explored, let alone resolved; rather they had been concealed behind vague and non-commital formulae and a host of contradictory statements.[23]

Of particular note in the report was analysis of the new media by social scientists and educational experts. Here moderately critical remarks were in evidence about the negative effects of the new media, and warnings were made about the effects of the introduction of private broadcasting, particularly cross-ownership of the press and broadcasting.[24] This section of the report was obviously set aside as an undisguised 'playground' for educationalists, social scientists, representatives of the churches and family associations, etc. It was only patchily followed up in the report's conclusion. Above all, the social scientists' work had very little effect on the final recommendations of the report. In the end, the commission advocated the introduction of broadband technology and private broadcasting, and the option of pilot projects was rejected. The state of Baden-Württemberg had to be allowed to launch the new media without having to go through the delays of a costly experiment.[25]

The government of Baden-Württemberg picked up on the recommendation to build an integrated broadband communications network. Conclusions were not drawn from the analyses of possible negative repercussions, nor were the commission's recommendations followed through into the details of policy. Baden-Württemberg decided in favour of the introduction of private broadcasting but without undue haste (the state media law only came into effect on 1 January 1986). Instead, the state pushed on with its planning for the introduction of other communications technologies, with the help of a further (not very influential) commission.[26]

The establishment of the EKM had diminished demands for other commissions that would cover the whole of the Federal Republic. The EKM's report was so designed that it could claim to have relevance and applicability way beyond the single state of Baden-Württemberg. With its moderately sceptical analyses of the effects of an expanded broadcasting system. It was even able to find acclaim among the opponents of private broadcasting. However, the protagonists of private broadcasting applauded the recommendations that had not been affected by such analyses.

Different political groups could identify with at least certain sections of the report. To this extent, it was well suited to become the basis of a public discussion, without further aggravating the controversies. The report reinforced the concentration of public debate upon broadcasting affairs. Since it had also addressed itself to the questions raised by other communications networks and services, however – though less thoroughly – it provided at the same time the basis for legitimation of the development of the new media beyond simply the narrow sphere of broadcasting.

Once again, the unanimity of the resolutions signalled the possibility of achieving a 'consensus' in questions about the new communications technologies; 'principled' opponents were clearly 'outsiders'. The measures that had already been taken by the Bundespost were evaluated for the most part positively, i.e. they were legitimized *ex post facto*. Fundamental alternatives were not elaborated. This final form of the report strengthened the impression that the development of the new technologies was a matter more of technological and economic determinism (*Sachzwänge*) than of political choice. In this way, the report was a further building block in the depoliticization of the issue of the introduction of the new information and communications technologies.

The inhibiting of overt political direction of the new technologies – the EK-IuK

With the KtK and the EKM reports the possibilities for consensus in communications policy were clearly exhausted. At the beginning of the 1980s many conflicts between the political parties were becoming sharper. The federal government under Chancellor Helmut Schmidt remained unsuccessful in combating the economic crisis, in particular unemployment. The conflicts within the governmental coalition (of SPD and FDP) were being fought out increasingly openly. The change of coalition partner by the FDP was fast approaching. At the same time, the public debate about growth, technology and ecology was intensifying. The polarization over the development of nuclear energy and over environmental protection, as well as the rise to political prominence of the 'Greens', was clear and demonstrable evidence of grass-roots dissension in the Federal Republic. This dissension made it more difficult, if not quite impossible, to achieve compromises on more specific questions. The force of these controversies spilled over into the debate about the new information and communications technologies. Evidence of a widespread fear of the possible development of a 'surveillance state' (*Überwachungsstaat*) could be seen particularly clearly in the mass movement against a national census. Its political momentum was only halted by the Federal Constitutional Court (Bundesverfassungsgericht), which in 1983 ruled the national census law to be unconstitutional.[27]

During such a difficult political period, the establishment of a further commission did not appear to be opportune. It carried the risk of aggravating conflicts and jeopardizing previous successes. Moreover, the conflict about media policy between the CDU/CSU and the SPD, as well as between the federal states and the federation, was being conducted more bitterly than ever. None the less, at this very moment the SPD parliamentary party in the Bundestag introduced the proposition to establish a parliamentary commission of inquiry (*Enquête-Kommission*).[28] The CDU/CSU, large sections of industry, most of the interest groups and associations, and above all every federal state were against the establishment of such a commission.[29] The federal states were jealous to protect their regulatory competence and thus apprehensive. The resistance of industry was based on the fear that a new commission would cause delays in the introduction and utilization of the new technologies. In fact, the SPD was staging a delaying action for reasons of media policy. The SPD did not want to promote private broadcasting, but sought to block it – hence the SPD's initiative to establish the commission. The CDU/CSU, however, soon warmed to the idea of a commission. The 'Union' parties saw in the recommendations of such a commission an opportunity to subject the SPD and the government to open public pressure about their media policy.[30] According to parliamentary rules, the CDU/CSU provided the commission's chairman.

The brief of the commission of inquiry was wide. It was to describe the problems of the new information and communications technologies from the point of view of law, particularly constitutional law, data protection and socio-political, economic, financial, technical and organizational questions, at both national and international level, and to elaborate recommendations for appropriate policy decisions.[31] The majority of appointees to the commission were parliamentarians; in addition, there were external (if also partisan) experts. The appointed membership was not limited to unconditional supporters of the new technologies. At the same time fundamentalist 'die-hard' opponents were absent. The introduction of the new information and communications technologies was considered by all members either as necessary or as unavoidable in practice on account of technological and economic developments.

Nevertheless, the membership of the commission was seriously divided on the question of whether the introduction of the new technologies should be accompanied by strict state regulations to prevent possible negative effects. The SPD and those scientific experts close to the SPD came out against 'non-regulation' and demanded legal measures designed to restrict any concentration of power, to provide data and consumer protection, to prevent 'de-skilling' at the work-place, etc.[32] The question of state intervention was fundamentally controversial. Unlike in the case of the KtK and the EKM this controversy could no longer be ignored, since either the new technologies had already been widely introduced or their introduction was imminent. If at all, state measures had to be taken immediately and without delay.

In addition, a second conflict was now superimposed in the form of a resumption of the media policy conflict about the broadcasting system. At the time of the establishment of the commission of inquiry, newly formulated ideas about the political influence of the media, especially broadcasting, had found a receptive audience among politicians.[33] Most notably Professor Elizabeth Noelle-Neumann projected the scientifically highly controversial theory of the 'spiral of silence'.[34] In the CDU/CSU the idea gained ground that the restructuring of the media landscape could be an important lever to electoral success, and that the development of broadband cable and satellite could provide an impetus for such a transformation of the structure of broadcasting, in particular by removing the monopoly of the public-service broadcasters. In contrast, the SPD adhered more or less solidly to the model of public-service 'integrational broadcasting' (*Integrationsrundfunk*). It was divided, however, in its evaluation of the inevitability or even desirability of a gradual 'opening-up' of the broadcasting system. The commission of inquiry's appointees were almost exclusively broadcasting specialists. Only a few had any expertise with regard to the whole range of information and communications technologies. Consequently, the conflict over broadcasting stood persistently in the foreground of discussion. Since the Bundestag has no regulatory competence in the field of broadcasting, however, the conflict had to be conducted in a different guise.[35] Protagonists of private broadcasting pleaded for the quick development of a broadband network using the readily available copper coaxial cable; by contrast, the SPD demanded that it should be constructed using only fibre-optic cable (which only later would be widely deployable).

The narrowing of conflict to the sphere of broadcasting was, at the same time, awkward for the SPD, as events were to reveal. In order to win time in the field of broadcasting policy, the SPD was pleading the case for an integrated services broadband communications network. This network was suited to facilitate a much faster introduction of the whole range of information and communications services. In this respect, however, the SPD had neither conducted a technology assessment programme nor worked out any precise ideas about the political formula for elaborating an appropriate legal, organizational and financial framework for such a development. The SPD had, so to speak, fallen into the political trap that had been lain in previous years when public debate had been limited to questions of broadcasting policy.

Nevertheless, political developments spared the SPD from becoming hopelessly ensnared. After the commission of inquiry had deliberated for a good year, the social–liberal coalition of SPD and FDP came at last to an end (in autumn 1982) and was replaced by a new coalition between the CDU/CSU and the FDP under Helmut Kohl. In the commission there followed a period of 'wait and see'. It culminated in a phase of open blockade by those members who were committed to the CDU/CSU. The reason was simple: the CDU/CSU had realized that from now on the SPD could use the commission for exactly the same purpose as previously they themselves had done – to make life difficult for the government. Until then, the CDU/CSU had been prepared to compromise on certain matters. Now, however, these compromises were felt to be restrictive – now that they themselves were in office in Bonn. For this reason the work of the commission of inquiry had to be terminated inconclusively. The SPD wanted to prevent this outcome. It wanted only to take the opportunity to steer public discussion towards the controversies about the new technologies – a discussion that the SPD had avoided as much as possible during the period when it had the responsibilities of governmental office.

A violent conflict followed within the commission of inquiry, less about substantive issues than about the question of how the commission's work should proceed. Eventually a difficult compromise was hatched: the section of the report that had been prepared so far was to be published in the form of a working document (called an 'interim report' or *Zwischenbericht*). At the same time, each side was also to be given the opportunity to express its dissent. As a result, findings that had already been formulated were now complemented by additional critical comments and objections. The whole affair was celebrated as a kind of ritual conflict for the benefit of the general public.

No longer were any policy recommendations decided. In this respect, the political victors of the confrontation were those political forces, i.e. the CDU/CSU and the communications industry, which desired, if possible, non-regulation or only very little regulation so that the new technologies might be left to the Bundespost and the market alone. The protagonists of non-regulation had succeeded in preventing the elaboration of alternatives. From now on, the Bundespost, together with industry, had a free hand to continue to introduce the new technologies.

The new centre-right government itself fell into the trap represented by the debate on broadcasting policy. The new Minister for Posts and Telecommunications Christian Schwarz-Schilling (CDU, formerly chairman of the parliamentary commission of inquiry) was first and foremost a media specialist and one of the strongest advocates of private broadcasting. In order to be able to introduce it as quickly as possible he pushed through the development of a copper coaxial cable network. In the process he encountered opposition from the electronics industry, which saw this as anachronistic and preferred fibre-optic cable. Since, in addition, the Bundespost proceeded to act in a very clumsy and unskilful manner, the progress of the cable programme was much slower in the following years than had been hoped. As a result, the breakthrough of private broadcasting was delayed – but so too was the speedy construction of a broadband network.

In none of the other commissions described in this chapter had there been such violent conflicts as in the parliamentary commission of inquiry, and in no other report were these conflicts documented so openly. At the same time, however, no other commission had had so little chance of producing effective recommendations. The change of government in 1982 had removed the latter opportunity. Moreover, during the period of the commission of inquiry, 1981–3, momentous and definitive decisions had in fact already been taken. Thus, on the very same day that the Bundestag had decided to establish the commission of inquiry the federal government had taken a far-reaching decision. This decision foresaw the expansion and digitization of the existing telecommunications network; it also foresaw the rapid construction of an integrated broadband fibre-optic communications network.[36] In the same political period, a decision was taken in favour of the federal-wide introduction of a new communications service – videotex (called *Bildschirmtext* in German).[37] Despite such decisions, however, the concrete shape of future developments still remained open in some important respects.

The scope of the parliamentary commission of inquiry for fundamentally determining the future course of policy and for making alternative recommendations was very narrow. All the parliamentary parties were united in the belief that the export dependence of the West German economy required that increased efforts be made in the area of technology policy (the 'Greens' entered the Bundestag in 1983). Industry demanded that the German domestic market should be considered as a demonstration market for its electronics products. Moreover, West German industry, in order to maintain its international competitiveness, had to face up to foreign competition. The West German market had therefore to be opened to Japanese, American and European products. The combination of the developments in technology, the internationalization of communications and the economic interest in larger markets set structural constraints on policy. If the information and communications technologies were to be exploited optimally for economic expansion in international markets and the modernization of the home economy, then the scope for political influence on the organization and management of the introduction of the new technologies was very slight. It has to be presumed that effective influence might only have been exerted as a result of consensus among all the powerful political forces, including the communications industry itself. Neither the CDU/CSU nor industry, however, had any interest in political intervention.

The violent conflict in the commission of inquiry symbolized the impossibility of organizing support for a political planning and management of developments in communications technologies. Moreover, by then it was probably already too late. The possibility had already been ruled out during the period of the KtK and the EKM. These commissions had agreed upon empty compromise formulae. Only after the most momentous and definitive policy decisions had already been taken did conflict break out openly within the parliamentary commission of inquiry. At the same time, however, it had primarily a ritual significance. From now on policies demonstrated on the public stage just how hard and uncompromising were the politicians' struggles over the issue – as were also their efforts to achieve consensus. On the other hand, the politicians were concerned to show that the demise of the commission of inquiry was not attributable to personal failings of its membership. Blame was laid at the door of the premature end of the legislative period – as a result of the collapse of the socio-liberal coalition – which resulted in much-increased pressure of business on the parliamentary timetable.[38]

Interim summary

As already mentioned at the start, the EK-IuK has had no visible consequences in the form of concrete political decisions. Occasionally the odd casual reference is made to its work in the course of scientific discourse or political discussions. In practice, however, political decisions have been taken without consideration of the commission's groundwork. The Bundespost has further developed its plans to extend its telecommunications services, including the digitalization of the telephone network, the transition from integrated digital network to ISDN and later the integration of the new cable broadcasting systems into the broadband network.[39] The Bundespost is currently working on the gradual realization of these plans.

Private commercial television is now allowed or at least tolerated in all of the *Länder*. The highest court in the land, namely the Federal Constitutional Court (Bundesverfassungsgericht), has accepted the constitutionality of the existence of a dual broadcasting system – the coexistence of a public-service broadcasting sector financed primarily by the licence fee and an advertising-based commercial broadcasting sector. The programmes of new private television and radio services can be received in all of the *Länder*. The future of the broadcasting system is no longer the object of any general public debate. It has become a matter of concern to small groups only. The construction of the copper coaxial cable system is proceeding apace,[40] if somewhat less rapidly than originally planned. The start of the first direct broadcasting satellite service has meanwhile been a disappointing technical failure; however, a new satellite is being prepared.

The further expansion of telecommunications as a technocratic and routine public policy problem: the Government Telecommunications Commission

As described above, important new directions have been taken and, quite clearly, the political way forward has been cleared for decisions about the expansion of telecommunications and broadcasting to be taken out of the realm of the public arena. For one important field of decision making, however, a further commission was established, to explore the question of the reorganization of the Bundespost and the liberalization of its services. More thematically, it was a matter of deciding about the whole structure of the telecommunications sector. This structure, in turn, shapes decisions about the fashioning of telecommunications networks and the services they carry and also the market for terminal equipment. Until now the Bundespost had enjoyed a predominant, largely monopolistic position in these fields. Without a doubt an important section of industry including the largest electronics concerns in the Federal Republic had profited from this situation. Now, however, the view was gaining ground that the Bundespost's monopoly and its bureaucratic rigidities were a significant hindrance to the further expansion of the market. Moreover, the West German telecommunications sector was almost bound to be influenced by the deregulatory policies being pursued at this time in many other industrial states.

The federal government therefore established the Government Telecommunications Commission (*Regierungskommission Fernmeldewesen*) (1985–8) with the task of analysing the relationship between private enterprise and the state-controlled Bundespost in the field of telecommunications. In particular, the commission's brief was to discover 'the best possible means of promoting technological innovation, the development and maintenance of international standards and the safeguarding of competition in the telecommunications market'.[41] Social policy aims, such as had still been a determining feature of the EK-IuK, no longer appeared on the agenda. The management of the future directions of telecommunications was reduced to the neutrally conceived goal of innovation, seen apparently as a purely pragmatic problem of standardization, and to the economic goal of safeguarding competition. In addition the commission was required to form the basis of a narrowly technocratic concept preconceived by the government to promote the development of information and communications technologies. The commission's membership was limited to leading politicians, from the spectrum of the established parties and not the Greens, and representatives of the concerned industries. In addition, there were three scientific experts whose close relations with industry and the economy were well known and who fundamentally agreed with the technocratic approach to the problem. The chairmanship of the commission was entrusted to one of the latter, Professor Witte, who had already chaired the KtK. Also with regard to the list of attached experts and organizations it was quite apparent that every effort had been made to exclude or marginalize any possible source of criticism. The commission's report was adopted by the great majority of its membership. However, it also contained special disclaimers of four members, for whom the foreseen liberalization did not go far enough, and from the representatives of the SPD and the German Postal Workers' Union who warned against individual aspects of the liberalization.

The recommendations of the commission were not radical. Instead they carried all the signs of a compromise, in the sense that competition was to be increased but at the same time the economic power and the politically leading role of the Bundespost was to be maintained as far as possible. According to the proposals of the commission the Bundespost should keep, albeit in loosened form, its network monopoly for the time being with the one reservation that it be subject to continuous assessment; in the event of the market not developing in a satisfactory manner, then the option was to be retained for abandoning the monopoly. In the field of telecommunications services, only the telephone monopoly should remain. Moreover, there should no longer be a monopoly of terminal equipment. The Bundespost should also undergo a fundamental organizational shake-up, in the course of which its commercial and administrative functions should be separated. In this way the commercial flexibility of the Bundespost should be increased but simultaneously the influence of the government on important questions of policy should be safeguarded. The commission's recommendations testified to an attempt at least partially to comply with the demands from the United States and the European Commission for a stronger liberalization of the West German telecommunications market.

On account of its specific brief and its delimited membership the commission was able to narrow its inquiry to an economic and technocratic perspective and largely to ignore the wider social significance of telecommunications. To this extent the same fundamental recipe for success was applied as had determined the KtK's activity. This held for the proposals to introduce changes – for instance in respect of the loosening of the Bundespost's network monopoly – only gradually. Also, by this strategy any potential for conflict was absorbed. The recommendations for a restructuring of the telecommunications market and a reorganization of the Bundespost were certainly highly political in nature; however, the cautious procedure and the exclusion of any explosive problematic dimensions insured against them fuelling any fundamental debate about the social uses and alternative structures of telecommunications. The development of telecommunications was reduced to a routine public policy problem, the processing of which was handled primarily from the perspective of increasing economic efficiency while at the same time respecting established structures.

The public had played little part in the commission's work. Moreover, the resultant governmental decisions to reorganize the Bundespost seemed only to be of particular interest to the experts and the consternation of the Postal Workers' Union. In due course, on 1 March 1988, the Bundespostminister published a draft Post Structure Law (*Poststrukturgesetz*) more or less exactly along the lines of the Commission's recommendations. In turn, on 11 May 1988, this draft was approved by the Cabinet and the Bill began its legislative passage through the Bundesrat and the Bundestag. Finally, on 20 April 1989 the Bill was voted into law by the Bundestag, still very much along the lines recommended by the commission, and it came into effect from 1 July 1989.

The implementation of the new technologies: legitimation by science and by law

The commissions described in this chapter had the task of preparing policy decisions. However, there was also potential for conflict at the level of the implementation of decisions. In this respect, too, special strategies for absorbing conflict and maximizing public acceptance were developed.

Legitimation by science: pilot projects

Typical of these strategies were the so-called pilot projects with their attached research studies. They served the purpose of easing the introduction of the new technologies and at the same time applying the legitimating artefact of scientific research to the problem.

Videotex

Chronologically, experiments were first conducted in connection with the introduction of videotex (*Bildschirmtext*). In 1980 two pilot projects were started, in Berlin and Düsseldorf. The Bundespost was experimenting with videotex, and both the Bundespost itself and the respective state governments concerned contracted out research to both commercial research institutes and universities.[42] The main purpose was to test the acceptance of videotex among private consumers and to examine its possible repercussions on other media. However, by mid-1981, long before the conclusion of this research, the Bundespost had already taken the decision to introduce videotex nation-wide from the middle of the following year.[43] The results of the research were not yet available; thus they were not the basis for policy.

In terms of substantive content and methodology the aims and tasks of the research and the pilot projects had not been drawn up in a way conducive to the thorough exploration of the social and political implications of videotex and its effects on other media. The investigations suffered from excessive pressures of time and from the requirement on the side of their client-contractors that they should continually receive detailed interim reports of progress. This requirement suggested clearly once again that the whole business was actually more a matter of proving that research activity was being conducted than of producing consequential research results. These structural conditions as well as the concrete agendas of the questions set for the research ensured that its purpose was cosmetic and purely affirmative. From an academic and scientific point of view this research was nevertheless fruitful. To some extent material was produced that could be used for later research, for example, for long-term investigation. Yet, future developments indicated that the 'wrong' question had been addressed. It soon became clear that *Bildschirmtext* had not been a success as a domestic appliance for the private household. Instead it had become an important means of communication in several spheres of social application, for instance in banking and insurance. However, these kinds of social application had not been the object of the research. For policy, the research was without consequence. None the less, the research projects represented to the general public the promise of careful inquiry. Who wants to fight against a scientifically conducted experiment? Public confidence in science was used in order to give the 'go-ahead' to videotex.

Private broadcasting

Videotex, however, had not troubled the public imagination very much. Such was not the case with private television, the introduction of which encountered considerable resistance. In this case, the KtK's recommendations to commence with pilot projects was really the ideal means of whittling down the opposition. The expansion of the broadcasting system requires a legal basis, according to West German constitutional principles. The standards that

West German constitutional law sets for broadcasting laws are high.[44] However, the legal constraints on 'experiments', designed to furnish the legislators with relevant experience and information upon which to base their decisions, are less strict.[45] Yet, once private television has been introduced – even if only on an experimental basis – it becomes politically difficult to do away with it later. The experiences of the pilot projects demonstrated that they were conceived by the federal states less as experiments than as means to achieve an easier introduction of private broadcasting. Correspondingly, the introduction of private broadcasting nation-wide was a preconceived decision; the policy-makers were not going to await the results of the experiments. It is evident from many different broadcasting systems in the world, that those broadcasters have the best chances of enduring success who are in at the beginning and who secure for themselves advantageous starting conditions in the competition that follows. Accordingly, the private broadcasters understood and made good use of the pilot projects as aids to their start-up operations.

The state laws establishing the pilot projects envisaged that the projects would be accompanied by academic and scientific investigations. The research, in other words, was given legally defined aims. Thus the effects on society and on the family, on existing broadcasting organizations and the press, on consumer behaviour, on costs and possible modes of finance, were all to be investigated. For the purpose of such research a special commission was established. Research contracts were awarded to commercial as well as university research institutes.[46]

The results of the research have remained without consequence. It is doubtful if the research was seriously conceived of as a means of providing a basis for policy making.[47] Four pilot projects, with a very limited number of participants, are presumably not well suited to the purpose of testing adequately broadcasting developments that are subject to the uncertain eddies of the economic market (and that require very large markets). Moreover, social effects and fundamental changes in the private sphere of the family or in the communications skills of the citizen do not lend themselves to examination in this manner. Further, questions of finance and organization can only be examined in a very limited manner indeed in such experiments, since permanent operations usually develop on a quite different scale from geographically and temporally limited tests. What is more, the research suffered because of a strong element of indirect and sometimes direct state influence exerted upon the entrusted institutions and personnel. Finally, preference was given to research methods that did not encourage assessment of complex relations and cross-effects. Clearly, the policy-makers did not bank on help from research in making their decisions; the direction of policy was clearly recognizable from the general introduction of private broadcasting before the completion of the experiments. The promise that policy would be informed by the research, however, impeded the mobilization of effective protest against the introduction of private broadcasting. It was then too late for protest.

The structural constraints and deterministic forces created by the condoning of pilot projects were so great that policy-makers were subsequently able to dispense with even the appearance of wanting to await research results. It is true that the research accompanied the pilot projects was carried through to its conclusion, although funds were diverted to this end from the licence fee revenues of the public-service broadcasters. However, further plans for research were buried. Above all, research with a wider ambit than the pilot projects was not undertaken. For this a new 'media commission of the states' (*Medienkommission der Länder*) had been established. Its work was prematurely terminated.[48]

The legitimating character of the research that was actually produced is clearly recognizable from the fact that it had been contracted predominantly to scientists, academics and research institutes that had a positive attitude towards the new technologies and/or towards their applications. Those with a critical attitude were simply overlooked. Moreover, the themes of the research were oriented towards 'affirmation'. A strategy that was already employed in the other commissions became quickly evident. Scientists and academics were considered desirable to the extent that they supported decisions already envisaged by the policy-makers; they were considered undesirable and were 'blacked' to the extent that they tended to formulate their own questions independently, to look for negative effects and to recommend alternative policy decisions.[49] Thus the criterion for the employment of science in policy making is the 'applicability' of the results for the legitimation of policy decisions which have themselves already been taken without the benefit of scientific expertise.[50]

Other research

Since the conclusion of the activity of the parliamentary commission of inquiry and the start of the pilot projects no further political requirement of special precautions for the absorption of resistance has been identified. In the meantime, even the SPD states have opened the way for private broadcasting. In this process of conversion, the decisive factor was not the conviction that commercialization would be without negative effects on the quality and diversity of programming. it was the insight that it was too late politically to offer an adequate defence against events. When the copper coaxial network is already partially constructed, the attempt to prevent the distribution of private programmes by this means gains the appearance of a form of censorship. When direct broadcasting by satellite comes, and if it is a success, there will be no effective means of obstructing the transmission of programmes. The activities of the European Commission – following the Green Paper on *Television Without Frontiers* of 1984 and finally resulting in the recent Council Directive of 1989 (see Chapter 5) – are contributing further to the opening up of broad-casting.[51] If SPD-governed states were to mount restrictions on private broadcasting, broadcasters would only site their operations in other states whilst their programmes would still be receivable everywhere. Instead, the SPD states have placed their hopes on giving preference to attracting broad-casters to locate their activities and thereby create employment opportunities and an indigenous communications industry. Economic policy calculations of advantage have therefore prevailed over broadcasting policy reservations.[52]

On the one hand, some of the new media laws of the states envisage conti-nued research.[53] On the other hand, there are no grounds for the assumption that such research might be any more consequential than previous research has been.

With the waning of the public discussion and the reduction of the problem-atic to technocratic and routine public policy questions the need for legitimating research fell away. Accordingly the later Government Telecom-munications Commission (*Regierungskommission Fernmeldewesen*) did not propose the establishment of any research projects. Even the suggested con-tinuous assessment of the network monopoly was unaccompanied by an pro-posal for scientific evaluation by experts. Moreover, during its period of deliberation the commission abstained from commissioning research, apart from submissions of a research institute of the Bundespost itself and two com-mercial research consultancy firms. No submissions or working papers from independent academic and scientific research organizations were requested.

The urgent social policy questions, however, were the object of research projects commissioned by the (SPD-ruled) state of North-Rhine Westphalia. This state has invested very considerable resources in technology assessment and with it engaged a notably large number of scientific and academic experts with critical viewpoints. Telecommunications is one of the areas studied. A comprehensive report has been produced which has formulated alternative proposals for the expansion of the telecommunications networks.[54] However, the work was commissioned so late that the report could only be presented after the conclusion of the work of the Government Telecommunications Commission. Thematically, it was much more broadly conceived than the pur-poses of the Government Telecommunications Commission. Its intention is to demonstrate the technology policy, economic, political, social and social psychological consequences of the policies currently being pursued to expand the telecommunications network and services. However, at present nothing indicates that the research report will measurably influence the political deci-sion-makers or stimulate the intended 'technology policy dialogue with the citizenry'.

Legitimation by law

In the process of changing the broadcasting system the states have had to pay particularly careful attention to the requirements of constitutional law. From a technical legal perspective, it was very difficult to introduce a form of private broadcasting that fulfilled the requirements of the Federal Constitutional Court. For instance, in the wake of the Federal Constitutional Court's ruling of November 1986, Lower Saxony had to revise its own legislation; in the same month the Bavarian Constitutional Court declared the Bavarian Media Experimentation and Development Law of 1984 unconstitutional. Legal regulations are also politically necessary with respect to public opinion. Commercial television had no tradition in the consciousness of the Germans. In order to heighten public acceptance, regulations recommended themselves that bore testimony to a state responsibility for the introduction of private broadcasting. In German political culture there exists a relatively high degree of trust in the regulatory power of the law. Therefore it would be correct to say that the conflict over the broadcasting system in the Federal Republic has also been a conflict over constitutional law. The courts have possibly had a greater significance for the development of the broadcasting systems than the parliaments (state and federal).[55]

Legitimation by law is therefore a further important concept. In this respect, however, the parliaments were at a loss about the type of regulation that, on the one hand, creates an opening of broadcasting to the economic market and, on the other hand, safeguards such goals as diversity, balance and freedom from manipulation.[56] The imagination of the legislators was limited. The German legislators have primarily taken on board the kind of regulations that have been developed abroad, especially in the United States by the Federal Communications Commission. In doing so, they have closed their eyes to the obvious failures of these regulations in the United States. In the latter, ineffectiveness, 'goal displacement', unwanted side-effects and many other shortcomings are more in evidence than positive achievements.[57] In the United States, deregulation is a reasonable conclusion to draw from the experience of failures of regulation in the field of commercial broadcasting. However, if the German parliaments were seeking to adopt this kind of regulatory policy, they were displaying a measure of helplessness. It is clear that regulations have been sought that do not hinder private broadcasting but that at the same time create the appearance of being able to prevent adverse developments. The American experience suggests that 'appearance' is all that will remain of such efforts. In this respect, the measures introduced in the Federal Republic can be counted as belonging to the category of the symbolic use of politics.[58] The regulations are a means of easing the transition to private broadcasting.

From all this, it might easily be concluded that the regulations can be weakened later – after the establishment of the new broadcasting order. Hints of this can already be detected. Thus, after long years of negotiation the Länder have agreed upon an inter-*Land* broadcasting treaty with a view to unifying the fragmented body of broadcasting law (according to which each *Land* has its individual regulatory framework). This was accompanied by a slackening of the regulations, for example in the field of advertising.

The dilution of further broadcasting regulations is probable. To this extent it must be assumed that the political responsibility of the democratically elected legislators will be considerably diminished. The European Commission's guidelines for broadcasting, adopted in the Council Directive of 1989 (see Chapter 5)[59] point in the direction of a reduction of broadcasting standards of regulation in Europe to a common denominator which lies considerably beneath the norms established by West German broadcasting law. If – as seems increasingly to be the case – broadcasting is considered to be an everyday economic product and broadcasting policy an element of economic policy making, then it seems reasonable to expect the reduction or removal of restrictions which disadvantage economically any given country's own domestic broadcasting industry. In a common European market it can be assumed that the West German broadcasting law makers will reorient themselves to the requirements operative in other countries. Since the political responsibility for this process of expedient accommodation to external factors will not reside at the national level (but at the European), it can be presumed that there will not be any widespread domestic protest. Under these circumstances, no further legitimation measures will be necessary. The transfer of the decision-making competence to Brussels thus signifies a political disburdening.[60] As the European Commission for its part is not dependent upon democratic legitimation in the same way as national governments are, the Europeanization of future developments will lead to a loss of legitimation requirements.

Similarly, for decisions relating to telecommunications more broadly than the single sphere of broadcasting national policy-makers have been disburdened of their responsibility as competences have shifted to the European Commission, which in its Green Paper concerning the development of a common market for telecommunications services and equipment[61] has presented far-reaching proposals for a strengthening of competition within a unified internal European market. Quite apart from this, in the Federal Republic decisions affecting the telecommunications infrastructure and its usages have traditionally been the preserve of parliamentary legislation to a very limited extent only. The Bundespost has long enjoyed general blanket authorizations allowing it to issue directives and orders in the form of so-called statutory decrees (*Rechtsverordnungen*) and administrative regulations (*Verwaltungsvorschriften*) without the participation of Parliament. Accordingly, the debate about the expansion of telecommunications services and the organizational reform of the Bundespost has been even further removed from the general political gaze than the dispute over the future of broadcasting.

Conclusion

Only the state media laws have aroused great public attention. However, under cover of the debates about these laws, and unnoticed, the definitive course was being set for the other applications of the new information and communications technologies. Media laws aside, the Bundespost, in its capacity as a state institution, has taken a number of technocratic decisions and established a number of administrative guidelines about the use of the new technologies. To this extent, the expansion of the communications network and the development of new communications services have not been left entirely to the economic market. After all, the Bundespost could hardly be expected to forfeit, of its own volition, the political and economic power that it had built up over decades. Moreover, this continuation of its regulatory power corresponded to the interests of an influential section of the electronics industry which sought economic benefits from collaboration with the Bundespost.

However, even here there has recently begun a drastic transformation. The Bundespost sees itself under industrial and international pressure to allow more competition within the field of telecommunications and to transform itself into a more commercial kind of organization which will have to assert itself in the marketplace. First steps towards organizational reform and the liberalization of the telecommunications market have been introduced.

The decisive factors in the policy of the Bundespost were calculations of business policy and also in part – such as in the area of broadcasting – the media policy preferences of the respective governing parties over the period under review. What received far too little consideration were social and political concerns about the consequences of the new media for the state, society and individual. The new media and the new telecommunications services have been introduced in the Federal Republic without any exploration of such questions within the framework of a technology assessment programme and without adequate public discussion about the desirability or acceptability of such developments. The official commissions and the associated research have served more to hinder than promote such a debate. Nevertheless – or even precisely for this reason – they have actually assisted the introduction of the new media in the Federal Republic.

Notes

This contribution was translated from the German original by Peter Humphreys.

1 *Verhandlungen des Deutschen Bundestags, 10, Wahlperiode* (Bonn: Bundestag-Drucksache, 1983), pp. 1140ff.
2 *Zwischenbericht der Enquête-Kommission 'Neue Informations- und Kommunikationstechniken'* (Bonn: Bundestag-Drucksache 9/2442, 28 March 1983).
3 Generally on this, see H. Paschen, K. Gresser and F. Conrad, *Technology Assessment*

– *Technologiefolgenabschätzung* (Frankfurt a.M.: Campus, 1978); C. Bohret and P. Franz, *Technologiefolgenbschätzung, Institutionelle und verfahrensmässige Lösungsansätze* (Frankfurt a.M.: Campus, 1982); and H. Hartwich, *Politik und Macht der Technik* (Opladen: Westdeutscher Verlag, 1986).

4 For an overview of the development, see H. Montag, *Privater oder öffentlich-rechtlicher Rundfunk* (Berlin: Spiess, 1978); and H. Bausch, *Rundfunkpolitik nach 1945* (München: Deutscher Taschenbuchverlag, 1980).

5 As examples of such arguments see K. Lenk, 'Informationstechnik als Machtverstärker', *Rundfunk und Fernsehen*, 32 (1984), pp. 330–40; P. Sonntag (ed.), *Die Zukunft der Informationsgesellschaft* (Frankfurt a.M.: Haag & Herchen, 1983); B. Mettler-Meibom, *Breitbandtechnologie* (Opladen: Westdeutscher Verlag, 1986).

6 V. Hauff and F.W. Scharpf, *Modernisierung der Volkswirtschaft, Technologiepolitik als Strukturpolitik* (Frankfurt a.M.: Europäische Verlagsanstalt, 1975); Bundes-ministerium für Forschung und Technologie (ed.), *Modernisierung der Volkswirtschaft in den achtziger Jahren, Ergebnisse eines Fachgesprächs im BMFT* (Düsseldorf/Wien: Econ, 1981); Bundesverband der Deutschen Industrie e.V., *Neue Informations- und Kommunikationstechniken und ihre gesamtgesellschaftlichen Auswirkungen* (Köln: Industrie-Förderung, 1982).

7 Mettler-Meibom, op. cit., p. 219.

8 On the various interests, see A. Zerdick, 'Oekonomische Interessen bei der Durchsetzung neuer Kommunikationstechniken', *Rundfunk und Fernsehen*, 30 (1982), pp. 478–90.

9 See, for example, R.S. Homet, Jr, *Politics, Cultures and Communication* (New York: Praeger, 1979), pp. 87ff.

10 Kommission für den Ausbau des Technischen Kommunikationssystems – KtK, *Telekommunikationsbericht mit 8 Anlagenbänden* (Bonn: Bundesministerium für das Post- und Fernmeldewesen, 1976).

11 Mettler-Meibom, op. cit., pp. 210f.

12 Ibid., pp. 218, 227.

13 Nevertheless, the development was to be kept open, see Empfehlung E 11, in KtK, op. cit., p. 122.

14 Empfehlungen E 9 and 12–15.

15 KtK, *Telekommunikationsbericht Anlageband 1, Bedürfnisse und Bedarfe für Telekommunikation.*

16 On the public reaction, see Bausch, op. cit., pp. 878ff.

17 On the background, see Bausch, op. cit., pp. 915ff.

18 On this debate, see Montag, op. cit.

19 See G. Friedrichs and A. Schaff (eds), *Auf Gedeih und Verderb, Mikro-Elektronik und Gesellschaft* (Wien: Europaverlag, 1982).

20 See Mettler-Meibom, op. cit., pp. 296ff.; Mettler-Meibom, 'Versuche zur Steurung des technischen Fortschritts', *Rundfunk und Fernsehen*, 31 (1983), pp. 24–40, especially 34ff.

21 See H. Kubicek and H. Rolf, *Mikropolis. Mit Computernetzen in die 'Informationsgesellschaft'* (Hamburg: VSA/VVA Grossohaus Wegner, 1985); Optek, P. Berger, H. Kubicek, M. Kühn, B. Mettler-Meibom and G. Voogd, *Optionen der Telekommunikation, Materialen für einen technologiepolitischen Bürgerdialog* (Düsseldorf: Ministerium für Arbeit, Gesundheit und Soziales des Landes Nordrhein-Westfalen/Programm Mensch und Technik, 1988), three volumes.

22 Expertenkommission Neue Medien – EKM – Baden-Württemberg, *Abschlussbericht*, 3 Bände (Stuttgart: Kohlhammer Verlag, 1981).

23 For a criticism, see W. Hoffmann-Riem, 'Ein Anlauf zu privatem Rundfunk, Analyse

der Vorschläge der baden-württembergischen "Expertenkommission Neue Medien"', *Zeitschrift für Rechtspolitik*, 14 (1981), pp. 177–85.

24 See EKM, op. cit., vol. 1, pp. 15ff., 105ff.

25 See Mettler-Meibom, op. cit., 1986, pp. 339ff.

26 See *Bericht der Expertengruppe 'Förderung Neuer Kommunikationstechniken (EKM)'* (Stuttgart: Kohlhammer Verlag, November, 1982).

27 Entscheidungen des Bundesverfassungsgerichts, vol. 65 (Tübingen: Möhr Verlag, 1984), pp. 1ff.

28 The motives lay less in the attempt to analyse the information and communications technologies more closely. Rather, the suggestion arose out of tactical considerations in order to ensure that the SPD might have the chairmanship in another commission of inquiry – into energy policy.

29 With regard to this and the following remarks, see especially Mettler-Meibom, op. cit., 1986, pp. 394ff.; W. Hoffmann-Riem, 'Schwierigkeiten interner Politikberatung', *Kritische Vierteljahresschrift für Gesetzgebung und Rechtswissenschaft*, 2 (1987), pp. 331–50; W. Hoffmann-Reim 'Schleichwege zur Nicht-Entscheidung. Fallanalyse zum Scheitern der Enquête-Kommission "Neue Informations- und Kommunikationstechniken"', *Politische Vierteljahresschrift*, 29 (1988), pp. 58–84; G. Vowe 'Interesse und Macht', *Zeitschrift für Parlamentsfragen* (1986), pp. 557, 564f.

30 Mettler-Meibom, op. cit., 1986, p. 399.

31 Printed in the *Zwischenbericht der Enquête-Kommission*, p. 2.

32 Concerning these problems see the publications quoted in note 5.

33 Hans-Seidel-Stiftung e.V., *Wahlkampf und Fernsehen* (München: Akademie für Politik und Zeitgeschehen der Hans-Seidel-Stiftung e.V., 1980); P. Radunski, *Wahlkämpfe, Moderne Wahlkampfführung als politische Kommunikation* (München/ Wien: Knoth, 1980).

34 E. Noelle-Neumann, *Die Schweigespirale, Oeffentliche Meinung – Unsere soziale Haut* (München: Piper, 1980). Professor Elizabeth Noelle-Neumann is Director of the Allensbach Institute für Demoskopie (the Allensbach Opinion-polling Institute). Since 1976 she had maintained that the SPD had retained power in national elections, against the CDU/CSU opposition, by virtue of the power of television. She was supported in this assertion by her colleague, Professor Hans Mathias Kepplinger of the University of Mainz, who conducted empirical studies to prove anti-CDU/CSU bias in television reporting. However, the claim was widely challenged by other social scientists in the Federal Republic. In order to give a theoretical basis to the alleged link between the (again alleged) partisan political preferences of television journalists and electoral behaviour in West Germany, she elaborated the theory of the 'Schweigespirale' (spiral of silence). According to this theory, there is a natural human behavioural propensity to want to conform to the majority opinion; those who are led to believe that they belong to the majority will express their opinions more boldly, while conversely those who are led to believe that their opinions are unpopular will usually be more reticent in expressing them. Correspondingly there arises a 'spiral process' whereby the presumed majority opinion strengthens in support during elections and the minority opinion weakens. A key part of this process is the signalling of alleged political preferences of the television journalists to the electorate. Her accusation is, effectively, that the definition of 'popular' opinion is manipulated by partisan television journalists.

35 *Entscheidungen des Bundesverfassungsgerichts* 12 (1962), pp. 224ff.

36 Decision of the federal government of 8 April, 1981, in *Zur Medienpolitik der Bundesregierung* (Bonn: Presse- und Informationsamt der Bundesregierung, 1981), pp. 63f.

37 See the synopsis of decisions of the cabinet sittings of 13 May and 24 June 1981 on the theme of media policy in the documents cited in note 36, pp. 8ff., 14.

38 *Zwischenbericht der Enquête-Kommission*, p. 3.
39 See Bundespost, *ISDN – Die Antwort der Deutschen Bundespost auf die Anforderungen der Telekommunikation von morgen* (Bonn: Bundespostminister für das Post- und Fernmeldewesen, 1984).
40 Data in Hans-Bredow-Institute (ed.), *Internationales Handbuch für Rundfunk und Fernsehen 1988/89* (Baden-Baden: Nomos Verlagsgesellschaft, 1988), p. A16.
41 *Bericht der Regierungskommission Fernmeldewesen, Neuordnung der Telekommunikation* (Heidelberg: R.v. Decker's Verlag, G. Schenck, 1987), p. 9.
42 See Wissentschaftlicher Beraterkreis, *Feldversuch Bildschirmtext* (Düsseldorf/Neuss), *Bildschirmtextbericht, Abschlussbericht* (Bochum). On the concept, see W.R. Langenbucher, H. Treinen and E.K. Scheuch, 'Zur wissenschaftlischen Begleitung des Bildschirmtextversuchs Düsseldorf/Neuss', *Rundfunk und Fernsehen*, 28 (1980), pp. 379–92, and the critical analyses of B. Mettler-Meibom, 'Kann Begleitforschung Technologien sozialverträglich machen? Das Beispiel Bildschirmtext', *Rundfunk und Fernsehen*, 33 (1985), pp. 5–20. For further comments see W. Degenhardt, *Akzeptanzforschung zu Bildschirmtext* (München: Verlag Reinhard Fischer, 1986).
43 Mettler-Meibom, op. cit., 1986, p. 14.
44 *Entscheidungen des Bundesverfassungsgerichts*, 57 (1982), pp. 295ff.
45 Ibid., p. 324.
46 An overview of the related research is given by U. Hasebrinck, 'Begleitforschung zu den Kabelpilotprojekten', in Hans-Bredow-Institut (ed.), *Internationales Handbuch für Rundfunk und Fernsehen 1988/89* (Baden-Baden: Nomos Verlagsgesellschaft, 1988), pp. B167–87.
47 See the critique by W. Hoffmann-Riem, 'Modellversuch als Scheintest. Zur geplanten Einführung der Kabelkommunikation in Ludwigshafen', *Zeitschrift für Rechtspolitik*, 13 (1980), pp. 31–8.
48 See B.P. Lange, 'Die Medienkommission der Bundesländer – Ein gescheitertes Unternehmen?', *Media Perspektiven* (1986), pp. 428ff.
49 See the case study by W. Hoffmann-Riem, 'Sachverstand: Verwendungsuntauglich? Eine Fallanalyse zur Politikberatung im Rahmen der Enquête-Kommission "Neue Informations- und Kommunikationstehniken"', in D. Grimm and W. Maihofer (eds), *Gesetzgebungstheorie und Rechtspolitik, Jahrbuch für Rechtssoziologie und Rechtstheorie*.
50 Generally, see U. Beck and C. Lau, 'Die Verwendungstauglichkeit "sozialwissenschaftlicher Theorien": Das Beispiel der Bildungs- und Arbeitmarktforschung', in U. Beck (ed.), *Soziologie und Praxis, Sonderband 1, Soziale Welt* (Göttingen, 1982), pp. 369ff.
51 European Commission, *Television Without Frontiers*, Green Paper on the establishment of the Common Market for broadcasting, especially by satellite and cable, COM (84)30 (Brussels: EC Commission, 1984); The Council of the European Communities, *Council Directive on the coordination of certain provisions laid down by law, regulation or administrative action in Member States concerning the pursuit of television broadcasting activities*, 5858/89 (Brussels: Council of the European Communities, 1989).
52 See W. Hoffmann-Riem, 'Internationale Medienmärkte – Nationale Rundfunkordnungen. Anmerkungen zu Entwicklungstendenzen im Medienbereich', *Rundfunk und Fernsehen*, 34 (1986), pp. 5–22, especially pp. 13f.
53 See, for example, R. Weiss and U. Hasebrinck, *Begleitforschung zur Medienentwicklung, Fragestellungen und Vorschläge für künftige Untersuchungen am Beispiel Hamburg* (Hamburg: Verlag Hans-Bredow-Institut, 1987).
54 Optek *et al.*, op. cit.; a short report is given by M. Mettler-Meibom, 'Postpolitik am Scheideweg?', *Media Perspektiven*, 7 (1988), pp. 409–20.
55 Note in particular *Entscheidungen des Bundesverfassungsgerichts*, vol. 12, pp. 205ff.,

vol. 31, pp. 314ff.; vol. 57, pp. 295ff.; vol 23, pp. 118ff.; vol. 24, pp. 297ff.; and vol. 39, pp. 159ff. (Berlin: Carl Heymanns, 1972); a short overview of the ruling is given in W. Hoffmann-Riem, 'Rundfunkverfassung als Richterrecht', in P. Glotz and R. Kopp (eds), *Das Ringen um den Medienstaatsvertrag der Länder* (Berlin: Volker Spiess Verlag, 1987), pp. 32–51.

56 A comparative survey of German broadcasting laws is given by R. Ricker, *Privat-Rundfunkgesetze im Bundesstaat* (München: C. Beck, 1985).

57 Overview in W. Hoffmann-Riem, 'Deregulierung als Konsequenz des Markt-rundfunks. Vergleichende Analyse der Rundfunksrechtsentwicklung in den USA', *Archiv des öffentlichen Rechts*, 110 (1985), pp. 528–76; D. le Duc, *Beyond Broad-casting Patterns in Policy and Law* (New York and London: Longman, 1986).

58 M. Edelmann, *The Symbolic Uses of Politics* (Urbana, IL: University of Illinois Press, 1964); on this also W. Hoffmann-Riem, 'Law, politics and the new media: trends in broadcasting regulation', *West European Politics*, 9 (1986), pp. 125–46.

59 See note 51.

60 This is not gainsaid by the fact that the *Länder* are protesting vigorously against the regulatory competence of the European Commission. To this extent, though, there is a determination to defend the fullest regulatory jurisdiction of the *Länder*.

61 COM (87) 290 Final (elsewhere printed as *Bundestagsdrucksache 11/930*).

Chapter nine

The political economy of telecommunications in France: a case study of 'telematics'

Peter Humphreys

This chapter focuses on the attempts by recent French governments to respond to a dramatic transformation of the telecommunications sector
brought about by a combination of technological, industrial and market
change. As a key to understanding developments in this field, the interventionist and mercantilist French state tradition is examined first. In particular,
the ongoing debate about the effectiveness of the characteristic *étatiste*
approach to industrial development is introduced. The question is raised
whether the prominent and mercantilist role of the French state can be maintained in the face of the recent pressures towards deregulation and state disen-
gagement. There follows an empirical overview of the respective roles of the
state and markets in French telecommunications policy over the last two
decades. Finally, the question of the efficacy of French telecommunication
policies is approached by means of a detailed case study of one very significant
grand project conducted by the state in the field of telecommunications, namely the 'telematics programme'.

Theoretical questions

The French state tradition

For years most academic observers have agreed with Shonfield that what distinguishes the political economy of France from that of most other advanced
industrial states is its 'strong state' tradition and its exceptional interventionist and *dirigiste* capacity.[1] Indeed, ever since the days of Colbert in the seven-
teenth century, the French state has periodically intervened very dramatically
in the economy in order to promote industrial development.[2] Moreover, the
French state has pursued a mercantilist political economy: in the words of
Zysman, the French state is 'accustomed to imposing its will on the market
place' and to pursuing political goals in industrial development 'to ensure that
French firms could defend the national position'.[3] At the core of this mercantilist tradition is a complex of entrenched, and typically 'French', attitudes to

the state: the state is held to be the 'primary unit of analysis' in international relations; the state is the expression of the national 'community', which can be traced back to Rousseau's ideas about 'general will' and 'social contract'; and the goals of state action are 'national power' (security) and 'external autonomy'.[4] The mercantilist political economy typically employs such instruments as controls on capital flows (e.g. through national ownership of banks and state-controlled credit), a high degree of state regulation of industrial activity, and the protection and promotion of 'strategic industries'. Indeed, throughout history the French state has encouraged economic nationalism, has resorted to protectionism and has been mainly concerned either with industrial catching up or more recently with achieving a position of industrial leadership. In recent times, technology has increasingly come to be seen as the key to the future success of French political economy.[5]

Ever since De Gaulle, a characteristic feature of the French approach to economic and technological modernization has been a commitment of the state to *grands projets* designed to re-equip the national industrial structure, to create new markets and to prime domestic industry for international competition. In the fields of defence, aerospace and energy very considerable success has manifestly resulted during the post-war period from highly voluntaristic 'Gaullist' programmes involving a massive mobilization of state resources. Typically the instruments of successful state action have been the provision of very generous subsidies to industry, an extremely nationalistic public procurement policy, and the promotion of industrial concentration, in particular the deliberate promotion of giant French 'national champions' which have typically been the beneficiaries of large public R&D funds and munificent public procurement contracts. Even the more 'liberal' economic programmes of French conservative governments have accepted the logic of the 'national champions' policy geared increasingly towards selected future-oriented and capital-intensive industries, such as telecommunications.

However, there has recently appeared in Britain another school of theories, that might be called 'revisionist', about the French state which argues that the French state has much less potential for autonomous and effective *dirigiste* action than is suggested by the conventional wisdom. Cerny has described this school's approach as that of the *état éclaté*.[6] Most notably, Hayward has fiercely disputed the implied claim of the *dirigiste* school that economic policy making is coherent, generally by directing attention to a significantly high degree of conflict within the state apparatus itself.[7] Similarly, the *état éclaté* theme has been adopted by Machin and Wright, who have also warned against ascribing too much autonomy and cohesiveness to the French state.[8]

A very interestingly allied perspective is offered by Rhodes who has applied the *état éclaté* approach to a broad-sweeping analysis of the modernization of French industry. In fact, Rhodes has taken the argument an interesting and important step further. Apart from pointing to the 'fragmentation' of the state, Rhodes has focused upon the increasing internationalization of production (and markets) which 'severely limit(s) the freedom for manoeuvre of national governments, rendering impotent or inappropriate traditional instruments of policy'. The latter point is, of course, particularly germane to the central theme of this volume. Moreover, following Cohen and Bauer, Rhodes has gone even further in challenging the received wisdom, by questioning the 'rational' policy-making role of the *grands corps*, the leading expert and managerial *cadres* at the heart of the French state. The conventional wisdom has been that these state officials, by their ability to move freely between the state administration, the financial sector, and the public and private sector firms, have supplied an important degree of coherence to state action which is strikingly absent in certain other systems (e.g. Britain). On the basis of his examination of the 'policy communities' and 'policy networks' across a number of sectors – including the field of information technology – Rhodes contests the notion of coherence and rationality within the French state. The state is not merely characterized by internal fragmentation, it is also composed of 'states within the state', whose lobbying power in pursuit of narrower organizational-political goals throws into question the whole notion of 'state autonomy' implicit in the arguments of the conventional school of thought.[9]

In the past, so Rhodes claims, the *grands corps* may indeed have been responsible for a certain degree of cohesive, rational and technocratic government, carrying important state *projets*, such as the nuclear energy programme or the high speed train (TGV) project, through to an enviable degree of success. However, it can also be argued that they have tended to become 'states within the state, . . . developing their own self-serving strategies and lobbying policy-makers for decisions in their favour'. Contrary to the claims of the *étatiste* myth, Rhodes claims, these technocratic experts are by no means always guided by the *interêt commun* nor are they always infallible in their judgements. In this respect, there is always a certain potential for non-rational decision making and conflicts with other legitimate interests.[10]

The state and the telecommunications markets

Another set of questions is raised by the current pattern of transformation of the telecommunications sector outlined in Chapter 1. In short, traditional interventionist instruments, such as have been typical of public policy in France, have come increasingly under question under the impact of fast-moving new developments in technologies and markets.

To recapitulate briefly the significant points: telecommunications networks are now at the heart of the computerization revolution; the rapid diffusion of computers has led to a 'convergence' of the data processing and communications sectors; in turn this has vastly expanded the scope of the telecommunications sector to include a proliferation of new transmission methods and services. The French have coined the term 'telematics' (*télématique*) to describe this convergence of advanced electronics, computing and telecommunications. As a result, a host of new information providers and users have combined to form a powerful lobby for sectoral deregulation of the monopolies of the traditional post and telecommunications operators (PTTs). Corporate business users have become more dependent than ever upon the supply of price-sensitive advanced telecommunications services. The new information providers and suppliers of value-added services, in particular, have mounted an increasingly effective challenge to the traditional monopoly of such services by the PPTs. The corporate sector, including powerful multinational companies, have lobbied more and more vocally for ways of reducing their costs and have called for a more cost-related structure of telecommunications tariffs and much greater freedom to connect new privately owned and operated value-added communications systems. By the same token, the PTTs have gained a poignant organizational-political motivation for seeking to secure their control, at least, of the supply and operation of the new value-added services.

However, the private commercial corporate actors are often highly mobile and have exerted their pressure by the unspoken threat to transfer their operations to less regulated and more commercial environments. At the same time, the technological convergence of computing and telecommunications has had the effect of opening up previously closely guarded telecommunications equipment markets to powerful new entrants from relatively unregulated sectors. In particular, the collapse of barriers between the telecommunications, office automation and data-processing sectors has enabled powerful computer and business automation firms like IBM to enter the field of telecommunications and transform the industry's culture and ecology. In fact, IBM has become a major player in the field of value-added services as well as equipment. IBM has been accustomed to a relative lack of regulation (in the field of computers) and has recently been exempted from regulation (by the US deregulation of telecommunications). Such firms are now formidable competitors for the traditional telecommunications operators.[11]

Moreover, the deregulation of telecommunications in the United States and Britain has set precedents for the departure from the traditional pattern of historically highly regulated, discrete national telecommunications industries, dominated by major public sector monopoly providers of the telephone network. The new 'model' being pursued in the United States and Britain aims to respond to the changing realities characterized by a proliferation of new telematic value-added services, new and highly diversified telecommunications markets, the breakdown of the 'natural monopoly' nature of telecommunications, new opportunities for more market-oriented and decentralized (firm-centred) technological innovation and, last but not least, the increasingly competitive and internationalized nature of telecommunications markets. More generally in Western Europe, reliance on comparatively small, fragmented and protected national public markets is increasingly widely being perceived as a significant handicap to growth, efficiency and competitiveness, as the general Europe-wide acceptance of the concepts behind, and increasingly also the practical implications of, the European Commission's efforts indicate (see Chapter 4). This new awareness is sharpened by the fact that European firms have begun to appear decidedly small in stature. Competition from giant US (and Japanese) producers, benefiting from a large domestic market and economies of scale, is growing fast.[12] In particular, the dismantling of the AT&T monopoly in the United States had a massive impact in Europe. As Tunstall and Palmer have put it, 'the divestiture [of AT&T] called into question the prevalent European concept of "natural monopoly", loosed AT&T into European markets, and enticed Europeans with an entry into the US market'.[13]

In the face of these dynamic changes, West European states have been faced by a difficult dilemma: should they open up national markets to competition, in order to reap in full the rewards of technological innovation, and give precedence thereby to the free development of the new value-added communications services in the cause of general economic competitiveness? This has been the course adopted by 'Reaganomics' and 'Thatcherism'. Alternatively, should they continue to give priority to supporting their national telecommunications manufacturing industries and protecting them from undue exposure to competition from more efficient overseas producers? State action to invest in ambitious programmes aimed at the domestic producers necessarily sits uneasily with the liberalization option. This dilemma has been succinctly summarized by a recent *Financial Times* article:

> Two camps appear to be emerging in the world of telecommunications ... defined along the dimension of liberalisation (the opening up of markets to competition). Wherever liberalisation has happened, it has acted as the cutting edge of the telecommunications revolution. Change has come fastest to the previously cosy and over-protected world of telecommunications in those areas where competition has been introduced. .... Yet liberalisation has also had its downside. Countries which are liberalising most quickly are also tending to lose market share in equipment supply by exposing their domestic companies to new competitors without compensatory opportunities overseas.[14]

Given their country's protectionist, mercantilist and *étatiste* traditions, and the post-war predominance of industrial modernization over the provision of services, French policy-makers have keenly felt the sharp edge of this dilemma. On the one hand, the mobility of capital in the context of the increasingly internationalized nature of the world economy has presented a new challenge to the statist approach typically favoured by the French. On the other hand, as seen, France in particular has always favoured policies to promote national industrial and technological 'independence' designed to avoid the risk of dependence on foreign supply and the attendant threat to national security.[15]

The purpose of the following empirical examination is twofold:

1 In the next section of this chapter we examine in overview the respective roles of the state and markets in French telecommunications policy as it has developed over the last decade and a half. In this respect, the main aim is to assess the pattern of change in the light of the debate about deregulation and the appropriate future role of the state in promoting adaptation to the imperatives of changes in technology and international markets. To what extent have traditional French mercantilism and *étatisme* given way to the 'global wave' of neo-liberalism?
2 In the final section of the chapter we examine an industrial case study, namely the telematics programme. Here the aim is to evaluate the efficacy of state intervention by means of *grands projets*. This should enable some conclusions to be drawn with respect to the debate between the 'conventional' admirers of the French 'policy style' and the 'revisionists' concerned to demythologize French *étatisme*.

French telecommunications policy in overview: from modernization of the telephone system to the telematic revolution

Telecommunications policy under Giscard d'Estaing

It is unquestionable that since the mid-1970s French policy-makers have become increasingly aware that telecommunications is a 'strategic' sector. Undoubtedly the most spectacular example of direct state action in the field of telecommunications policy has been that conducted by the governments serving under President Giscard d'Estaing (1974–81) to modernize and expand the notoriously backward French telephone system. During the period 1975–80, a massive state investment programme of FFr140 billion was carried out by the Direction Générale des Télécommunications (DGT), the branch of the state administration responsible for telecommunications. The main instruments used were direct subsidies and public procurement contracts, which went mainly to French telecommunications 'national champions' like Thomson and CIT-Alcatel, and also a massive R&D programme in the field of public switching, financed to the tune of 70 per cent by the DGT. This promethean research effort was largely conducted by the Centre National d'Etudes des Télécommunications (CNET, the DGT's research laboratory).

During the 1970s, the DGT began to install the world's first fully digital exchange, the E 10 system, developed by the CNET. Between 1970 and 1981 the French telephone system grew from a mere 4 million to no less than 17 million subscribers. By the late 1970s, the main beneficiary of this policy – CIT-Alcatel – had already gained a leading world position in digital switching for telephone networks. By a characteristic mobilization of state resources, it appeared that French industry, in this single field of information technology at least (the computer industry continued to be a disappointment), had successfully reconquered the domestic market.[16] Moreover, as a result of this programme of massive investment during the Giscard presidency, by 1989 France could boast of having the 'world's most highly digitized telephone network with 71 per cent of its intercity switching equipment now digital'.[17]

This successful programme appeared to prove the merits of the traditional state-led model of modernization. Significantly, it also did much to boost the prestige of the DGT and of the *Grands Corps des Ingénieurs des Télécommunications*. As a result, the latter was elevated from its traditional 'third-rank' status to rival that of the influential élite *Corps des Mines* and *Corps des Ponts et Chaussées*.[18] The DGT did indeed now begin to assume the attributes of a very powerful 'state within the state' (as the Rhodes thesis suggests). Towards the end of the Giscard d'Estaing presidency, the DGT and the telecommunications *Corps* began to assert themselves as a very powerful lobby *vis-à-vis* government. Notably, they feared that the imminent completion of this first *grand projet* in the field of telecommunications would remove the legitimation of the huge investment capacity that the DGT had meanwhile acquired. The search began in earnest, and government was effectively lobbied, for a follow-up *projet* that would ensure the status of the DGT and the *Corps* into the 1980s and 1990s. This 'administrative rationale' therefore helps to explain the origins of the next *grand projet* in the field of communications, namely the telematics programme (*Plan Télématique*), as is explained in the last section.

The telematics plan also emerged from another very important initiative taken during this early period: namely, the establishment of a government expert commission to examine the question of communications policy in the light of the rapid advances that were beginning to become very evident in the field of information and communications technologies. This commission produced in 1978 the influential Nora–Minc report which caused a nation-wide stir. On the one hand, the report's analysis and recommendations were much criticized for their technocratic approach and an alleged submission to technological determinism. On the other hand, the report had an unmistakable mercantilist message and, in this respect, played an important role in focusing attention on the strategic importance of the issues at stake: in particular the internationalization of communication; the power of the multinationals (especially IBM); and the importance of telematic telecommunications networks as the future nervous system of the advanced 'post-industrial' economy. The report emphatically characterized telecommunications as a 'strategic industry' and warned, in drastic terms, about the danger of loss of national sovereignty (mainly to IBM). It called for a comprehensive national strategy to meet the challenge of American domination in telematics.[19]

Telecommunications policy under the Socialists (1981–1986)

The statist approach

The French Socialists, coming to power in 1981, took the message of the Nora–Minc report to heart. One of the first acts of the Socialists was to establish the 'Farnous Commission' (La Mission Filière Electronique) to identify the specific needs of the electronics industry. In March 1982, this commission submitted a report to the Minister of Research and Industry in which it reiterated the importance of advanced electronics to the French economy. It recommended a 'redeployment of the electronics industry' so that the industry should play a central role in France's 'emergence' from the economic 'crisis' (la sortie de la crise). Like the earlier Nora–Minc report, the Farnous report too had a distinctly mercantilist and nationalistic emphasis, pointing to the need to reaffirm 'national independence', the need to create and secure employment in France and to prevent the loss of employment opportunities to foreign producers, and the need for a 'global strategy' for the recovery of the industry (redressement da la filière), which should aim to place French industry among the world leaders by the year 1990. As a result of this report, the telecommunications industry was now given a central role in a highly étatiste national plan for the filière électronique (PAFE), which according to President Mitterrand was designed to enable France to catch up with the United States and Japan. The PAFE, in the words of one expert, was 'perhaps the most important manifestation of the voluntaristic industrial ambitions expressed at the beginning of the Mitterrand presidency'.[20]

Accordingly, the Ministry for Research and Industry, then under the direction of the highly nationalistic Jean Pierre Chevènement, gave the PAFE a key place in the ninth Five-Year Plan (1984–8). The PAFE foresaw a total expenditure of FFr140 billion between 1982 and 1987, of which FFr60 billion was to come directly from the state.[21] Moreover, no less than 40 per cent of the total amount was to be devoted to developments in telecommunications. Significantly, defence and telecommunications were the only areas of French comparative advantage within the advanced electronics filière. Accordingly, the French Socialists aimed to make telecommunications the 'locomotive' of its programme for modernization both in the wider field of information technology (dominated by the Americans and the Japanese) and in the closely related field of audiovisual equipment (dominated by the Japanese). The DGT was therefore given the task of leading the whole electronics filière towards greater international competitiveness. In line with Socialist doctrine, the leading firms in the filière (notably Compagnie Générale d'Electricité (CGE), Thomson and Compagnie de Constructions Téléphoniques (CGCT)) were nationalized. The explicit mercantilist aim was to 'reconquer' domestic markets and to develop an 'economic strike force' in order to attack foreign markets. In order to prepare French domestic industry further for the task of attacking international markets, in 1983 the French Socialists merged the telecommunications operations of Thomson into CIT-Alcatel (the telecommunications subsidiary of CGE) in order to consolidate and rationalize national resources and to give France a major presence in the international markets.[22]

By means of nationalization and long-term industrial 'strategic' planning, the French Socialist government aimed to co-ordinate and promote rationalization and exploit 'synergies' between national producers in the information and communications technology sectors. In one very important respect, the distinctive *filière* strategy marked a significant break with the Giscardian approach to modernization. The latter too had hinged upon encouraging French 'national champions', but by encouraging them to concentrate on exploiting market niches (*créneaux*, such as digital telephonic switching technology, as described above). By contrast, the *filière* strategy was far more ambitious: it aimed at no less than the integration and promotion of a whole industrial sector. The Socialists held that the *créneaux* strategy had involved abandoning too much of the economy to rapid decline. The *filière* strategy, however, sought to advance on a very broad front, by exploiting synergies and aggressively promoting strategic 'poles' with 'upstream' and 'downstream' benefits. Moreover, the new strategy placed far greater emphasis on creating user demand for new information technology services.

Typically, these 'poles' took the form of ambitious 'technology push' programmes (*grands projets*), which might be seen as *micro-filières* themselves since they would have these all-important 'upstream' and 'downstream' effects. Characteristically, the Socialists had no qualms about mobilizing massive state resources to promote 'national champions' and to help them to establish a firm base for an 'assault' on international markets by supplying an internal market for these programmes. It was in this context, then, that the French Socialists adopted the telematics programme as a second generation initiative to modernize the French communications infrastructure (in fact, the first steps had already been started under the previous Giscardian governments – see p. 206). The telematics programme was an archetypal and important element of their wider strategy for the *filière électronique*.

Statism reassessed

However, the PAFE soon proved to be far too ambitious a venture, in common with many other areas of the early period of French Socialist policy making. The general disappointments of this period have been well documented elsewhere. To summarize briefly, in the absence of the expected upturn in the world economy, French 'go-it-alone' reflation soon resulted in rising inflation, balance of payments problems and runs on the franc. The French Socialist government struggled to salvage their programme by means of repeated devaluations of the currency, but by 1983 they had had to resort to deflation and 'austerity'. It was now recognized that their major spending programmes, both for social and industrial policies, had been far too ambitious and had now to be reined in. In this new climate, the DGT began to view its key role in the electronics *filière* as an embarrassment rather than an honour: indeed, it had become little more than the milch cow of the *filière électronique*. Worse still, the DGT's resources were now raided to help out the state budget, which had become overstretched by the Mauroy government's social programmes. The PAFE itself suffered from a chronic lack of coherence and co-ordination which again, like the Socialist project more generally, resulted from its over-ambitious breadth and scope. The symbolic grandeur of its vision proved to be an obstacle to its translation into practical policies. The DGT itself fell victim to the internal 'fragmentation' of the French state and was unable to supply a useful co-ordinating role in fields that exceeded its narrow range of competences. In practice, the PAFE fell victim to the internecine bickerings and crossed purposes of a whole range of public agencies and ministries.[23]

Moreover, the twin pressures of financial constraints and new industrial requirements led to some significant modifications in the direction of privatization and liberalization. During the period of the Fabius premiership (1983–6), there occurred a significant change of tack regarding the government's attitude towards the respective roles of the state and the market. After 1983, with the U-turn towards general budgetary *rigeur* ('austerity'), the Socialist government became much less enthusiastic about *étatisme* and voluntarist industrial policies. By the end of the Socialists' period in office, the important role of the 'market' was beginning to eclipse 'politics' in the language of government: for example, Prime Minister Laurent Fabius actually recommended a degree of denationalization while President Mitterrand himself summed up the new mood by announcing '*c'est l'enterprise qui crée la richesse*'.[24] In line with this general reassessment of economic policy, the Fabius government introduced a significant number of steps in the direction of increasing private enterprise in the telecommunications sector. A certain amount of competition was introduced by the DGT in the markets for terminals, headsets, and customer premises equipment. However, crucially, no action was taken to liberalize the telecommunications sector properly by opening up the increasingly important market for value-added services. As will be seen, the spearhead of French strategy for this particular field of enterprise was to remain, at least under the French Socialists, the state-led telematics programme.

The most significant change of tack under the Fabius government was the wider realization that French firms, whether national champions or not, were often unable to meet the requirements of the domestic market, in terms either of simple production capacities or of technological sophistication. The focus of the Socialists' technological modernization programme therefore progressively switched towards the promotion of international collaboration. The grand foreign economic policy aim of asserting 'independence' *vis-à-vis* the Americans and the Japanese could still be achieved by broadening French mercantilism to include a 'European' dimension, with France supplying leadership of course. Thus, the Fabius government took a lead role in calling for European collaboration in R&D. The French Socialist government of Laurent Fabius now gave enthusiastic support to the European Commission's RACE, BRITE, and Esprit programmes and played a major role in launching the wider European Eureka programme. The latter programme was presented, in symbolic terms at least, as a specific response to President Reagan's 'star wars' initiative. More prosaicly, Eureka provided an opportunity for Mitterrand and his Socialist government to maintain the credibility of their grand strategic goal of 'technological renaissance' by the simple expedient of spreading the costs among France's European partners. The fact that Eureka was not a European Community (EC) programme – indeed, the EC was highly unenthusiastic about the initiative – and that it had been launched by Mitterrand himself helped to maintain the image of French leadership. (Naturally, the latter was also a potent political message designed to bring domestic electoral rewards in the forthcoming legislative elections of 1986). Nevertheless, this 'Europeanization' of innovation policy marked a significant switch away from the earlier emphasis on an 'all-French' strategy by means of a traditional emphasis on nationalist *grands projets*. As one analyst has put it, 'by 1985, the French Socialist government appeared to acknowledge that the pursuit of national independence in innovation policy had become prohibitively expensive and competitively impractical for a country the size of France'.[25]

Telecommunications policy under the Chirac government (1986–1988)

Neo-liberal rhetoric

The trend towards a more market-oriented policy which had thus already become evident under the Fabius government appeared to be confirmed when, in March 1986, national legislative elections brought to power a conservative coalition government of Gaullists and Liberal Conservatives (RPR/UDF) under the premiership of Jacques Chirac. In the approach to these elections, the conservatives had presented the electorate with an uncharacteristically neo-liberal programme, which, as far as the Gaullists were concerned, promised to mark a considerable break with their *étatiste*-interventionist and mercantilist tradition. Moreover, both the PTT and the Industry Ministry, which was ultimately responsible for the PTT, now found themselves in the hands of prominent neo-liberal Liberal Conservatives, respectively Gérard Longuet and Alain Madelin, both members of the

Gaullists' main coalition partner, the independent Republican Party (PR). Accordingly, the DGT's key role under the Socialists in the promotion of industrial policy for the *filière électronique* seemed to be set to change dramatically.

The new government now embarked upon a general economic programme of privatization of nationalized industries, ending price and capital controls, easing foreign exchange restrictions and introducing financial and industrial deregulation. Equally, the Chirac government seemed to be determined to revolutionize the field of telecommunications. Apparently impressed by the telecommunications reforms that had meanwhile occurred in the United States, Britain and Japan, PTT Minister Longuet now indicated that the situation in France had to be adapted in tune with international developments. As one of his first acts, Longuet removed the competence which the Socialists had given to the DGT for directing industrial policy in the *filière électronique*. In line with the EC's concern to separate regulatory and industrial activities in the approach to the internal market of 1992, the new conservative government also now took steps to remove the DGT's regulatory competence and transfer it to an 'independent' new authority, symbolically entitled the National Commission for Communication and Liberty (CNCL). Moreover, very dramatic change was promised by the drafting of a deregulatory telecommunications law and the announcement that it would be enacted by the end of 1987. This law foresaw the transformation of the status of the DGT (from early 1988 onwards renamed France Telecom) from that of a powerful arm of the French administration into that of a private company, which, although still state controlled, would operate with a much greater degree of commercial autonomy rather like the French railway or electricity utilities.[26]

In practice, however, change proved to be gradual rather than dramatic. In particular, the French state continued to play an important, if moderated, role in guiding the direction of change. By the end of this rather short, as it turned out, period of conservative rule, very little real progress had been made towards telecommunications reform. In particular, the CNCL had proved itself to be a very weak instrument of regulation, its 'independence' from the state was highly questionable (indeed it became the object of a damaging scandal on this account) and the proposed deregulatory law appeared to be no nearer enactment than when the conservatives had come to power. In the latter connection, the government appeared to be most reluctant to antagonize powerful vested interests. The trade unions, and more significantly for the purposes of this chapter, the very powerful *Corps* of telecommunications engineers, had made their opposition to the government's more radical deregulatory plans very evident indeed. In addition, very clearly French political culture and the mercantilist national ideology had placed a major constraint upon the Chirac government's aim to depart from traditional nationalist and protectionist practice. Finally, the government's energies had meanwhile been diverted from regulatory reform by the need to handle some important developments in the international markets.

The privatization of Compagnie Générale d'Electricité and Compagnie de Constructions Téléphoniques

The new government's priorities to privatization and increased competition in French domestic markets was immediately put to a serious test by pressures of 'internationalization' which involved the government in making major strategic decisions about the future of individual French telecommunications companies. As seen, the French Socialists had aimed to strengthen France's competitive position in international markets by a policy of building up national champions even (indeed deliberately) at the cost of pluralism in French markets. However, as suggested, it had quickly become doubtful whether French firms, even if their telecommunications operations were rationalized and merged into giant concerns like CGE–Alcatel–Thomson, would be able to provide a strong enough base for an effective assault on world markets. As seen, by the time that the Chirac government came to power there seemed to be an overwhelming rationale for a move from 'Francization' towards 'internationalization': in other words, towards making further alliances, either within the Continent or in North America (or Japan), in order to spread development costs and gain new market opportunities.

In July 1986, CGE announced that it intended to acquire the telecommunications activities of the American multinational ITT. Significantly, the latter had a large number of operations across Europe, including in West Germany where its subsidiary SEL was the Bundespost's second largest supplier after Siemens. This deal had clearly mercantilistic attractions: it would make CGE, at a stroke, the dominant telecommunications manufacturer within Europe and the second largest in the world, clearly capable of challenging AT&T (United States) and NEC (Japan) in world markets. However, rather than promoting competition, it would consolidate the 'quasi-monopolistic' position of CGE (CIT-Alcatel) within the French domestic market. Moreover, it would seriously stretch CGE's financial resources and weaken its balance sheet at a highly critical time when the company was approaching privatization under the Chirac government's programme. Significantly, despite the free-market rhetoric of the new conservative government, the ultimate decision did not rest with CGE's president Georges Pebereau nor with the company's shareholders (following privatization): it still required formal government approval. In the outcome 'politics' (mercantilism) clearly prevailed over 'markets' (the best conditions for privatization; domestic competition policy). With very little hesitation, the Industry Minister Alain Madelin gave his government's approval for the deal on wider industrial policy grounds – 'the pursuit of political goals in industrial development' – namely the strategic aim of promoting French manufacturing prowess in world markets.

That the French state would continue to intervene in markets whenever strategic considerations dictated was soon confirmed by the 'Byzantine politicking' that surrounded the privatization and sell-off of another French company, the ailing state telecommunications company CGCT. In fact, the latter question quickly became a hugely symbolic issue of national importance which went right to the core of the conservative government's 'neo-liberal' strategy. Ironically, the issue had arisen, in large part, as a legacy of the previous Socialist government's *étatiste* strategy to reorganize the *filière électronique*. The Socialists had hoped that their nationalizations and other interventionist measures to reorganize the French telecommunications sector would increase indigenous output enough to cover, more or less, the increased domestic demand. However, even in the area of telephonic switching equipment, a field in which France had quite evidently already gained comparative advantage (thanks to the earlier Giscardian government's policies), French industrial capacity had shown itself not to be strong enough to support an entirely nationalistic industrial strategy such as the Socialists had hoped to pursue. The giant telecommunications conglomerate which the Socialists had formed, namely CIT-Alcatel, had soon proved itself to be incapable alone of meeting the increased demand for new switching equipment. For its part, the DGT had always been bitterly opposed to becoming reliant upon a single supplier. Moreover, as suggested, the strengthening of CIT-Alcatel's stranglehold in the French domestic market for switching equipment as a result of the CGE takeover of ITT seemed to contradict the new Chirac government's concern to introduce more (not less) competition into French markets. There was a problem for the new government, however, in seeking to ameliorate this state of affairs. France's only remaining indigenous supplier of digital exchanges, the state-owned CGCT, which had access to a very modest 16 per cent of the French public switching market, was by now in serious financial trouble and patently failed to present a realistic 'national' solution to the problem. Consequently, the Chirac government decided that a suitable foreign firm had to be chosen to provide the DGT with a second source.

The Chirac government itself was any way committed to privatizing CGCT as part of its wider neo-liberal programme. Now the main issue became which of four powerful foreign bidders – AT&T/Philips (United States/Netherlands), Siemens (West Germany), Northern Telecom (Canada) and Ericsson with Matra, Bouygues and Banque Indosuez (Sweden/France) – should the French state allow to buy the firm. There is irony in the latter point: for indeed it was the French state, and not the free market, which, despite the conservative government's neo-liberal rhetoric, played the key role in settling the affair. Moreover, the issue quickly assumed a 'high political' character, reflecting the politicization of international telecommunications markets generally. In this respect, it appeared that the French were by no means alone in adopting an essentially mercantilist stance to markets.

The US government exerted very considerable diplomatic pressure in favour of AT&T's bid. Indeed, the US authorities even threatened to block the access of Siemens to the US market if the latter were to gain control of CGCT. Nor were the French spared similar threats. American distrust of the French was already considerable in view of the leading role of the French government in promoting a European alternative to 'star wars', namely the Eureka initiative. Moreover, they had become very suspicious of French efforts to steer the EC towards a (neo-mercantilist) 'fortress Europe' strategy for 1992. Accordingly, they let it be known that they would have little difficulty in justifying trade reprisals against French companies. For its part, the West German government insisted that Siemens should obtain CGCT as a *quid pro quo* for the major access to the West German market acquired by CIT-Alcatel by dint of Alcatel's (CGE) take-over of ITT. The French were made aware that an adverse decision would compromise Alcatel's new interests in West Germany. However, in the face of these diplomatic pressures, the French government turned down the bids from AT&T and Siemens (and Northern Telecom) in favour of a 'Swedish solution'.

This decision clearly reflected the French state's strategic (mercantilist) evaluation of the negative consequences of allowing a major industrial rival (i.e. either the United States or West Germany) to gain important access to the French market. In particular, the French were very sensitive to the 'threat' posed by AT&T, which was clearly poised to sweep the liberalized post-1992 European market, a fact which made the American bid a very real potential obstacle to the French state's own manifest ambitions for its national telecommunications industry. AT&T had already gained a very considerable presence in Europe by virtue of its unequal collaboration with Philips. If allowed further penetration into Europe, AT&T would be in a uniquely advantageous position, as an international carrier, to exploit exciting new markets for services as well as equipment by dint of being able to benefit from compatibility of equipment supply. Moreover, a number of studies had indicated that AT&T was unrivalled in its technical, managerial and financial expertise.[27]

If the latter point meant that the AT&T bid was the obvious choice of the 'market', then the former points evoked the logic of 'politics'. In ruling against the AT&T bid, the French state simply deemed it to be 'politically impossible'.[28] By choosing Ericsson and Matra, supported by Bouygues and Banque Indosuez, the French state backed what was at least partially a 'national' solution, at the same time underpinning the future of another strategic French company – Matra was a French national champion with an important stake in the arms industry. Moreover, Ericsson was the second largest supplier of telephonic switching equipment in Europe after Alcatel. As a result of this choice, the French state therefore consolidated the French domination of this particular market in Europe. The deal also gave the French access to a technology in which they were highly interested but in a lamentably weak position, namely radiotelephony.[29] At the same time as fulfilling the mercantilist objectives of French state policy, the deal could be presented as a quintessentially 'diplomatic' solution which should mitigate the problem of 'jilted suitors' and diminish the risk of trade reprisals from either the Americans or the West Germans. The Swedish solution allowed the French to appear to be acting out of a concern to be even-handed in its industrial dealings with its two most important political partners. Thus, the French might posture as the 'virtuous' party while at the same time indulging in an act of 'high political' brilliance designed to leave them the undisputed winner from the affair!

Thus, in late 1987, the government sold CGCT for FFr500 million to a consortium composed of the French national champion Matra and Ericsson. Very interestingly, Ericsson was allowed to gain management control but the neo-liberal conservative government's privatization laws still only granted the foreign firm a maximum stake of 20 per cent. Matra took 49.9 per cent with the rest taken by a joint holding company of the other French financial interests involved. The latter 'non-market' measure made even more transparently evident that the conservative government's resolve to play a less interventionist role had failed the test of practice in a very important area of telecommunications policy, namely the question of industrial take-overs. The government's choice had been very clearly directed by the same strategic role of the state as the Socialists before them. Only the state, not the market, could be trusted to act so as to safeguard and strengthen French markets.

However, as Tunstall and Palmer have pointed out:

> one trade and political cloud darkened [the] European horizon . . . : the European Economic Community Commission, battling to control Community-wide mergers, was hostile towards anticompetitive acquisitions.[30]

Yet even here, the French could legitimately claim that both these almost Machiavellian moves exceeded the bounds of the Commission's jurisdiction: after all, ITT was an American company and Ericsson was Swedish. Moreover, the French could argue that the CGCT sell-off, to a very powerful European (if not 'Community') telecommunications firm, marked a very considerable *de facto* step towards the liberalization and internationalization of the French telecommunications industry and markets desired by the Commission.[31] However, the French state had confirmed the worst suspicions of the Americans about French, and indeed European, duplicity and neo-mercantilism. The affair was guaranteed to accelerate the American state's own designs to counter the Europeans by pushing for an 'international model' for telecommunications standards and procurement within the auspices of the GATT (see Chapter 1).

The liberalization of the market for value-added networks

As suggested, by the end of their period of incumbency, even the French Socialists had been compelled to face up to the reality that mercantilist and nationalistic policies would have to be adapted, at least, to the exigencies of
France's 'medium-sized' status in the global political economy – hence the
shift from 'Francization' to 'Europeanization', a policy goal manifestly shared
by the conservative coalition in its choice in favour of Ericsson in the CGCT
affair. By now, French policy-makers were becoming increasingly aware that
the neo-liberal tide of international telecommunications developments was
being propelled, to an important extent, by the demands of international markets beyond their direct control. To maintain a narrow focus on domestic markets, even as a springboard for a later 'attack' on foreign markets, was like
'putting the chicken before the egg'. In particular, very powerful international
business interests were now demanding access for price-competitive, innovative and 'customized' value-added services. Such services, it was beginning to
become apparent, were more likely to thrive in liberalized regulatory environments than in PTT-dominated markets.

Very significantly, in France, in direct contrast with the United States and
Britain, the field of value-added services had remained the preserve of the all-
powerful DGT. More specifically, this field of activity had been developed in
the embrace of the DGT's telematics plan. As suggested, this plan had been
developed in the first place as part of the Socialist government's industrial
strategy for the filière électronique. Moreover, as will be seen later, the DGT
had thereby been able to control the development of this highly promising
field of communications services (this, in turn, was a very significant factor for
the domestic 'success' of the telematics plan). On the one hand, the latter had
fulfilled one of the main aims of the Nora–Minc report in that it had
prevented the French market for both equipment and services becoming
dominated by foreign firms. On the other hand, however, it had also by now
become clear that overreliance on this state-led industrial policy programme
had incurred significant costs. Quite apart from the huge financial outlays, it
was becoming apparent that, despite her comparatively early recognition of
the strategic importance of telematics, France was now in danger of becoming
isolated in respect of international flows of information. In addition, France
was in danger of falling behind in the race to attract international investors in
new communications services. In other words, the old French priority to
manufacturing industry had indeed had a negative impact on French competitiveness in services.

Therefore the conservative government was now forced to introduce one
very important measure of liberalization. Before the electoral defeat of 1986,
Longuet finally took the step of opening up the DGT's coveted markets for
value-added services to private sector competition. Despite the failure to
enact the wide-sweeping deregulation promised by their neo-liberal rhetoric,

this single important act of liberalization by the conservative coalition could be seen as a highly significant admission of the inadequacy of the traditional mercantilist industrial strategy for telecommunications. As will now be seen, it testified to the distinct limitations of the 'jewel in the crown' of the statist approach to telecommunications modernization, namely the DGT's *grand projet* for telematics, which will now be examined in more detail.

A case-study of an industrial *grand projet*: the telematics programme

The following *grand projet*, conducted in the field of telecommunications in the decade from the late 1970s to the late 1980s, can be seen as part of the established tradition of state industrial intervention in France. Diana Green has eloquently summarized the relevant instruments of this approach, of which the telematics programme is a classic example:

> French governments have traditionally adopted a non-market approach to technological development, with emphasis on supply: the state determines the technology, selects or creates the firm(s) suited to its development, creates guaranteed demand for the product and/or assumes a significant share of the financial burden of development in an initially protected market . . . [32]

To rehearse the general context, the telematics programme formed part of the mercantilist efforts by the French state, in particular the DGT, during the period of incumbency of the Socialists, to modernize the French communications sector. Its purpose was in large part to provide indigenous French industry with captive markets, in order to protect and strengthen the domestic economy, and also to furnish the country with a powerful base for an assault on foreign markets. As Mayntz and Schneider have put it:

> The French videotex introduction strategy resembled very much the traditional French mercantilist orientation where the control of industry is used for the achievement of political goals. In fact, within the tradition of the French *grands projets* the *annuaire électronique* [electronic telephone directory] was used as an instrument of a general industrial policy, which was geared to challenge the American hegemony in the field of information technology.[33]

However, in line with the argument presented by Rhodes, this *grand projet* might also be seen as a novel attempt by the DGT, a sectional interest within the French state, to 'control' technological and market developments for its own organizational-political advantage. Beyond giving a straightforward account of this *grand projet*, the aim of this section is to judge the underlying motives, the 'rationality' and the efficacy of such an ambitious state-led programme.

The evolution of the telematics programme

The French telematics programme was actually officially introduced by an interministerial committee of the Raymond Barre government under President Giscard d'Estaing on 22 November 1978, when the committee decided to establish a videotex pilot-project at Vélizy near Paris. Since the early 1970s the CNET had been working towards creating an advanced data transmission system marrying the telephone system with personal computers, in an attempt to emulate British Telecom's revolutionary Prestel system. At that time, Prestel had appeared to be a highly promising technological break-through and the French were both alarmed and impressed by Britain's early lead in the field.[34] During the 1970s the DGT came to view the promotion of videotex – as the technology was generically known – as a highly promising industrial *grand projet*, which would provide the first stage in developing a future 'common carrier' network for the new value-added services that were at the heart of the telematic revolution. In the teeth of the international wave of deregulation and liberalization, which seemed everywhere to be challenging the traditional PTT monopolies, the DGT was concerned both to safeguard its 'common carrier' monopoly status and, even more ambitiously, to ensure thereby its future control of the promising new value-added services as well. The development, by the DGT, of a *grand projet* for telematics, along the lines of videotex, seemed to promise a neat solution to this problem. Moreover, the DGT and the *Corps des Ingénieurs des Télécommunications* had additional, more immediate and compelling motivations.

As already suggested, as the completion of the *grand projet* to modernize the telephone system had approached during the end of the Giscard presidency, the DGT had become increasingly preoccupied with the search for new markets for the telecommunications industry in order to legitimize its huge acquired investment capacity and to safeguard jobs.[35] In fact, the moment had been highly propitious for the DGT and its engineers. Because of its successful modernization of the telephone system during this early period of the telecommunications revolution the DGT had assumed a wholly new image. It was now widely hailed as an efficient and modern part of the state administration. At the same time, the Nora–Minc commission had just been established to enquire into the future development of the communications system and the *Corps des Ingénieurs des Télécommunications* was very well represented among its members. As a result, the DGT had been able to influence the commission's outcome substantially: the Nora–Minc report. It was therefore hardly surprising that this report argued forcefully that, as a matter of the greatest urgency, the public authorities should take a new interest in the national telecommunications sector, as the only means to control the computerization of France in the face of the international power of IBM.

As a result of its new-found authority and influence, the DGT was very easily able to win the support of the Industry and PTT Ministries. Moreover, as a result of its highly profitable telephone service, the DGT now commanded massive resources of its own, having a *budget annexe* (an independent budget), a massive annual turnover (of FFr96 American billion in 1985) and a huge investment capacity (of FFr31 American billion in 1985). The all-powerful Finance Ministry was therefore all the more favourably disposed to accept the DGT's plans. Finally, both Simon Nora and Alain Minc, the authors of the famous report, were very influential in the latter Ministry, being members of the prestigious *Corps des Inspecteurs des Finances*, and at the same time had patently 'networked' with the representatives of the DGT on the commission.

However, very quickly it also became important to legitimize the telematics programme – called Télétel – *vis-à-vis* other social actors. During 1979–80 the DGT's technical experiments in Brittany and the suburbs of Paris caused a significant degree of controversy and opposition, mainly from the press. The press had been quick to see the potential impact of the 'new media' (and videotex was seen as a potential mass medium) on its own advertising revenues.[36] The press amounted to a powerful lobby, particularly *vis-à-vis* the conservative parliamentary majority of the period. Moreover, there was also a certain amount of social opposition to the new medium, largely from the civil liberties lobby which saw it as a potential threat to privacy. The economic logic was also questioned on the grounds of cost: a prominent professor of computer studies attacked the DGT's plans for being both too 'centralist' and too expensive. Greatly to the chagrin of the DGT, Professor Bruno Lussato published a best-seller which argued forcefully for a private and decentralized development of the new telematic services (such as was to occur spectacularly in the United Kingdom following liberalization).[37]

The fact that the problem of very considerable political opposition was, in the event, quickly solved in the DGT's favour against these other legitimate concerns can indeed be explained, at least partly, in terms of Rhodes's thesis: the special advantages which the *grands corps* are able to mobilize as a powerful and privileged lobby 'within the French state' and, in particular, their monopoly of expertise'. As soon as the French Socialists came to power with an ambitious and highly nationalist and mercantilist programme for French economic renewal, the DGT capitalized on this interventionist industrial policy orientation of the new government. To be more precise, the DGT presented the telematic programme to the new Socialist PTT Minister, Louis Mexandeau, as a highly promising instrument for opening up new markets for the domestic French telecommunications industry. The DGT presented the telematics programme as a key *filière* (or 'micro-*filière*) itself, with 'upstream' and 'downstream' benefits within the larger electronics *filière* in which it had, as seen, assumed a leading role. Hardly surprisingly, Socialist policy-makers, themselves largely devoid of technical expertise, proved to be most receptive to the DGT's technocratic message that telematics presented an important opportunity to reconquer key areas of the *filière électronique*, most notably on the hardware equipment side.

In the second place, the DGT was itself able, by dint of its huge resources and relative autonomy of action within the French state, to skilfully adopt some key measures of its own to deflate and incorporate the opposition and legitimate the technology in the eyes of the general public. First of all, the DGT now deployed its massive financial resources to give special financial inducements to the press companies in order to help them develop their telematic services.[38] More importantly still, the DGT also developed a highly sophisticated marketing approach to win over the general public. In the latter connection, the DGT hit upon an ingenious method of fulfilling two aims: first, winning over the mass public, and second, creating a mass market for the new components and services. Quite simply, the DGT ensured the future domestic success of the telematics plan by deciding to supply the terminal – called Minitel – free to the general public. Moreover, it was in the unique position of being able to legitimize the huge cost of such a 'non-market' strategy. The new telematic terminal was introduced as the means to provide an 'electronic telephone directory' (*annuaire électronique*), which, in turn, was presented as both an exercise in rationalization of costs and a means to increase the range of services offered by the DGT.[39] The 'electronic directory' would allow the user to consult the Minitel terminal, linked to the telephone network, to obtain the information that had until then been provided by the normal printed telephone book. Accordingly, the DGT announced that it planned to distribute around 30 million free Minitel terminals over a 15-year period. By its largesse – giving the terminals away *en masse* – the DGT was engaging in a dual exercise of 'technology push' and policy 'legitimation'. Because the DGT could literally afford to wait for a long period before the new network became profitable. It was additionally in a unique position to create a new market.

However, another important feature of the *Télétel* programme was that, unlike foreign videotex systems, it was deliberately an 'open' system: in other words, the DGT now allowed service providers freely to connect the host computers of their choice, ranging from PCs to mainframes.[40] In this respect at least, it did mark a significant departure from the traditional PTT-centred model of service provision. However, this too had advantages for the DGT, which was thereby spared the costs of running its own data banks and information retrieval systems; this option also pre-empted any domestic pressures to challenge its network monopoly. Moreover, the DGT could still exert an important degree of indirect control over the new services: it had complete control not just of the network but also over the determination of standards and the supply of telematic terminals! Therefore this model of co-operation with private commercial actors could be seen as an ingenious way of adapting the telecommunications monopoly to the exigencies of the new, expanding and more competitive industry structure while pre-empting any really radical change. This approach could also be presented as 'decentralist', which neatly gelled with the current thrust of French Socialist ideology.

In order to simplify billing, the DGT deliberately adopted a uniquely innovative, but essentially very simple, tariff system called the 'Kiosk' for remunerating the service providers; it aimed to maximise both the number of services provided and the use of the medium. The Kiosk system did not require the users to subscribe to any particular service; instead users were given free access to a Kiosk of service providers and then were simply charged for the call. Part of this charge was then handed over by the DGT to the respective Kiosk service provider. This system allowed cheap and easy access to a wide range of different *à la carte* services. Undoubtedly, the system of 'pay-as-you-use', together with the free distribution of the Minitel terminal, helped to maximize consumer usage of the system and give the programme an important early impetus.[41]

A critical evaluation of the efficacy of the telematics programme

Indeed, the French *Télétel* programme quickly achieved an astonishing and unique degree of success at least on the domestic front. It supplied a captive market for those national firms which were the beneficiaries of the DGT's contracts to bulk manufacture the Minitel terminals, namely Thomson, Alcatel and Matra. It also provided a great stimulus to the domestic computer, components and software industries. Furthermore, it soon led to a prolific growth of new service providers: offering, for example, electronic mail, banking ('tele-banking') and other financial services, travel reservations, train and airline schedules, traffic information, property and stock market information, access to manifold data banks and a host of other on-line services. In addition, numerous local authorities and public agencies established their own information services. Moreover, all this led to the creation of much new employment. According to one estimate, the manufacture of the terminals permitted industry to create 1,800 new jobs while between 6,000 and 7,000 new jobs were created in the companies providing services. A further 2,400 new jobs were created in the software sector and between 1,200 and 1,400 in the DGT (France Télécom) itself.[42] The number of terminals taken up by citizens passed the 90,000 mark in December 1983; a year later the figure exceeded 500,000. By early 1987, more than 2 million French households were using the videotex terminal Minitel. By the end of 1987, nearly 3.5 million Minitel terminals had been distributed, generating a usage of more than 52 million hours of connection. One year later, well over 4 million Minitels accounted for 60 million hours of connection.[43]

However, a number of significant questions have to be asked about the efficacy of the French telematics programme. After all, it was very expensive indeed. According to a recent report by the *Cours de Compte*, the total cost of videotex by the end of 1987 was around FFr8 billion, not counting the very considerable R&D costs. However, the DGT's receipts from the spectacularly high usage of the system did not exceed FFr3 billion. Indeed, the report of the *Cours de Compte* expressed considerable concern that, 'five years after the effective introduction of videotex, the profitability of the *Télétel* programme appear(ed) uncertain . . . '.[44]

Obviously, at one level the *Télétel* programme has to be evaluated as a simple exercise in industrial policy: according to this criterion, Thomson, Alcatel and Matra would certainly deem it a resounding success. The manufacture of the Minitel, which might effectively be counted as a massive subsidy to French industry, amounted to 80 per cent of this enormous investment by the DGT.[45] The point is, of course, that there are wider criteria than the simple argument between the rationales of profitability and industrial subsidization.

The original aim of *Télétel* had been to supply the public with information services. In the meantime the French Socialist economic policy-makers had become concerned, above all, that it should become the provider of new corporate value-added services. In the event, the latter expectation was only partially met. By 1987, around one-third of Minitel terminals were to be found in offices or other business premises.[46] Disappointingly, however, business usage of the system remained largely a domestic affair. International corporations appeared to be unimpressed by the system. Moreover, it soon transpired that the French mass public were the main customer of the system, the main attraction of which proved to be as a simple medium for electronic mail (*messageries*), carrying messages often of a very personal kind. By the summer of 1984 the explosion in this much more prosaic usage of the system had actually caused an overloading of the telephone service. This seemed to highlight a weakness of the system, namely its lack of a more commercial orientation, and the absence of alternative means of delivery to that owned and operated by the PTT. Moreover, by opting for the Kiosk system, in order to entice mass usage, the PTT had evidently risked overburdening its basic telephone service.[47]

In addition, it can be persuasively argued that France may not have been nearly so far sighted, as has been often claimed (mainly by the French themselves), in backing videotex as its chosen *entrée* into the 'information society'. For the reasons explained, in particular the deployment of a system architecture which allowed the DGT to pursue its own organizational-political goals – namely, consolidating and expanding its network monopoly – the DGT's *Télétel* system clearly favoured universality, namely the mass public uses of the technology, over specialization and the more sophisticated 'customized' requirements of the corporate sector. The number of functions capable of being provided by the Minitel was distinctly limited because of its very basic character (it was an 'unintelligent' terminal). Furthermore, British experience (Prestel) had demonstrated that videotex was fast converging with a wide range of other office information and communication systems. In Britain, videotex had to compete with a growing plethora of different systems and networks fulfilling similar – and often far more sophisticated – functions in the services market. To a large extent, this was the result of British deregulation and privatization policies.[48]

During the same period that the DGT was pouring its resources into the videotex programme (and also an abortive 'third generation' plan for fibre-optic cable systems), liberalization in Britain had resulted in a veritable explosion of the, previously very small, private value-added networks (VANs) market. In fact, value-added networks had developed much more vigorously in Britain than elsewhere in Western Europe, where videotex-type systems remained within the PTT's orbit. In addition to the public videotex system (Prestel), over 700 VANs of myriad designs were licensed in the period 1981–6. As a result, business users from all over Europe had come to evaluate Britain as far more competitive in value-added services than France. Consequently, foreign multinationals were clearly favouring Britain rather than France as the main location for their European operations.[49]

Even greater disappointment resulted from the patent failure of the French *Télétel* system to gain successes for the *filière électronique* in international markets. The domestic market had been created by a non-commercial strategy (giving the Minitel terminals away). However, this meant that the system had a fatal flaw: the DGT had had to develop a very basic and inexpensive terminal. The Minitel was essentially an 'unintelligent terminal', unattractive to markets like the American and British ones, where there was already a very wide diffusion of 'intelligent terminals' in the shape of the microcomputer. On the one hand, the fact that the Minitel terminal was necessarily relatively unsophisticated and inexpensive had helped to socialize the user into acceptance of telematic information services, as even the otherwise critical report of the *Cours de Compte* readily admitted (this too was part of the DGT's gambit). On the other hand, a cynic might suggest that the *Télétel* programme's domestic success could be explained very simply by the fact that France was actually a comparative laggard, considerably behind other countries such as the United States and Britain, in the applications of the microelectronics revolution. Accordingly, it was hardly surprising that *Télétel* was able to establish itself easily in relation to microcomputers. The *Télétel* programme was a strategy of computerization that, at home at least, appeared to be particularly original and 'successful'. Abroad, however, where the development and usage of private microcomputer systems was much more impressive, the programme's merits were more questionable. Microcomputers could be just as easily interconnected as Minitel terminals by means of the public telecommunications network, but under more liberal regulatory regimes so too could they by means of a growing array of alternative commercial systems. The French, by contrast, were essentially limited to the use of a centralized network with comparatively 'unintelligent' terminals![50] Charon and Vedel have suggested that, while the *Télétel* programme restricts market penetration by foreign hardware manufacturers and foreign service providers, it ' . . . may [also] hamper the access of users and of French software companies to the increasingly globalised information market . . . '[51] Even more ominously, Mayntz and Schneider have pointed out that ' . . . monolithic videotex systems which we can today observe in France [and Germany] may [even] *disappear* in an array of overlapping and competing services, as seems already to be happening in Britain' (emphasis added).[52]

Ironically, the strategy of giving French domestic industry a captive market, the programme's first goal which was successfully achieved, may therefore explain, in large measure, its failure to achieve its more ambitious second goal, namely success in international markets. In fact, the former goal was arguably a disincentive to the successful pursuit of foreign markets by French firms. As Diana Green has succinctly put it, *Télétel* provides . . . an example of a truth which French governments seem to have difficulty in grasping: that the strategy of supplying a product, irrespective of demand for it, does not work in competitive markets'.[53]

As suggested at the end of the preceding section of this chapter, growing awareness of the inadequacy of a PTT-controlled market for value-added services was undoubtedly a major factor behind the Chirac government's decision finally to liberalize this singly important field of telecommunications activity.

Conclusion

The following broad conclusions can be drawn from this inquiry.

1 French communications policies, under successive governments, have displayed a degree of consistency to the extent that the state has sought to 'impose its will on the marketplace' (our, or to be more precise Zysman's, definition of mercantilism).

2 Nevertheless, under the impact of technological and market developments, principally internationalization, there has recently been a significant reassessment of the realistic scope for state action. This has involved a move away from traditional mercantilism towards an important degree of liberalization. However, state action still displays strong elements of neo-mercantilism, the corollary of which is that, in France at least, liberalization would appear to have certain well-defined limits.

3 The traditional approach to industrial policy, by means of *grands projets*, is less likely to bring success in a sector which is increasingly about internationalized information 'flows' and where such policies would appear to involve a trade-off between industrial and service sector benefits.

4 The conventional wisdom about the nature, essential 'rationality' and the

efficacy of state action in France has to be re-evaluated along the lines of Rhodes's thesis about the important role of bureaucratic lobbies internal to the state (here the DGT).

The first point hardly requires further comment. The theme of the continued role of 'politics' is best illustrated by the Chirac government's evident commitment to strengthening French national champions in international markets, a concern which overrode domestic concerns about the success of privatization and competition in domestic markets. The 'guardianship' role of the French state in respect of the activities and fate of French companies in international markets is confirmed by both the CGE takeover of ITT and the sell-off of CGCT. Indeed, under the Chirac government French telecommunications manufacturers came to occupy a dominant position within the European market, a fact that may yet bring the French state into conflict with the European Commission.

The second point is more complex. The main lesson learnt by the French state was that it had to adapt its habit of 'imposing its will on markets' to take into account the constraints set by 'internationalization'. This involved developing new instruments of action. The main problem at the heart of the Socialists' ambitious mercantilistic strategy for the *filière électronique* was that it was a national strategy which failed to take into account that the sector was becoming increasingly internationalized. This internationalization 'made unrealistic hopes of market reconquest across the whole *filière*'.[54] However, the French response was hardly defeatist: in this chapter it has been suggested that the French state has reacted in what might still be described as a 'neo-mercantilistic' manner – on the one hand by attempting to broaden out its mercantilism to the European level (Eureka; French ideas of a 'fortress Europe') and on the other hand by intervening politically in the process of company strategies for international mergers and take-overs (CGCT). This would appear to suggest that, despite new constraints, there is still some scope for mercantilism. At the same time, the failure of the Chirac government to match neo-liberal rhetoric with concrete practice was graphically illustrated by the absence of any dramatic deregulation and liberalization of the DGT's (France Télécom's) telecommunications monopoly.

The third and fourth points relate to the evidence supplied by the case study of the French videotex programme. The French videotex programme can be seen as a classic example of statist voluntarism designed to give the French telecommunications industry a much needed fillip. Undoubtedly, the French Socialist government saw in videotex a splendid opportunity to repeat, by the same voluntaristic approach, the spectacular success achieved by its Giscardian predecessor in the field of digital exchanges, only this time it was to have a knock-on effect for the wider *filière électronique*. Its aim was clearly to translate the 'mercantilist' message of the Nora–Minc report into industrial practice. Undoubtedly, the French electronics industry benefited from the very

223

generous DGT contracts for the Minitel terminals. Indeed, the programme seems to confirm the French state's traditional mercantilist predisposition to favour industrial modernization over the provision of services and thereby promote national industrial and technological 'independence' designed to avoid the risk of dependence on foreign supply. However, as seen, this may well have incurred significant costs in view of the increasing importance of competitiveness in corporate telecommunications services in an increasingly internationalized world economy which itself is more and more dependent on unrestricted information flows and highly sophisticated user demands.

The fourth, and final, point is a closely related one. The examination of the case study of telematics confirms the thesis advanced by Rhodes about the nature of French *étatisme* and, in particular, the role of the *grands corps*. In this case, the *grand corps* of telecommunications engineers in the DGT was able to latch onto the political ideology of the French Socialist government in the pursuit of its own organizational-political goals. At one level, the telematics programme clearly reflected the ideological centrality to French governments of national technological and industrial 'independence'. At another significant level, it reflected the transparent fact that the traditional state monopoly provider of telecommunications networks and services, the DGT, had grasped a new opportunity for commercial and institutional advancement under French Socialism. As suggested above, it can be argued that the resultant policy was not necessarily an entirely 'rational' one or to rephrase the latter remark, the policy may have had a distinct rationality in the domestic context, but this was not the case in the context of the international marketplace.

This strategy ensured that the DGT remained in control of the development of the telecommunications network, it retained complete control over both standards and equipment supply (the Minitel terminal), and thereby it could also maintain an indirect control of value-added services, as it had always intended. Moreover, both standards and equipment remained 'strictly French'! However, as a result, it has been suggested, France remained relatively undeveloped in the field of corporate applications of the microelectronic revolution. The French public may, as it has been widely claimed, have been socialized by *Télétel* into an early acceptance of the communications revolution, but by means of a 'dumb' terminal with distinctly limited applications. By contrast, in the United States and Britain, the microcomputer was experiencing much more rapid public diffusion. The result was that these foreign markets remained uninterested in the *Télétel* system which had the character of a novel but distinctly limited domestic phenomenon 'for the French only'.

One final comment is in order. If, until the end of the 1960s, French telecommunications policy could be thought of – and was thought of – exclusively in domestic terms, this situation is clearly undergoing very dramatic change: international political economy is now the prime concern. On the one hand, this chapter has illustrated the very strong position that French producer firms have come to occupy in international markets and especially within Europe. This seems to suggest that French telecommunications policies have been remarkably successful. However, the chapter has also described that this mercantilist approach has distinct limitations and indeed has incurred some unintended consequences in the context of an internationalized sector in which information flows and corporate business services are at least as important as the traditional industrial concerns. In particular, it appears that French policy-makers have had to – and, it is the author's belief, will continue to have to – modify their perceptions of what is at stake in the telecommunications sector with respect to the mix of priorities given to manufacturing and such services. Moreover, without a doubt, this one day will have to involve a major rethink of the role of the key actor in the sector, namely the DGT (France Télécom).

Nevertheless, there has already occurred a significant change of emphasis, from strengthening the role of the public sector and indulging in traditional industrial voluntarism towards an increasingly extensive opening of the telecommunications sector to private commercial interests. This is a more realistic and pragmatic approach which involves, rather than 'imposition of political will on markets', a subtle and more equal balance of the two.

Notes

This chapter is based partly upon a research project, entitled *Public Policies for the New Communications Technologies*, funded by an ESRC grant under the programme ESRC/CNRS 'Exchange Scheme for Social Scientists 1988–89'. The section on French videotex owes much to the work of Thierry Vedel who kindly allowed the author to see a number of draft papers prepared for the workshop *The Development of Interactive Videotex: A Cross-national Comparison*, which took place at the Max-Planck-Institut für Gesellschaftsforschung, Cologne, 15–16 December 1988. The author was a discussant at this workshop and he would also like to take this opportunity to express his thanks to Volker Schneider (who organized the workshop).

1 Andrew Shonfeld, *Modern capitalism: the Changing Balance of Public and Private Power* (London: Oxford University Press, 1965); for a later variation on this theme see Peter Hall, *Governing the Economy: the Politics of State Intervention in Britain and France* (Cambridge: Polity Press, 1986).
2 Kenneth Dyson, *The State Tradition in Western Europe* (Oxford: Martin Robertson, 1980).
3 John Zysman, 'Between the market and the state: dilemmas of French policy for the electronics industry', *Research Policy*, no. 3 (1975), pp. 312–36, at 314–15. For an account of the instruments of French state action see John Zysman, *Governments, Markets and Growth: Financial Systems and the Politics of Industrial Change* (Ithaca, NY: Cornell University Press, 1983).

4 Stephen Gill and David Law, *The Global Political Economy* (Brighton: Harvester Wheatsheaf, 1988), in particular Chapter 3.

5 Diana Green, 'The political economy of information technology in France', in J. Gaffney (ed.), *France and Modernisation* (Aldershot: Gower, 1988), Chapter 7, p. 125.

6 Philip Cerny, 'Public policy and the structural logic of the state: France in comparative perspective', *West European Politics*, 10 (1) (January 1987), pp.128ff.

7 Jack Hayward, *The State and the Market Economy: Industrial Patriotism and Economic Intervention in France* (Brighton: Wheatsheaf, 1986).

8 Howard Machin and Vincent Wright (eds), *Economic Policy and Policy-making under the Mitterrand Presidency, 1981–84* (London: Frances Pinter, 1985). However, the revisionist views of the editors are by no means shared by all the contributors to this volume.

9 Martin Rhodes, 'Industry and modernisation: an overview', in John Gaffney (ed.) *France and Modernisation* (Aldershot: Gower, 1988), pp. 66–95, 67 and 71; S. Cohen and M. Bauer, *Les Grands Manœuvres Industrielles* (Paris: Belfond, 1985).

10 Ibid.

11 Organisation for Economic Co-operation and Development (OECD), *Telecommunications; Pressures and Policies for Change* (Paris: OECD, 1983).

12 Jeremy Tunstall, *Communications Deregulation. The Unleashing of America's Communications Industry* (Oxford: Basil Blackwell, 1986).

13 Michael Palmer and Jeremy Tunstall, 'Deregulation and competition in European telecommunications', *Journal of Communications*, 38 (1) (Winter 1988), p. 60.

14 David Thomas, 'The liberalisation debate: conflicting views on competition', *Financial Times*, 19 October 1987, p. 11.

15 K.W. Grewlich, 'Telecommunications in European perspective', in S. Wilks and M. Wright (eds), *Comparative Government Industry Relations* (Oxford: Clarendon, 1987), p. 251.

16 Rhodes, op. cit., p. 72.

17 George Graham, 'French telecommunications system: world's most digitalised network', *Financial Times*, International Telecommunications Survey, 19 July 1989, p. XIII.

18 Thierry Vedel, 'Les ingénieurs des télécommunications', *Culture Technique*, no. 12 (March 1984), pp. 63–79.

19 Simon Nora and Alain Minc, *Informatisation de la Société* (Paris: Documentation Française, 1978); also published in translation as *The Computerisation of Society* by the MIT Press, Cambridge, MA, 1980. This report was prepared by several committees composed of numerous experts from public administration and industry, including the telecommunications sector. Information technology subsequently became the subject of an extensive public debate in the press.

20 Jean-Louis Moynot, 'The Left, industrial policy and the *filière électronique*', in George Ross, Stanley Hoffmann and Sylvia Malzacher (eds), *The Mitterrand Experiment* (Cambridge: Polity Press, 1987), pp. 263–76, 263.

21 Ibid., p. 264.

22 See Peter Humphreys, 'Telecommunications modernisation in Britain, France and West Germany', *Manchester Papers in Politics*, no. 6 (1988), p. 5.

23 Rhodes, op. cit., p. 83.

24 Howard Machin and Vincent Wright, 'Economic policy under the Mitterrand presidency', in Machin and Wright (eds), op. cit., p. 3.

25 See John Peterson, 'Eureka and the symbolic politics of high technology', *Politics*, 9 (1) (1989), pp. 8–13, 9.

26 See Rudolf Popischil, *Ansätze zur Neuorganisation des französischen*

Fernmeldewesens, Diskussionsbeiträge zur Telekommunikationsforschung No. 39 (Bad Honnef: Wirtschaftliches Institut für Kommunikationsdienste der Deutschen Bundespost, May 1988).

27 *Oxford Analytica*, Daily Brief, 19 March 1987.

28 Ibid., 23 April 1987.

29 Peter Humphreys, op. cit., p. 6.

30 Michael Palmer and Jeremy Tunstall, op. cit., p. 67.

31 Paul Betts, 'Catching up with the rhetoric of change', *Financial Times*, World Telecommunications Survey, 19 October 1987, p. VI.

32 Green, op. cit., p. 126.

33 Renate Mayntz and Volker Schneider, 'The dynamics of system development in a comparative perspective: interactive videotex in Germany, France and Britain', in R. Mayntz and T.P. Hughes (eds), *The Development of Large Technical Systems* (Frankfurt/Main and Boulder, CO: Campus Verlag and Westview Press, 1988), Chapter 10, pp. 263–98, 284.

34 For a history of the technical development of French videotex see Alain Giraud, 'Une lente émergence', in Claire Ancelin and Marie Marchand (eds), *Le Videotex: contributions aux débats sur la télématique* (Paris: Masson, 1984). For an almost 'heroic', and very nationalistic, account of both the origins and later development of the telematics programme see Marie Marchand, *La Grande Aventure du Minitel* (Paris: Librairie Larousse, 1987).

35 The number of employees in the French telecommunications industry started to fall from 1977 onwards. Having risen from 50,000 in 1970 to 94,000 in 1977, it dropped steadily from 91,000 in 1978 to 80,000 in 1980, 72,500 in 1982 and 70,000 in 1984. *Source*: Thierry Vedel.

36 *Cours de Compte, Rapport au Président de la République*, Paris, June 1989, p. 36.

37 Bruno Lussato, *La Défi informatique* (Paris: Fayard, 1981).

38 According to Thierry Vedel, the DGT gave support amounting to at least FFr17 million between 1982 and 1985, mainly for software.

39 *Cours de Compte*, op. cit.

40 *Télétel Newsletter*, Special Issue, no. 2 (1987), p. 4.

41 *Cours de Compte,* op. cit., pp. 36–7.

42 Jean-Marie Charon and Thierry Vedel, 'Videotex in France', paper prepared for the workshop *The Development of Interactive Videotex: A Cross-national Comparison*, Max-Planck-Institut für Gesellschaftsforschung, Cologne, 15–16 December 1988, p. 32.

43 *Cours de Compte*, op. cit., p. 37.

44 Ibid., pp. 36–44, esp. pp. 37, 40. Also see Charon and Vedel, op. cit., p. 31. The latter suggest that the videotex programme cost around FFr2 billion per annum.

45 Charon and Vedel, op. cit., p. 32.

46 *Télétel Newsletter*, op. cit., p. 6.

47 In the Télétel system, user terminals (the Minitels) are connected to the public switched telephone system, while most host computers (of the service providers) are attached to the Transpac packet-switching network. In June 1985 the entire system 'crashed' due to overload.

48 Mayntz and Schneider, op. cit., p. 294.

49 See Kevin Morgan and Douglas Webber, 'Divergent paths: political strategies for telecommunications in Britain, France and West Germany', in Kenneth Dyson and Peter Humphreys (eds), *The Politics of the Communications Revolution in Western Europe* (London: Frank Cass, 1986), p. 59.

50 Charon and Vedel, op. cit., p. 41.

51 Ibid., p. 40.
52 Mayntz and Schneider, op. cit., p. 268.
53 Green, op. cit., p. 133.
54 Rhodes, op. cit., p. 85.

Chapter ten

Conclusion

Kenneth Dyson and Peter Humphreys

The overall thesis of this volume has been that 'politics matters' in the development of communications policies and that the international political dimension is increasingly important. Politics matters in three main senses: institutions, their philosophies and their self-interests, shape the development of communications policies, at national and international levels; 'policy networks', within which institutions from the public and private sectors interact in a structure of dependent relationships, have their own rules and characteristics that give a dynamic to communications policy development, independent of the impact of governmental ideology on the one hand or of technology and markets on the other; and requirements of legitimation influence the nature of policy reform. These political factors combine to endow detailed variations in communications policies with significance. Accordingly, the volume has been concerned with such issues as the degree of autonomy and capacity for aggrandizement of international organizations such as the International Telecommunication Union (ITU) and the European Community (EC) (Chapters 2, 4 and 5); the relationship of strategy and structure as governmental ideologies interact with institutions and policy networks in communications policies nationally (e.g. Chapters 7 and 9) and internationally (e.g. Chapter 6); and the problems of legitimation and their implications for policy development (Chapters 7 and 8). In particular, institutional self-interest remains a powerful factor. Thus the enthusiasm of West European PTTs for the integrated services digital network (ISDN) is best understood against the background of their interest in controlling both the impact of the entry of computing companies into the telecommunications sector and the impact of American companies in Europe.

Above all, broadcasting and telecommunications have been elevated to a 'high politics' of international diplomacy (see notably Chapters 6 and 9). Policy networks have been altered as a territorial shift occurs in the arenas in which communications policies are made and the constraints of external pressures on these networks are more powerfully felt. Once-stable policy networks are destabilized by new entrants, and old partners – like PTTs and national telecommunications equipment suppliers – are freed from old dependencies. The mutual benefits of once exclusive and privileged relations are no longer so clear. Yet factors of institutional structure and the inherited characteristics of policy networks have not fundamentally changed. The national dimension of communications policies has not become an epiphenomenon of the international context. Dominant patterns of relations within domestic/national policy networks seem to be resilient to fundamental change.

In the chapters in this volume we have examined the nature of policy change in the communications sector from two perspectives: of national institutional structures and policy networks as they have had to deal with an increasingly important international dimension of market and technological change, and of international institutions as their role has been reassessed and redefined. In this respect the emphasis is on the public institutional frameworks and the policy networks within which policy issues and problems (discussed in Chapter 1) have been debated and policies have been formulated and applied. Such an approach has the value of being sensitive to the specifically political, cultural and historical elements in communications policy development as international institutions and national policy networks seek to accommodate and remould the mounting technological and market pressures under which they must operate. It reveals how international institutions and national policy networks have been beset by divisive and destabilizing forces in the 1980s. The prominence of new issues like liberalization has led the state and new groups to find it useful to modify the rules of the game and change relations which have become obsolete or unsuitable or are thought to be politically counterproductive. Ideological change and the restructuring of policy networks are, after all, major themes of the volume.

At the same time, additional to institutional self-interest, the character of policy networks has been decisive. The degree of centralization and concentration of state action shapes strategic action, by providing opportunities for or constraints on specific types of policy action. Here Chapters 7 and 9 are instructive. Also, the opportunities or difficulties that policy networks present for corporate actors remain important. Just how easy is it for telecommunications users and service providers to counteract the influence of telecommunications manufacturers? Underlying the continuing influence of policy networks on policy development are operational requirements of effective management and administration, notably of co-ordination and control, of intelligence gathering and of policy implementation. Policy networks provide a context within which policies can be renegotiated more or less informally and harmoniously. In this sense communications policies are not simply a story of new laws on liberalization and their application. They are above all a story of the refashioning of policy networks and the impact of institutional self-interest.

The political economy of communications policies

It has become apparent in this volume that the development of communications policies must be seen in the context of international political economy. Also, the chapters underline the weaknesses of established theories of the international political economy, notably the theories of neo-liberalism and neo-mercantilism. These theories share in fact a common weakness: they exaggerate the extent, continuity and consistency of the particular trends of change that they seek to emphasize, and they take a one-sided and deterministic view of their implications. Neo-liberalism exaggerates the supremacy of markets over politics; neo-mercantilism exaggerates the supremacy of politics over markets. In reality politics and markets are more interdependent, and their relationship more complex, than either theory is prepared to concede. This relationship is mediated by factors of culture, history and administration, which find their expression in the character and operation of institutional structures and policy networks. National and international communications policies reflect not only the interaction of contrasting and changing views of the relative importance of neo-liberal and neo-mercantilist policy measures. They are also informed by specific factors of institutional structure and interest and the character of policy networks. Neo-liberal and neo-mercantilist theories of the international political economy are in this respect too simplifying and static to embrace the forces at work in the development of communications policies adequately.

In drawing attention to the cultural, historical and administrative context of communications policies, the focus on institutional structures and policy networks highlights important empirical objections to the neo-liberal model. According to neo-liberal theory, a functional logic or evolutionary process is producing a convergence of communications policies amongst all technologically and economically advanced societies.[1] The fundamental impulse in long-term communications policy development is the universal and unavoidable exigencies of international technological and market rationality associated with the emerging 'information society'. Deregulation is the policy model most consistent with the functional imperatives that a rationally operating information technology and economy impose and towards which an evolutionary convergence is taking place. Elite leadership, like that of Thatcherism in Britain, is the key political process through which this decisive historical change is effected. In this perspective an Anglo-American axis can be expected to dictate the pace of regulatory change in Western Europe.

A notable feature of the theory of the 'information society' is that it has been advanced by neo-liberals who claim to offer an alternative objective basis for political and policy judgements to Marxists. Liberal values of competition, enterprise and choice are justified on functional and evolutionary grounds. They are revealing themselves in the course of communications policy development as the values most consistent with the logic of technology and industrial structure. Correspondingly, the evolutionary process eliminates unworkable ideologies of governmental intervention which are doomed to disillusionment and failure. Such a fate awaits French governments that attempt to place state interests and 'national independence' above the logic of communications markets. In this sense neo-liberalism argues not only that sovereignty is 'at bay' but also that traditional ideological conflicts based on class are coming to an end. Ultimately politics does not matter, except as an instrument to effect necessary change in the interests of international competitiveness (a 'heroic' function) or as a source of dysfunctional consequences like corporate bankruptcies, reduced investment and lost jobs.

By contrast, neo-mercantilism emphasizes the subordination of markets to politics and the role of states as actors pursuing independent political purposes.[2] Motivated by a political interest in economic security and self-sufficiency, states *choose* communication policies – whether or not to deregulate, and how to regulate, and which technologies to back. States structure and even create markets, giving priority to 'national champions' and to the quality of national infrastructural provision in communications policy. According to neo-mercantilist theory, the state has its own purpose for wanting to develop domestic production capacity and skills, namely to underpin its own long-term political influence as an actor on the world scene. Accordingly, communications policies seek to maximize the dependence of others upon one's self and to avoid developing dependencies upon others by a combination of subsidies, quotas and other barriers to entry. Behind these neo-mercantilist policies of tariff and non-tariff protection are powerful domestic electoral pressures and the need to manage the complexity of external changes that threaten disruptive effects on sensitive national economies. Whatever the ideology of the government, its intervention in communications is bound to remain intensive. In this sense neo-liberalism tends to be of greater rhetorical than practical significance; deregulation is a mask. Furthermore, deregulatory pressures within the international political economy represent the effort of particular states to reinforce their power and influence. Behind efforts to propagate the neo-liberal model of deregulation are not so much technological and market imperatives as political purposes. Neo-mercantilism replaces the functional logic of neo-liberalism with a teleological account of regulation. Regulation is shaped by the imperative of an independent political purpose, directed at advancing the public interest.

A critical perspective on neo-liberal and neo-mercantilist accounts of regulatory change in communications must recognize the important insights that they yield. Neo-liberalism underlines the impact of technological and market change on public policy. Policy-makers are confronted by powerful structural changes that present themselves as objective forces. Neo-mercantilism stresses the subjective determinants of behaviour and reminds analysis that actors can play an independently important role in making and changing communications markets. The major limitation of both theories is that they over-look the continuing vitality and resilience of policy networks and institutional structures as independent factors in communications policy. Neo-liberalism offers an account of communications policy development that is based on a narrow, oversimplifying and unrealistic conception of economic rationality. Communications policy is understood as involving the maximization of only those objectives that can be satisfied through market exchanges. In reality West European communications policies remain concerned about the provision of collective goods, like universal access to basic telecommunications and broadcasting services, and about communications as cultural policy, with an emphasis on 'quality' and 'standards'. They have had to grapple with the paradoxes of rationality; collective provision versus individual preference, and cultural versus economic criteria. The problem with neo-mercantilism is that regulatory change has not been a story of far-sighted policy-makers imposing some grand political purpose. The overwhelming impression is of muddle, incompleteness and delay, with special interests in a position to shape the scale and pace of change. 'The state' is too internally divided and too 'penetrated' by external actors to be the unit of analysis. Equally, the market is not an abstraction to be detached from what governments choose to do.

Realism involves the recognition that actors are embodied in policy networks and institutional structures and that policy networks and institutional structures are increasingly embedded in complex and deep-seated changes within the international political economy. Within this fast-changing environment policy actors are attempting to establish an 'advantageous' control and influence, shaped not least by strategies of institutional aggrandizement. A persuasive account of the development of communications policies must, accordingly, emphasize that the communication 'revolution' has involved a redistribution of power within policy networks, as the resources (such as technical, financial, organizational and legal) available to actors have changed. Correspondingly, power and conflict within policy networks, and the constraints that they impose, have been central to the development of communications policies. Policy outcomes have varied across countries, with no West European country simply following American experience of deregulation. The specific combinations of political and economic interest and the contrasts of institutional and cultural frameworks have militated against simple policy convergence. Politics and culture do, accordingly, matter as much as they ever did. However, no single political or cultural imperative is at work within European communications policies in the way that neo-mercantilist accounts would suggest.

The telecommunications 'revolution'

Renaud (Chapter 2) describing the ITU notes how the academic study of international relations has shifted from a focus on the state as the basic unit of analysis to theories of 'interdependence'. According to these theories, state actors are no longer the only actors, and not necessarily the most important. The ITU is clearly a very important international organization, being both the largest and the oldest surviving. For Renaud the central question is whether the ITU has become a global actor in its own right or whether it is essentially an arena for conflicts of interest amongst states. Has the ITU achieved a degree of autonomy from its member states? To what extent have the latter had to relinquish sovereignty? And how successfully has the ITU taken advantage of the challenge of the telecommunications 'revolution' to pursue organizational aggrandizement? Werle and Schneider ask similar questions about the EC.

Renaud draws on 'functionalist' theory to explore the extent to which the ITU might be said to have transcended or 'undermined' the primacy of national interests. Because of the pressing need that states have to negotiate about telecommunications in the interests of international trade, functionalist theory would lead one to expect that the ITU would provide an excellent example of how co-operation in 'low politics' could spin a global cobweb of ties based on technical rationality. Functionalism stresses that international organizations like the ITU will necessarily grow in relative importance *vis-à-vis* states as the latter are confronted with the need to adapt to an increasingly complex and interdependent world. This integration at the level of low politics releases a dynamic that modifies 'high politics'.

Renaud's historical sketch of the ITU seems to go some way to support the functionalist argument. The rise of capitalism and the growing internationalization of trade during the last century and a half led to a considerable development of the ITU's basic functions of standardization and regulation. In the increasingly interdependent world economy associated with the telecommunications revolution the potential role for such an international organization is greatly increased. In fact, Renaud finds major empirical problems with the functionalist argument. In the 1980s the sheer scope and unpredictability of change in telecommunications, combined with increasingly fierce international competition, has injected a new note of disharmony – in another word, politics – into the ITU. Politics has been further intensified by a more diverse set of players as a concomitant of the break-up of the traditional state telecommunications monopolies. The ITU has become an arena of conflict, in particular between industrialized countries at different stages of development in telecommunications and in deregulation and motivated by considerations of national interest. This process was most clearly revealed in the preparations for, and during the proceedings of, the World Administrative Telegraph and Telephone Conference (WATTC-88). The United States and Britain, supported by important business interests, sought to influence the ITU to resist its regulatory reflex, whilst many West European countries, especially France, and Japan opposed deregulation. Also, large manufacturing companies in Western Europe, such as Siemens, Thomson, Ericsson and Cable and Wireless, have used the ITU as a means of pursuing their own economic interests, notably trade with the Third World, to the disadvantage of American companies.

Whether states are for or against deregulation, they – and transnational companies – are less disposed than ever to perceive the ITU as an autonomous actor. The ITU faces a more serious challenge in adapting to a more dynamic and complex sector than functionalism would suggest. After over a century of expansion, its global regulatory regime is being supplanted by bilateralism in key areas. At the same time, new global information services, for instance for financial markets, are over stretching its resources and leading to a serious questioning of its competences. In particular, at WATTC-88 the pro- and anti-deregulation camps were drawn into major conflict over the question of whether the ITU should regulate new specialized networks and new value-added services. Renaud suggests that there might even be a conspiracy of de-regulators to diminish or destroy the ITU, and he raises the question of the subsequent impact on users. The eventual outcome of WATTC-88 was in fact a compromise which seemed to accommodate many of the pressures for a liberal regulatory regime, especially for new private networks. This development can be taken as evidence that the ITU is capable of pragmatic adaptation to ensure its survival. As an international organization it has managed to sustain itself and to absorb deregulatory pressures. However, it can also be seen as a sign that, in the face of political pressures for deregulation, the ITU's regulatory powers are set to decline in scope. The politics of the ITU involves a reassessment by powerful states of the advantage that they gain from the organization. Functionalism's prediction that the ITU will have an impact on high politics through its operation at the level of low politics would seem to be disappointed. The opposite has occurred: as a result of technological and economic challenges, telecommunications policy has assumed the character of high politics for states, with consequent dangerous tensions within the ITU. The ITU has been locked in a web of 'economic statecraft', as states have sought to pursue neo-liberal or neo-mercantilist policies or to combine them in different ways.

In Chapter 4 on the EC and telecommunications policy, Schneider and Werle focus on the same question: has the EC become more than just a regime, born out of conflict and compromise amongst member states, to emerge as a corporate actor in its own right? Here the context is different. A supra-national dimension is built into the EC in the form of the independent authority that the European Commission, the European Parliament and the European Court of Justice possess. There is also the treaty obligation to pursue 'an ever closer union', whilst the Single European Act of 1987 includes provision for majority voting in the Council of Ministers for measures completing the internal market. In the case of the EC Schneider and Werle clearly show that EC institutions have operated as corporate actors pursuing regime change, not least by dramatizing the scale of the external challenge in telecommunications to the member states. The EC has itself been important in raising telecommunications to the status of high politics and initiating policy change. It has also acted as a source of pressure for deregulation of West European markets, in particular coming into conflict with France. In effect, the EC institutions have used the challenge of the telecommunications revolution to strengthen the position of the EC *vis-à-vis* member states. Following the Green Book of 1987, a series of major telecommunications decisions followed: in May 1988 the Commission directive on terminals liberalization; in June 1988 the Council resolution on the objectives of telecommunications policy based on the Green Book; in October 1988 the proposal for a directive on the opening of telecommunications procurement markets; in April 1989 the Council resolutions on co-ordination of ISDN introduction and standardization in information technology and telecommunications; in June 1989 the publication of the Commission directive on liberalization of telecommunications services, leading to a major confrontation with the French government; and in August 1989 the proposal for a Council directive on the implementation of open network provision (ONP). There were even indications that the European Commission might consider taking a national government to the Court of Justice over breach of the EC's competition principles.

The transformation of European telecommunications policy becomes even clearer if the integration process in the EC is compared with that in the European Conference of Postal and Telecommunications Administrations (CEPT). CEPT's origins lay in the functional requirements of technical co-ordination. However, it remained essentially a 'soft' regime with a technical orientation – to facilitate cross-border communication. CEPT was tailored to the limited requirements of co-ordinating highly protectionist national policies, in short to low politics. The development of a more dynamic EC telecommunications policy, as industrial policy, was related to a perceived need for more concerted policies in response to the threat from American and Japanese companies. The chemistry was provided by the fusion of the elevation of telecommunications to high politics at the national level with the European Commission's arguments that national responses were inadequate to cope with the scale of the challenge.

In Chapter 3 Komiya shows that in the case of Intelsat high politics has been operative from the outset, with satellites being recognized by governments to be of strategic importance. Even so, for a long period of time, Intelsat operated a system of utilization charges that reflected a conception of it as an international co-operative, reflecting the needs of dominant PTTs. In the 1980s high politics resurfaced when the Reagan Administration decided to break its alleged monopoly by authorizing the launch of five private satellite systems. Komiya shows the extent to which the argument for competition in satellite systems was couched in terms of foreign policy, trade and national security. The motivations of the Reagan Administration were a mixture of foreign policy concerns and politico-economic goals. The United States no longer perceived that its foreign policy aims could be fulfilled through an organization in which its power had become much diluted. Additionally, the Reagan Administration had become convinced that Intelsat had become inefficient, unresponsive to the need to innovate and incapable of meeting the new demand for specialized and enhanced telecommunications services. Behind this conviction lay the Reagan Administration's supply-side strategy to increase the overall competitiveness of the American economy and in the process to favour the international expansion of its communications, computer and aerospace industries. As in the case of the ITU, mercantilism was a powerful ingredient in the behaviour of national governments, exposing Intelsat to the turbulences of high politics. Policy was being driven at least as much by national political interests as by an objective logic of international economic liberalism.

In Chapter 9 on the relative importance of the state and markets in the development of French telecommunications policy Humphreys shows just how important institutional factors and the character of national policy networks can be for policy development. The French state sought to play a central interventionist role in creating and managing telecommunications markets (e.g. videotex) so that national producers could gain a leading place amongst European companies. Even under Chirac (1986–8) policy was driven less by liberalization than by mercantilism. Behind this mercantilism was not so much a coherent state strategy as powerful vested interests pushing for organizational aggrandizement, notably the *grand corps* of telecommunications engineers. Such interests, including the electronics industry, could exploit the potential centralization and concentration within the policy network to develop mercantilist strategies on their behalf. At its best French telecommunications policy achieved a unity of strategy and structure; at worst, it foundered on a clash between what was rational for the *corps* and the requirements of the international economy (as with the *Plan Télématique*). The policy network seemed to display remarkable resilience in the face of both governmental change and international market pressure.

Hoffmann-Riem, in Chapter 8, examines the question of the means by which states legitimate the introduction of new communications technologies and services. In West Germany it is clear that the Bundespost has had considerable success in influencing the debate about these issues, not least in the interest of damage limitation to its own institutional interests. Also, with respect to the broadcasting dimension, the West German *Länder* (states) have played a similar leading role. Technocratic policy legitimation emerges as a main characteristic of West German communications policy sectors, along with the mercantilist ambitions of the individual *Länder* as they compete for political profile and investment in the communications sectors. Behind the devices of legitimation (expert commissions, pilot projects etc.) and the mercantilism it is once again possible to discern the interplay of special interests, as specific political and economic interests seek to take advantage of the new constellations of power that have been created by the communications revolution.

The broadcasting 'revolution'

In Chapter 5 on the EC Papathanassopoulos both complements and extends the argument of Schneider and Werle. By focusing on the EC's policies towards broadcasting he is able to show that, whilst its policies appear to be adaptive and increasingly dynamic, in the case of broadcasting the EC faces enormous difficulties in dealing with the international pressures for liberalization. Muddle and procrastination result from the inability of the EC to reconcile conflicting trends in the absence of adequate political authority to act. On the one hand, member states increasingly recognize that unilateral action is no longer adequate, given the increasing interdependence of broadcasting markets. There is consequently a growing acceptance that collective regimes are required. On the other hand, EC policy bargaining and outcomes are dictated by domestic political and economic structures and interests. In short, the drift towards a collective EC regime in communications policy is accompanied by a continuing central role for the member states in policy development. As Dyson (Chapter 6) also emphasizes, Papathanassopoulos argues that broadcasting has seen a renationalization of policies rather than an effective EC regime – a phenomenon more consistent with a neo-mercantilist than a neo-liberal explanatory model. Papathanassopoulos also stresses the consequent disproportion between effort and results in the EC policy process. Policy making for broadcasting at the EC level is characteristically reactive and incremental, disposed to muddle through on the basis of complex and shifting compromises rather than to comprehensive and radical policy making. The combination of economic and political complexities with linguistic divides and cultural variety suggests that the role of broadcasting as an integrator of Europe is likely to prove modest. It is clear from a comparative reading of Chapter 4 by Schneider and Werle and Chapter 5 by Papathanossopoulos that the EC has been more successful in extending its role both as regime and as actor in telecommunications than in broadcasting.

In Chapter 7 on Britain Negrine provides an example of 'inward-looking' broadcasting policy. He offers two explanations for the exercise in radically restructuring British broadcasting in the 1980s. On the one hand, a series of neo-liberal policy initiatives, culminating in the 1988 White Paper *Broadcast-*

ing in the 1990s: Competition, Choice and Quality, might seem to suggest that policy was a response to the functional imperatives of new technologies and international markets. On the other hand, the British government's policy initiatives can be interpreted as the national pursuit of a political ideology, neoliberalism as the handmaiden of mercantilism. The former explanation plays down the role of politics, whilst the latter gives politics pride of place. Negrine concludes that, despite the functional imperatives – the internationalization of television production and trade, the new international mobility of capital in the sector, and trans-frontier broadcasting – British broadcasting policy in the 1980s has remained a peculiarly domestic concern. It has failed to address the vast international changes in the political economy of broadcasting. Domestic politics seems to be the prime mover of policy. Ideology has elevated competition into an end unto itself, treating culture as an epiphenomenon of policy and avoiding the complexities of the evolving international dimension of the political economy of broadcasting.

The insularity of British broadcasting policy can in part be explained by Britain's traditional structural position in the international political economy of broadcasting. To some extent because of the quality of its programmes, and to an even greater extent because of the size of the English language world market to which it has easy access, British broadcasting has long been a world-class player. Among European countries it has been uniquely able to penetrate the huge American market. By comparison, European markets have not mattered much to British broadcasters because of linguistic and cultural barriers. Britain has also not been exposed to aggressive media neighbours in Western Europe, for the same reason. In short, the international orientation of British broadcasting and its accumulated expertise in this area has not disposed a neo-liberal government to develop a strong international dimension to policy. In the age of satellite broadcasting, notably Astra, this missing international dimension to policy could be revealed as complacency.

In analysing Luxembourg's central role in the development of commercial broadcasting in Western Europe Dyson (Chapter 6) stresses the importance of structural, historical and ideological factors for an understanding of what happens in 'policy networks'. This chapter is also a study of the interactive nature of policy developments in Luxembourg, France, Belgium and West Germany and of the complex interaction of national and international dimensions in broadcasting policy. The pivotal position of Luxembourg in Europe meant that its broadcasting sector was embroiled in high politics in an often spectacular manner. This high politics involved in particular France, where neo-mercantilism emerges as a central policy model explicable by reference to structural, historical and ideological factors. Luxembourg's pursuit of neo-liberalism in broadcasting policy emerges as a key factor in revealing the limitations of French neo-mercantilism in this sector. The neo-liberalism of Luxembourg is closely linked to major structural characteristics, notably the country's insignificant internal market, its dependence on inward investment and its high degree of penetration by foreign interests. In short, it is a classic case of a 'small country in world markets'. At the same time Dyson reveals the hidden hand of mercantilism behind the neo-liberalism of the Luxembourg government. Dependence on a very circumscribed range of industries with comparative advantage disposes government to act on behalf of those industries. Indeed, the inheritance of a commercial broadcasting tradition meant that the Luxembourg government did not need to engage in sweeping liberalization measures. The central characteristic of Luxembourg broadcasting policy was a new activism of the government in the 1980s.

Dyson also highlights the inseparability of regulation and the market. Markets are not to be understood as autonomous factors, existing outside an institutional and policy framework on which they exert a deterministic effect. Markets can be shaped and even created by institutional structures and policies. Humphreys' study of the French videotex programme provides a good illustration in similar vein. Dyson shows how, in the case of France and Luxembourg, governmental actions have shaped commercial broadcasting markets and influenced the behaviour of firms. Equally, regulatory tools have been adapted to cope with new market problems, as in the efforts of the Luxembourg government to maximize Luxembourg's presence in the new satellite broadcasting market and of the French government to control access to new commercial broadcasting markets in France. West European broadcasting policy illuminates the limitations of both markets and regulation, neither of which proves as rational in practice as its advocates promise. As Dyson emphasizes, in a context of ignorance and uncertainty about technological choices and market demand and about the international dimension of policy decisions, both market operators and regulators have been overwhelmed by events.

Politics, markets and communications policies

This volume has underlined the difficulties that follow when political economy bases its analysis on the dichotomy of politics and markets. Both neo-liberalism and neo-mercantilism assume the 'externality' of the state from the market; the state is either 'nightwatchman' or champion of the national interest.[3] One perspective enlists economics in the service of politics, the other reverses the subordination; one reifies the state, the other reifies the market. The reality of both the market and the state is that each is composed of a plurality of institutions. Markets are many and diverse in scale, rate of change and institutional characteristics, being shaped not just by technology and internationalization but also by national cultural and institutional patterns.[4] States are also internally fragmented and compartmentalized, with institutions that sometimes behave like 'a state within a state'. They are the site of conflicts, not least of opposing institutional self-interests. The 'autonomy' of the state and of the market belongs to the realm of political symbolism and is more appropriately the object of analysis than a tool of analysis.

Accordingly, a neo-pluralist approach offers a much more adequate basis for empirical research on public policy. By this means it is possible to examine in a more detailed manner the way in which institutions and policy networks respond to market and technological changes. This volume has shown that communications policies reflect the complex interdependence of market and politics. A range of variables has affected policy development, generating an international variation of policies. Amongst these variables market forces and technological changes have been important in destabilizing institutional arrangements and policy networks. In broadcasting, and more especially telecommunications, they have helped to modify the perceptions of policy-makers about the options that they face. At the same time the specific characteristics of institutional arrangements and policy networks have shaped the degree to which pressures for liberalization have been accommodated.[5] In Britain the authority enjoyed by the Prime Minister in cabinet was decisive, allied to the institutionalization of a counterweight to Whitehall culture in the form of ITAP. In France, by contrast, the authority of France Telecom and of the *grands corps* was central to policy development and was linked to very different constraints and opportunities. Neither a logic of the market nor a logic of the state has been in evidence. Communications policies have been contingent on the complex configurations of market forces, technological changes, institutional self-interests and realities of dependence within policy networks that are specific to individual cases.[6] These policies have achieved a degree of stability and effectiveness to the extent that strategy has rested on a firm bedrock of supportive institutional structure. Where strategy and structure have been difficult to reconcile, problems of implementation have bedevilled policy and compromised success. A central conclusion is, accordingly, that there is no one single strategy for success in communications policy. Success depends on the strength and adequacy of a reforming coalition within a policy network to implement a given strategy.

A second major conclusion is that policy development, especially implementation, is increasingly bound up in the internationalized nature of the political economy of communications. National policies are compelled to encompass the behaviour of foreign governments, of international institutions and of multinational companies. Faced by the complex realities of interdependence, governments have to make more difficult choices about how to maximize national advantage – in particular, whether to attract internationally mobile capital by 'deregulation' or whether to back 'national champions' that are prepared to invest in national communications infrastructure. As we have seen, these choices are not made autonomously, and their character has been conditioned more by changing perceptions of institutional self-interest than by governmental ideology. The facts of interdependence have been important in reshaping perceptions of institutional self-interest during the 1980s.

At the same time the concept of interdependence needs to be refined to reflect the imbalance of international power in communications. The interdependence of Western Europe, and the EC in particular, with the United States and Japan in communications has been asymmetrical.[7] This particular fact of interdependence has influenced the nature of policy responses in Europe, often profoundly, as this volume shows. Several chapters have revealed that, by dint of its economic power and technological leadership, the United States has managed to transform the agenda of the international political economy of communications towards deregulation to match the domestic characteristics of its own economy. The outcomes of the assertion of American power are by no means clear-cut, however. Neo-pluralist characteristics of the international political economy are apparent in the emergence of countervailing power, whether by medium-sized countries like France, by France's major role within the EC or by pressure within the ITU. 'Asymmetrical' dependence has revealed itself most profoundly in the role of the United States as the initiator of agenda change, to which the EC and its member states have had to respond. At the same time external threat has given a powerful weapon to the European Commission, to PTTs and to national broadcasters in their pursuit of institutional aggrandizement. The politics of broadcasting and telecommunications in Western Europe are accordingly more active and complex (rather than less) and fraught with economic consequences.

Notes

1 See, for example, C. Kerr, *The Future of Industrial Societies* (Cambridge, MA: Harvard University Press, 1983); W. Dizard, *The Coming Information Age* (London: Longman, 1982); and A. Toffler, *The Third Wave* (New York: W. Morrow, 1980).
2 See, for example, R. Gilpin, *The Political Economy of International Relations* (Princeton, NJ: Princeton University Press, 1987).
3 S. Gill and D. Law, *The Global Political Economy* (Brighton: Wheatsheaf, 1988).
4 See, for example, P. Hall, *Governing the Economy: the Politics of State Intervention in Britain and France* (Cambridge: Polity Press, 1986); J. Zysman, *Governments, Markets and Growth: Financial Systems and the Politics of Industrial Change* (Oxford: Martin Robertson, 1983); and R. Hollingworth and L. Lindberg, 'The governance of American industry', in W. Streeck and P. Schmitter (eds), *Private Interest Government* (Beverly Hills, CA: Sage, 1985).
5 For an example of the 'new institutionalism' in policy research see F. Scharpf, 'Policy failure and institutional reform: why should form follow function?', *International Social Science Journal*, no. 38 (1986), pp. 179–89. For the concept of policy networks see P. Katzenstein (ed.), *Between Power and Plenty* (Madison, WI: University of Wisconsin Press, 1978); J. Zysman, op. cit.; and S. Wilks and M. Wright, 'States, sectors and networks', the 'Conclusion' in S. Wilks and M. Wright (eds), *Comparative Government–Industry Relations: Western Europe, the United States and Japan* (Oxford: Clarendon Press, 1987), pp. 274–313.

6 G. Lehmbruch *et al.*, 'Institutionelle Bedingungen ordnungspolitischen Strategie-wechsels im internationalen Vergleich', in M. Schmidt (ed.), *Staatstaetigkeit* (Opladen: Westdeutscher Verlag, 1988).

7 R. Keohane and J. Nye, *Power and Interdependence: World Politics in Transition* (Boston, MA: Little, Brown, 1977).

Index